Google™
Docs
4Everyone

Steven Holzner and Nancy Holzner

que®

800 East 96th Street,
Indianapolis, Indiana 4624(

Google™ Docs 4 Everyone

ISBN-13: 978-0-7897-3936-0
ISBN-10: 0-7897-3936-4

Library of Congress Cataloging-in-Publication Data

Holzner, Steven.
  Google Docs 4 everyone / Steven Holzner, Nancy Holzner.
    p. cm.
  Includes index.
  ISBN-13: 978-0-7897-3936-0
  ISBN-10: 0-7897-3936-4
  1. Google Docs. 2. Integrated software. 3. Word processing. I. Conner, Nancy, 1961- II. Title. III. Title: Google Docs for everyone.
  TK5105.885.G66H65 2009
  005.5--dc22
                        2008054405

Printed in the United States of America

First Printing: February 2009

Trademarks

Warning and Disclaimer

Bulk Sales

Que Publishing offers excellent discounts on this book when ordered in quantity for bulk purchases or special sales. For more information, please contact

U.S. Corporate and Government Sales

1-800-382-3419

corpsales@pearsontechgroup.com

For sales outside of the U.S., please contact

International Sales

international@pearson.com

Associate Publisher
Greg Wiegand

Acquisitions Editor
Michelle Newcomb

Development Editor
Steve Schafer

Managing Editor
Patrick Kanouse

Project Editor
Mandie Frank

Copy Editor
Language Logistics, LLC

Indexer
Ken Johnson

Proofreader
Leslie Joseph

Technical Editor
Vince Averello

Publishing Coordinator
Cindy Teeters

Designer
Ann Jones

Compositor
Bronkella Publising LLC

Contents at a Glance

Table of Contents

About the Authors

Steven Holzner is the award-winning author of many books. His books have sold more than two million copies and have been translated into 18 languages around the world. He's been a contributing editor at *PC Magazine* and has been on the faculty of MIT and Cornell University, where he got his PhD.

Nancy Holzner writes and edits tech books from her home in central New York state on topics ranging from Google Apps to WAN optimization to Zoho. She is also a novelist (mystery and urban fantasy) and has worked as a medievalist, an English teacher, and a corporate trainer. Nancy holds a PhD from Brown University.

Dedication

Steve: To Nancy, of course!
Nancy: To Steve, with so much love.

Acknowledgments

This book has two authors, but it exists thanks to the hard work of many people. We'd like to thank Michelle Newcomb for discussing the initial idea for this book and offering support throughout its writing—thanks especially for your patience, Michelle. Developmental editor Steve Schafer helped us to shape the chapters and add clarity to the text. It's always a pleasure to work with tech editor Vince Averello, who's diligent in double-checking instructions and technical details. Thanks to Chrissy White for her thorough copyedit. And thanks also to project editor Mandie Frank for keeping things moving throughout the production cycle.

We Want to Hear from You!

As the reader of this book, *you* are our most important critic and commentator. We value your opinion and want to know what we're doing right, what we could do better, what areas you'd like to see us publish in, and any other words of wisdom you're willing to pass our way.

As an associate publisher for Que Publishing, I welcome your comments. You can email or write me directly to let me know what you did or didn't like about this book—as well as what we can do to make our books better.

Please note that I cannot help you with technical problems related to the topic of this book. We do have a User Services group, however, where I will forward specific technical questions related to the book.

When you write, please be sure to include this book's title and author as well as your name, email address, and phone number. I will carefully review your comments and share them with the author and editors who worked on the book.

Email: feedback@quepublishing.com

Mail: Greg Wiegand
         Associate Publisher
         Que Publishing
         800 East 96th Street
         Indianapolis, IN 46240 USA

Reader Services

Visit our website and register this book at www.informit.com/title/9780672330322 for convenient access to any updates, downloads, or errata that might be available for this book.

Introduction

Welcome to Google Docs!

Since its introduction in 2006, Google Docs has changed the way people think about office productivity tools—first word-processing documents and spreadsheets and then slideshow-style presentations (which made their Google Docs debut in 2007). Unlike traditional productivity applications, which you buy, install on your computer, and later upgrade yourself (for an additional fee), Google Docs' applications are Web-based. That means your documents, spreadsheets, and presentations are stored on the Web, and you can access them from anywhere you have an Internet connection and a Web browser. Imagine the possibilities: No more having to remember to transfer a file from your desktop computer to your laptop before you hit the road. No more wondering whether the version you're working on is the current version. No more having to back up all your documents—because Google's got you covered.

And if you sometimes need to work when you're offline, Google's got you covered there, too. When you install Google Gears (Chapter 3 tells you how), you can work on your documents and view your spreadsheets even when you're not connected to the Internet. Using Gears to work offline is optional; you don't have to install it to use Google Docs.

But one of the greatest advantages of Google Docs is the ability to share your documents with others—and collaborate on them in real time. If you've ever collaborated by emailing a flurry of files or waiting for someone else to check a document back into a central repository (so you can have your turn), you'll love collaborating in Google Docs. When you share a document with some collaborators, those people can sign in and work on the document whenever they want, from wherever they are. Multiple collaborators can work on a document at the same time. All edits happen to the current version of the document, so you never have to worry about working on an out-of-date file. (If someone makes edits you need to undo, you can roll back to a previous version using Google Docs' revision history feature.)

Best of all, Google Docs is free. Yes, you heard that right—it won't cost you a penny to use. There's nothing to install on your computer, and Google takes care of fixing bugs and updating the applications.

It's no wonder that organizations—including GE, L'Oreal, the District of Columbia, and Google itself—are evaluating or switching to Google for their productivity tools. And it's no wonder that millions of individuals are choosing Google Docs to create, edit, and store their documents. Given that you are reading this introduction, you've probably done the same (or are thinking about it). Whether for business or personal use, this book will help you get the most out of Google Docs.

A Quick Overview of This Book

Google Docs lets you create and work with three kinds of documents:

- Word-processing documents—From letters, memos, or reports to the Great American Novel, documents are anything that you might create with a word processor such as Microsoft Word, OpenOffice.org Writer, WordPerfect, and so on.

- Spreadsheets—Whether you're creating a schedule, tracking your stock portfolio, figuring out your household budget, cataloging your wine collection, or something else, you can use a Google Docs spreadsheet. A spreadsheet is a grid of columns and rows you can use to organize information and perform calculations on that information.

- Presentations—A presentation is a series of slides that you show in sequence. Traditionally, Microsoft PowerPoint has been the most popular presentation program.

After an introductory chapter to get you started with Google Docs, this book is organized by the different kinds of documents and what you can do with them:

- Chapter 1, "Getting Started with Google Docs," tells you how to create a Google account (a must for using Docs), how to use the Google Docs home page to organize and search your documents, and how to maximize your efficiency to make Google Docs work with iGoogle, Google's personal and highly customizable start page.

- Chapter 2, "Starting Word Processing," takes you through the steps of creating and saving your first document in Google Docs. The chapter also covers the basics of formatting text and shows you how to use helpful keyboard shortcuts and print a document.

- Chapter 3, "Formatting Documents," goes beyond the basics. Topics in this chapter include formatting documents, using templates to create preformatted documents, importing existing documents into Google Docs (and exporting your Docs documents to another program, such as Word), using Google's research tools, and editing documents when you're not connected to the Internet.

- Chapter 4 is titled "Taking Your Docs to the Next Level: Lists, Tables, and Insertions," and that's precisely what this chapter is about. Create and format bulleted and numbered lists; insert and edit tables, pictures, and links; and create a table of contents.

- Chapter 5, "Sharing and Collaborating on Documents," explains the how-tos of sharing a document with viewers (who can read a document but not make changes to it), collaborators (who can both read and edit a document), or both. If you've never collaborated on a document in real time before, the chapter explains how that works. Finally, we look at Revision History, which lets you find and compare previous versions of a document—a great feature if a collaborator makes changes you don't like.

- Chapter 6 introduces Google Docs spreadsheets (which is why it's called "Introducing Spreadsheets"). After a quick discussion of spreadsheet design, the chapter moves right into creating your first spreadsheet in Google Docs. From there it covers spreadsheet templates, formatting, working with multiple sheets, and the basics of working with data.

- Chapter 7, "Spreadsheets: Formulas and Charts," shows you how to power up your spreadsheets using formulas and functions, as well as how to display a spreadsheet's data graphically by creating charts and using gadgets (a gadget is a self-contained mini-program that you can put on a Web page).

- Chapter 8, "Sharing and Collaborating on Spreadsheets," covers such topics as publishing a spreadsheet on the Web, inviting others to view or collaborate on your spreadsheet, creating forms others can use to add data to a spreadsheet, and working with a spreadsheet's revision history.

- Chapter 9, "Introducing Presentations," tells you everything you need to know to create a professional-looking slideshow presentation. The chapter begins with some pointers for designing an effective presentation and then takes you through the steps of creating your first presentation. From there, you learn how to add slides and fill them with elements—text, lists, images, shapes, and videos. The chapter discusses how to import individual slides or entire presentations, as well as export a presentation so you can work on it in PowerPoint, print it out, or save it to your computer.

- Chapter 10, "The Main Event: Sharing and Viewing Presentations," covers what presentations are all about—sharing them with others. Whether you want to bring others in to help you design the presentation, show the presentation to a live audience, or publish the presentation on the Web, this chapter tells you what you need to know.

 Google frequently asks users for feedback and feature requests—and they're almost constantly updating their applications in response. Because of these frequent updates, you may find that some of the pages and steps on the live applications differ from what you see in this book.

A Word About Security

If you're used to storing your files locally on your own computer, the idea of "cloud computing"—accessing programs and storing files using the Internet—might feel a bit uncomfortable. The question is an important one: Is Google Docs secure?

When you create a document in Google Docs, that document and any information in it is private. No one can look at that information unless you explicitly grant them permission to do so by sharing the document or publishing it on the Web. Google stores your documents on its own secure servers. Any information that you store in your Docs documents, spreadsheets, and presentations is *not* accessed by search engines. That means your private info won't appear in search results. The only exception to this is if you (or one of your collaborators) have published the document and posted its Web address on a public site—in that case, your info is already out there in public on the Web, where search engines can find it.

Keep in mind that Google uses Docs for its own staff—that shows the company believes in the security of its data.

Of course, security is also up to you. Make sure that your password is a tough one to crack (using a combination of upper and lowercase letters, numbers, and punctuation marks), and don't share that password with anyone else. Take care in choosing those with whom you share your documents. And if you're using Gears to work offline, be aware that anyone who uses the computer on which you've installed Gears can see your offline documents.

Technical Requirements for Using Google Docs

To use Google Docs, you need to have a computer that can connect to the Internet and a Web browser. Table I.1 lists the combinations of operating system and Web browser that work with Google Docs.

Table I.1—Operating System–Web Browser Combos That Support Google Docs

Operating System	Web Browser
Windows XP or Vista	Chrome
Windows NT, XP, or Vista	Internet Explorer 6 or higher
Windows NT, XP, or Vista	Firefox 2.0 or higher
Linux	Firefox 2.0 or higher
Mac OSX 10	Safari 3
Mac OSX 10	Firefox 2.0 or higher

 If you're a Mac user and you want to download Gears to work with documents offline, you must use Mac OSX 10.4—earlier versions won't work with Gears.

Besides having one of the operating system–browser combinations shown in Table I.1, you need to make sure two more things are in place before you can use Docs:

- Enable cookies—A cookie is a piece of text that's stored on a user's computer by a Web application for later use. Cookies are used for authentication, session tracking, and maintaining specific information about users. You need to have cookies turned on in your Web browser for Google Docs to work. Google offers a handy guide for turning on cookies in a variety of Web browsers at www.google.com/cookies.html.

- Enable JavaScript—JavaScript is scripting language that the Web browser can run. In Google Docs, it lets you open a document in a new window, create a table of contents, and use Docs reference tools, among other things. If you're not sure how to enable JavaScript, check your Web browser's Help files.

Getting Started with Google Docs

When most people think of the programs they use to do their work—word processors, spreadsheet programs, and presentation software—they think of programs that live on their computers and store files there, too. If you want to share a report with a colleague, for example, you probably email the file. If you make a few tweaks in the meantime, you have to email it again. And if your colleague needs to make a change, he will have to email the document back to you to incorporate those changes. Before you know it, you've got half a dozen different versions of the file. Or maybe you want to take a spreadsheet on a business trip. If you forget to put it on a flash drive or otherwise transfer it to your laptop, you're out of luck while you're on the road.

Google Docs has changed all that, revolutionizing the world of office productivity tools—those programs you use to create documents, spreadsheets, and presentations. With Google Docs, your documents are stored on the Web, so you can access them from anywhere you can connect to the Internet and fire up a Web browser. (And thanks to Google Gears, you can now view and edit documents even when you're *not* online.)

Even better, you can give others access to your documents so they can view or edit documents in real time. That means any changes you make to the document show up immediately in everyone else's version—so you don't have to worry that the document's current version got lost in a blizzard of email attachments. Real-time collaboration also means that you can work on the same version of a document with others—so Tom in Topeka, Susan in Salinas, and Harry in Houston can all review and contribute to a document at the same time. (And if an overzealous editor messes things up, you can always roll back to an earlier version.)

Best of all, Google Docs is free. It doesn't cost you a penny for the convenience, masses of storage space, and sharing and collaboration tools Docs offers. And there's just no way to beat a deal like that.

This chapter gets you started with Google Docs: how to create a Google account; how to use the Google Docs home page; and how to set up another free Google service, iGoogle, to create a Google Docs–centric home page.

A Google Account: Your Passport to All Things Google

There are lots of ways you can get started with Google Docs. Someone may invite you to collaborate on a document they created. Or maybe you have a Gmail account and you clicked the top-of-screen Documents link to see what that's all about. You might even have gone directly to http://docs.google.com and signed up for Docs there.

But perhaps you're completely new to the world of Google applications—maybe you've used Google to search the Web or Google Maps to get driving directions, but you've never used any Google program that made you sign in, such as Docs, Gmail, Calendar, Sites, Talk (Google's instant-messaging program), and so on. If that's you, the easiest way to get started is to create a Google account of your very own and use that as your launching pad for Google Docs and any other Google applications that interest you.

If you have Gmail or a Docs account, you already have a Google account. It's worth taking a minute to explore the Google account to see what you can do there—the following sections will be your guide.

Signing up and Signing in

Let's get right down to business. To create a Google account, send your Web browser to www.google.com/accounts. This lands you on a page that looks like the one in Figure 1.1. If you've signed up for Gmail, Docs, or another Google application, you can sign in here using your Google username and password. Otherwise, click the Create an Account Now link below the sign-in box.

When you click Create an Account Now, Google opens the Create an Account page so you can do just that. Here's the information Google needs to create your account:

■ **Your current email address**—If, for example, you use johndoe@myemail.com, type that in here.

 It's a good idea to create your Google account by creating a Gmail account. That way, your email account and your Google Docs account are already linked. To get Gmail, go to http://mail.google.com and click the Sign Up for Gmail link.

■ **Choose and reenter a password**—Your password must be at least eight characters long. You don't want anyone else to access your account, so don't use anything obvious like your birthday or street address. The best passwords—that is, the hardest to guess—are a combination of letters, numbers, and punctuation marks. As you type in your password, Google gauges its strength—when Google says the password is strong, you'll know you've got a good one.

Figure 1.1
Click the link to create your Google account.

 In case you come up with a password so good that even *you* can't figure out what it is, go to the sign-in page at www.google.com/accounts and click I Cannot Access My Account. On the Help page that opens, click I Forgot My Password. Google opens a page where you can type in your email address. Do that and click OK. Next is a verification page; type in the letters you see and click Submit. Google sends an email to your registered email address with a link you can follow to reset your password.

- Remember Me on This Computer—If you want Google to fill in your username for you when you sign in on the current computer, check this box.
- Enable Web History—By default, this box is checked when you create a new account. Web History aims to make your Web surfing more personalized by making it easier to find pages you've visited in the past and tailoring your search results to past searches and site visits. If Web History isn't for you, uncheck this box. You can always turn Web History on (or off) later, after you've created your account.
- Location—Google wants to know where you're based; choose a country from the list.
- Verification—To make sure that you're a living, breathing human being (and not some kind of rogue robot program crawling the Web), Google asks you to read and interpret a random series of letters in an undulating font. Type the letters you see into the text box. And don't worry about upper or lowercase; it doesn't matter here.
- Terms of service—It's worth taking a minute to read Google's terms of service and privacy policy (links to each opens the fine print in a new window) before you sign up, so you know what you're agreeing to.

When you've filled out the form (and double-checked all your info), click I Accept. Create My Account. Google sends a verification email to the address you gave, so fire up your email program and check your inbox. Open the email (it's called, not-so-imaginatively, Google Email Verification) and click the link it contains. (If the link doesn't work, copy it and paste it into your Web browser's address bar.) This takes you to a page that activates your Google account.

Congratulations! You're now the proud owner of the world's newest Google account. Click the link (and read on) to see what your Google account has to offer.

What Can I Do with a Google Account?

After you've created a Google account, you can access it at any time by going to www.google.com/accounts and signing in. Or if you're using Google Docs, you can zip right over to your Google account by clicking Settings, Google Account settings.

 After you've created a Google account, you can also sign in directly to any Google service using Google username and password. For Google Docs, go to http://docs.google.com.

When you first create an Account, your Google Account page will look something like the one in Figure 1.2.

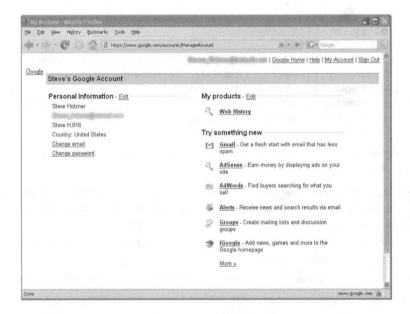

Figure 1.2
Your Google Account page provides centralized management for your account.

Unless you signed up for your Google account by another route (such as by signing up for Gmail or another Google service), you probably don't have anything under My Products on the right-hand side of the page. Don't worry; that'll change soon.

Let's take a look at what's on your Google Account page, moving from left to right:

- Personal Information—This lists info that you gave Google when you created the account, such as your name, email address, and location. Here's where you can edit your information, change your password, and more (see next section).
- My Products—As you add Google services, such as Gmail, Google Docs, Picasa Web Albums, and so on to your account, they appear in this section.
- Try Something New—Here Google lists other services and programs you might want to try. Click More » at the bottom to see the whole, humongous list.

As the following sections explain, your Google account is the centralized management center for all you do with Google. For example, if you change your name, you don't have to change it in each separate application; just go to your Google Account page and change it once. Or if you want to try out a cool new Google service you've heard about, you can sign up for it here. The next section tells you more.

Managing Your Google Account

Now that you've got a Google account, you'll probably want to fine-tune your information or add some apps. You've come to the right place: Sign in to your Google account to tweak your personal info, see which apps and services are associated with your account, or try something new.

Changing Your Account Information

People change, so the information on your Google account isn't set in stone. For example, you might want to change the name on your Google account—maybe you got married or decided that *Thomas* sounds more professional than *Tommy*. Perhaps you've moved to a new time zone and want your documents' timestamps to reflect that.

To change the personal information for your Google account, go to your Google Account page (www.google.com/accounts). Next to Personal Information is an Edit link. Click that.

The page that opens lets you add or edit this information:

- First name
- Last name
- Nickname
- Zip code
- Country
- Time zone

In addition, you can associate another email address with your Google account (besides the one you used to sign up). Why would you want to do this? If you use more than one email address— say one at work and a different one at home—this can save you a few headaches. For example, say you got an invitation to share a Google Docs document, but it was sent to your home email address, and your Google account is based on your work email address. Associating both addresses with your account lets Google figure out that you're still the same person, no matter which email address you use.

 If you create a Gmail account from your Google Account, your Gmail address automatically becomes your primary email address for the Google account. The email address you used to open the Google account becomes a secondary, associated address.

Adding and Launching Google Applications

Google offers tons of services and applications, and it seems like they're always brewing up new ones. To see and sample Google's current services, go to your Google Account page and in the Try Something New section, click More ».

The More Google Products page is a mammoth list of a Google services. Click the name of any service to go to its home page. If the service is one that requires sign-in, Google takes you to a sign-in page that has your username already filled in. Type your password and click Sign In—and you're all signed up! Some applications may require a little bit of additional information before they take you to the app's home page.

The next time you go to your Google Account page, the new application you signed in to automatically appears in the My Products section. Click the name of any of your products to launch it.

 You can also launch Google Docs by going straight to its sign-in page at http://docs.google.com and signing in there. And check out "iGoogle and Google Docs," coming up in this chapter, to learn how you can keep an eye on your documents and open Google Docs from your iGoogle page.

Getting Familiar with the Google Docs Home Page

Okay, so you've got a Google account, and you've set it up the way you want it. Now you're ready for the big time: Google Docs. Google Docs has three main components:

- A word processor
- A spreadsheet editor
- A presentation editor and viewer

Whether you're plugging figures into a spreadsheet, checking spelling in a memo, or inserting a photo into a slide, you're still using Google Docs. And you manage all those different kinds of documents from one place: the Google Docs home page. To get there, head to http://docs.google.com. If you're not already signed in to your Google account, sign in here, using the email address and password you use for your Google account. This gets you to the Google Docs home page, shown in Figure 1.3.

There's a lot to see on the Docs home page, but it's divided into four main sections:

- A search box at the very top of the page next to that colorful Google logo.
- A left-hand menu that lets you organize and display your documents in various ways.
- The Docs list in the center of the page shows recently created or saved documents, along with information about each, such as who created it, who's sharing it (if anyone), and when it was created or last saved.
- A toolbar that stretches across the top of the Docs list and offers various actions related to your documents: share, move, hide, delete, and so on.

The Docs home page is where you go to find and open a document. It's also where you organize all the documents in your account. And that's what we discuss next.

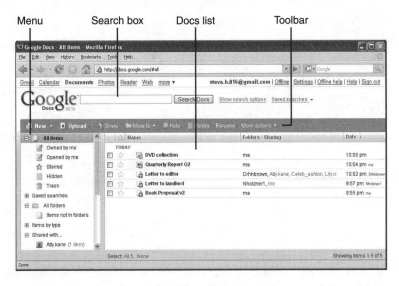

Figure 1.3
The Google Docs home page shows a list of recent documents.

Organizing Your Documents

In Google Docs, you can store your documents in folders. First things first, though: You need to create some folders to hold the documents. To do that, click New, Folder. Google immediately creates the folder, calling it New Folder, and adds it to All Folders in the left-hand menu.

Of course, it's not going to be very easy to find your documents if you've got two dozen folders and all of them are called New Folder. So before you do anything else, rename the folder Google has created. Right-click the new folder and from the context menu that appears select Rename. The screen changes to look like the one in Figure 1.4. The folder's current name appears, highlighted, in a textbox at the top of the page. Type in the folder's new name and add a description if you want (it's optional). Click Save to save the renamed folder.

 For a fast way to rename a folder, click the folder's current name in the left-hand pane. This makes the screen change to look just like the one in Figure 1.4, allowing you to type in a better name.

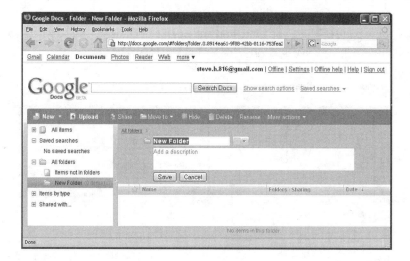

Figure 1.4
Renaming a folder.

 To create a subfolder for an existing folder, click the top-level folder first, and then click New, Folder. Google puts the new folder inside the one you clicked.

Giving a Folder a Color

Here's a neat trick that makes it a cinch to find the folder you're looking for: Assign colors to your folders. That way, when you're scanning the list of folders, the one you want will jump right out at you. Pick green for financial documents, red for love letters—anything that makes those important folders easy to remember and easy to find. It's like sticking color-coded labels on your folders. Google applies the color you choose to the folder's name, giving it, for example, dark blue letters on a light blue background.

To pick a color for a folder, find the folder you want in the All Folders list and right-click it to open a context menu. Put your cursor on Change Color, and a flyout menu appears, as shown in Figure 1.5. This flyout shows a couple dozen color combinations you can use to label the folder. Click one to select and apply it.

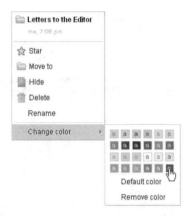

Figure 1.5
Use color to label a folder and make it stand out.

Documents in a Folder—or Two or Three...

An empty folder may have a lot of potential, but it's not much good in helping you find a document. Now that you've got some folders, start filling them up. Click All Items to show all your documents in the Docs list. Then select a document you want to put in a folder by checking the little box to the left of its name. Repeat to select more documents if you want.

Next, click Move To. This opens a dialog box that lists all your folders by name. Click a folder to select it and then click Move to Folder.

"Hey!" you may be thinking. "How come my documents didn't move?" If you look, they're still there on the Docs list. The only difference is that they now have a folder's name to the right of the document's name. But if you click the folder to open it, there's the document inside, right where you told Google to put it. What's going on here?

Google just performed a little magic, that's what. Unlike on your desktop or laptop computer, where files live in a specific location on the hard drive, Google Docs documents live on the Web. What you're putting into a folder is really just a pointer to the document, *not* the document itself. And that means that you can put the same document in more than one folder, as Figure 1.6 shows. When you put the same document into multiple folders, you can open it from any folder (just click its name), work on it a bit, save your changes—and the document is changed across the board, no matter which folder you opened it from or how many folders it's in.

Consider the possibilities: You've just written a draft of a letter to the editor publicizing the annual Rutabaga Festival. Which folder do you file it in: Letters to the Editor? Rutabagas? Festivals? With Google Docs, you can put it in all three. And when you open the Rutabagas folder, edit the draft, and save your changes, the letter is updated in all three folders, so you'll never work on an obsolete draft by mistake.

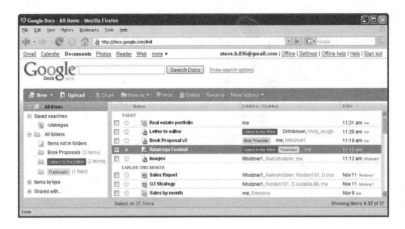

Figure 1.6
Documents, such as the highlighted one, can be in more than one folder.

Marking Important Documents

Another way to identify documents you want to find easily is to give important documents a star. On the Docs list, to the left of each document's name is the outline of a star. When you mark the document with a star, that star gets filled in with bright yellow to highlight it.

To mark a document with a star, select the document you want—or select a whole bunch of them by checking the checkbox to the left of each document's name. Click More Actions, Star, and Google turns on the stars for the documents you chose. Later, if you want to remove a star, select the document and click More Actions, Unstar.

 To see only those documents you've marked as important, expand the left-hand list's All Items section (by clicking its plus sign) and then click Starred. The Docs lists shows all the documents you've marked with a star—and only those documents.

Finding a Document

When most people think about Google, they think first about the powerful search engine that searches billions of Web pages and finds the results you're looking for, all in a tenth of a second. So it should be no surprise that Google brings the power of its searches to the documents in your Docs account.

You can do a quick search of all your docs—word-processing documents, spreadsheets, and slideshow presentations—by typing your search term in the box at the top of the Docs home page and then clicking Search Docs. Google zips through all your documents and returns a list of those that contain your search term.

Ninety percent of the time, that'll probably be all you need to do to find the document you're looking for. If you need to fine-tune your search, however, click Show Search Options to the right of the Search Docs button. This displays the options shown in Figure 1.7.

Use these options to search more precisely:

- Has the words—What word or words are you looking for? Type them here.
- Named—If you want to search documents' titles only, use this field.
- Type—Looking for a particular kind of document, such as a spreadsheet or a form? Choose the kind of document you're looking for here.
- Search—If you want to restrict the search to certain groups of documents, use this drop-down to make one of these choices: Owned by Me, Starred, Hidden, or Trash.
- Search folders—Click this button to open a box listing all your folders and then choose the folder you want to search. Or if you're pretty sure the document isn't in a folder, you can select Items Not in Folders.
- Sharing—This option lets you search by a document's sharing status. The choices are Any, Private (not shared), Shared by me, Shared with me, and Published.
- Shared With—If you know that the document you're looking for is one that you share with a particular colleague, friend, or family member, you can search by that person's email address.
- Owner is—If someone shared a file with you and you know who created the file, search by that person's email address here.
- Date—Choose either the date the file was last changed by someone or the date you last opened the file. You can also choose a date range using the "within" field. So you might, for example, search files that you last opened within the past three days or within a week of a particular date.

When you've set your search parameters, click Search Docs. Google returns a list of documents that meet your criteria.

Saving Your Search Results

When you've searched for a particular set of documents, it can be convenient to save the results. That way, there's no need to repeat the search later if you need to find similar documents in the future.

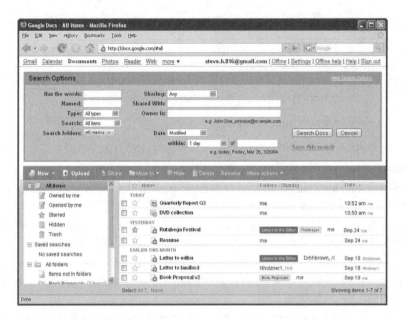

Figure 1.7
Fine-tune your search to narrow your results.

If you want to save a search, you need to have the Search Options box (Figure 1.7) displayed. Then after you've done the search, click the Save This Search link (it's just below the Search Docs button). This opens the New Save Search dialog box. Give the search a name and then click OK. Google saves the search and adds it to the Saved Searches list on the left. Later, if you want to look through the list of results for this search, click its name.

 After you've saved a search, you can rename it or fine-tune its parameters further and save it as a new search.

iGoogle, You Google, Everybody Googles

Before we get into the meat and potatoes of Google Docs—how to work with documents, spreadsheets, and presentations—it's worth taking a quick detour into another Google service, one that dovetails with Docs and makes your life that much easier. We're talking, of course, about iGoogle.

If you've never used iGoogle, you'll be glad you discovered it. And if you've already set up your own iGoogle page, did you know that you can keep an eye on your Docs list, open Google Docs, even create a new document or form right from your page? iGoogle works together with Google Docs to up your productivity—no extra effort required.

What's an iGoogle Page?

Your iGoogle page is your personalized starting point for exploring the Web. You can use it to search, of course. After all, this is Google we're talking about. But iGoogle offers a lot more. iGoogle is just waiting for you to load it up with gadgets: mini-programs that you can use right on the page. By adding gadgets to your iGoogle page, you can keep an eye on the weather forecast, see what's playing at the local movie theater, look up words in a thesaurus or dictionary, scan the latest headlines, chat with friends, and more. Best of all for Google Docs users, you can see what's happening with your documents and even open Google Docs, right from your iGoogle page.

Ready to customize your own iGoogle page? Read on to find out how.

Setting up iGoogle

To get started designing your custom iGoogle page, point your Web browser to www.google.com/ig. (Too many letters? Typing www.igoogle.com will get you to the same page.) If you're not already signed in to your Google account, click the Sign In link and then sign in. A brand-new iGoogle page, waiting for your touch, appears, looking something like the one in Figure 1.8. This page gives you a preview of what an iGoogle page can look like and lets you start customizing.

Figure 1.8
Start customizing your iGoogle page by choosing interests and selecting a theme.

The Create Your Own Homepage in Under 30 Seconds box has three sections:

▪ Select Interests—Choose topics that interest you by checking their boxes: News, Technology, Music, Sports, and so on. Each topic becomes a tab full of related content on your iGoogle page.

▪ Select a Theme—Make your iGoogle page pleasing to the eye by selecting a theme that combines artwork and a color scheme.

▪ Choose Location—Select your region and (if relevant) type in your zip code to localize your iGoogle page (for weather, movie times, etc.).

When you're ready, click See Your Page to set up your iGoogle page with the selections you've made.

 Don't worry about setting up your iGoogle page just so right now. You can always change your selections later.

Customizing Your Page

Figure 1.9 shows what a typical iGoogle page looks like. At the top is the familiar Google search box, along with a theme (if you chose one). If you selected categories of interest in the setup box, these appear as tabs on the left-hand side of the page. (There's always a Home tab here.) To the right of the tabs are gadgets that hold various kinds of content: news headlines, local movies and weather (based on your zip code, if you gave it), YouTube videos, the current date and time, and more. Each tab has specialized content chosen by Google and based on the interests you gave when you set up iGoogle.

 Beneath each tab's name is a list of gadgets on that tab. Click any gadget's name to display just that gadget. Click the tab's name to bring back all the other gadgets on that tab. If you prefer not to see each and every gadget listed, click the minus sign to the left of a tab's name to collapse the list.

One of the great things about iGoogle is that it's endlessly customizable. Don't like the location of the weather forecast? Move it. Don't need a clock? Get rid of it. Prefer the BBC to CNN? Change it. How your page looks and the content it holds is entirely up to you.

Moving a Gadget

To move a gadget to a different spot on the page, simply click the gadget's title bar and drag it to the new location, letting go of the mouse button when the gadget is where you want it. As you drag the gadgets, other gadgets on the page rearrange themselves to make room. Of course, you can drag-and-drop those, too.

Figure 1.9
Your iGoogle page comes preloaded with content.

Adding Gadgets

Google starts you off with a pretty good selection of gadgets, but there are thousands more to choose from. To see what's available and choose from that vast selection, click the Add Stuff link on the right to open a page like the one in Figure 1.10.

This page displays currently popular gadgets. Click any gadget's title to learn more about it, including comments and reviews from people who've used it on their iGoogle pages and suggestions for similar gadgets.

You can also browse gadgets by categories (Editor's Picks, News, Communication, Fun & Games, and so on). Find a category in the left-hand list and click it to see what it holds. Or use the upper-right search box to find gadgets related to a specific topic, such as travel or fashion.

When you find a gadget you want to try, click its Add It Now button to put it on your iGoogle page. And when you're ready to go back to iGoogle, click the upper-left Back to iGoogle Home link. (Google likes to place new gadgets in the top-left slot of your iGoogle page, so look for it there.)

Adding a Theme

Just as you can customize the content of your iGoogle page, you can also customize its look. When you select a theme, you choose an image for the top of the page and a color scheme for the rest of it.

Figure 1.10
There are thousands of iGoogle gadgets to choose from.

As with gadgets, there are about a gazillion themes to choose from. To see what's on offer, click Change Theme from <Name of Theme> (with your current theme's actual name in place of *Name of Theme*); on the page that opens, click Themes. You can browse themes by Hottest, Most Users, or Newest—just click the category you want to look at.

 Some themes have been created by artists and designers specifically for iGoogle. To take a look, choose Artist Themes.

Click a theme's name to learn more about it—a comment from the creator, maybe, and user reviews. When you find one you like, click Add It Now to try it on iGoogle. If you don't like it, just start the process over. You can change your theme as often as you like.

 Can't decide which theme you want? Try the Theme of the Day (you can search for it by that name), which displays a fresh, new theme each day. If one of the daily themes really grabs you, click Keep This Theme (to the right of Get Artist Themes) to make it permanent.

Adding Tabs

In iGoogle, tabs are pages that hold different content. For example, you might have one tab to follow your favorite sports teams, another to keep an eye on news headlines, and another to link to your Google apps. You can put anything you want onto a tab—just add and customize gadgets as described earlier in this chapter.

To add a tab, click the down arrow to the right of your currently selected tab. This opens the Add a Tab dialog box, shown in Figure 1.11. Give the new tab a name. If you want, Google will look at the name and pick content based on it—loading up a tab named Movies, for example, with reviews, local show times, a list of the week's most popular films, DVD releases, and so on. If you want Google to choose content for you, leave the I'm Feeling Lucky box checked. If you'd rather select your own content, uncheck the box. Click OK to create the tab.

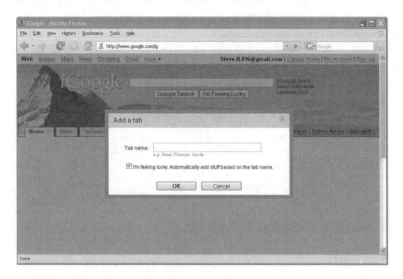

Figure 1.11
It's easy to add a new tab to your iGoogle page.

Working with Tabs

After you've added some tabs, you can work with them in various ways: change the layout, share all or some of the content, give each tab its own theme, and more. Click a tab to select it, and then click the down arrow next to its name; a menu appears, giving you these options:

- Edit This Tab—Click this option to open the Preferences page where you can rename the tab, share or delete the gadgets that comprise its content, select a new theme (for this tab only), or change the tab's layout.

- Share This Tab—When you choose this option, the Send Tab to a Friend dialog box appears. Here, you can choose your favorite gadgets and then enter a friend's email address and optional message to send a link to your page, which your friend can add (whole or in part) to her own iGoogle page.

- Delete This Tab—This option does just what it says. Click it and then click Delete This Tab to confirm, and the tab is gone.

- Add a Tab—As you saw in the previous section, this option creates a new tab for your page.

Oops! Delete the wrong tab by mistake? Before you panic, look at your iGoogle page's header. You'll see a message that looks something like this: *The "Movies" tab has been removed. Undo. Close.* Click Undo to restore the tab, just the way it was.

iGoogle and Google Docs

Your iGoogle page can serve as a command center for your Google Docs account. With the right gadgets in the right places, you can have Google Docs (and any other Google services you use) at your fingertips. Keep an eye on your email, see recently edited documents, chat with colleagues or friends, open a document (or create a new one), even search your documents—all from your iGoogle page. Figure 1.12 gives you an idea of the possibilities.

Figure 1.12
Gadgets can centralize your Google programs and services.

Google Docs Gadget

This gadget, the upper-right gadget in Figure 1.12, gives you a window into your Google Docs account, even when you don't have Docs open. The gadget lists documents, spreadsheets, presentations, and forms that have recently been saved in your Google Docs account. This means that if, for example, you've shared a document with someone, you can see when he or she worked on it. Click the name of any document to open it in a new window.

Finding and Viewing Documents

Looking at the most recently saved documents is one way to view your Google docs in this gadget. But there are other ways to view your Docs list that you might find helpful. Click Show and then choose from these options:

- Opened by me—Shows only those documents you've opened recently.
- Owned by me—Shows only documents that you created.
- Starred—Shows only documents that you flagged as important in your Google Docs account.

 If the document you're looking for doesn't appear in the gadget, click either All Docs (in the lower-right part of the gadget) or Google Docs (in the gadget's title bar) to open Docs in a new window.

If you're looking for a particular document and you don't see it in the list, use the search box at the top of the gadget. Type in a word or two, and Google scans the titles of the 100 most recent documents in your account. No luck? Just press Enter. Google searches the titles and text of *all* your documents and displays the results in a new window.

 You can display up to nine documents in the Google Docs gadget's docs list. To change the number of documents showing in the gadget, click the down arrow in the gadget's upper-right corner and choose Edit Settings. The gadget expands to show a Documents to Display list. Click the list and choose how many documents you want the gadget to show: 1 to 9. Click Save to save this setting.

Creating a new document

You can also create a brand-new document right from the Google Docs gadget. Click New, and a context menu appears. From that menu, choose the kind of document you want to create: document, form, presentation, or spreadsheet. Google creates the document and opens it in a new window. It also adds the newly created document to the list that appears in the gadget.

Google Shortcuts Gadget

You can see this gadget in the middle of the top row in Figure 1.12. As the name implies, this gadget gathers shortcuts to several popular Google services, so you can launch any of them from iGoogle. Just click, and the application you chose opens in a new window. (The Google Docs icon is the one that looks like a pencil and some paper, fourth from the left in Figure 1.12).

Gmail Gadget

Gmail dovetails nicely with Google Docs. If you have a Gmail account, the Gmail gadget (the upper-left gadget in Figure 1.12) gives you an at-a-glance look at what's currently in your Inbox. Click any email message to open it in a new window. Click Inbox or Gmail to open Gmail in this window. Click Hide Preview if you'd prefer the gadget not to show the sender, subject line, and opening of emails in your Inbox. Click Compose Mail to open another window and start writing an email.

Google Talk Gadget

With Google Docs, not only can you share and collaborate on some kinds of documents, you can also chat about them with your collaborators as you work. Upcoming chapters explain how to chat with others while you're working on a spreadsheet or viewing a presentation. But you can also add the Google Talk gadget to iGoogle and chat from there. (You can see the gadget in the middle of Figure 1.12.) A collaborator who's working on a shared document or spreadsheet, for example, can easily contact you to ask a quick question, even though you're not currently working on the same doc.

After you've added the gadget, you can invite others to chat with you. Simply type an email address into the Search, Add, or Invite box and then click Invite to Chat. Google sends the person an invitation, which he must accept before you can add him to your list of contacts.

 When someone invites you to chat, you get a message in Talk saying something like this: "joesmith777345@gmail.com wants to add you as a friend. Add as a friend?" Either click Yes to enable chat with that person or click No to reject the invitation.

With some friends and contacts in your list, you can start chatting. First, pay attention to the other person's status—the symbol to the left of his or her name:

- A green circle means the person is online and available to chat.
- A red circle with a white line through it means that the person is online but busy. (You can still try launching a chat, but the other person might ignore you.)
- A gray circle with a white x in it means the person is unavailable for chatting, offline, or not signed in to Talk.

To set your status (from available to busy, for example), click the down arrow just under your name. A menu appears that lets you set your current status. You can even write a custom message—for example, instead of *Busy*, you might write something like *Working on the final edits for the Smith report*. Choose a status to apply it to Talk. Now all your friends and colleagues will see this status by your name in their contacts list.

To start a chat, make sure that the person you want to chat with is online and available to chat and then click his or her name. The gadget changes to look like the example in Figure 1.13. A new tab opens with your chat partner's name at the top and a chat area at the bottom. Have your say by typing a comment or question into the text box at the bottom (next to the smiley face). Press Enter to display the comment in the chat area. When the other person replies, the comment appears below yours—and back and forth it goes.

 If you need a little help expressing your feelings, click the smiley face at the bottom of the Talk gadget. This opens a menu that gives you a range of emoticons, from happy and laughing faces to angry, doubtful, cool, and devilish ones.

Figure 1.13
Here's the Google Talk gadget in action. Click the pop-out icon (circled) to open the gadget in its own window.

 As Figure 1.13 shows, the Google Talk gadget allows group chatting. When you've got a chat going on, click Group Chat to open your contacts list. Choose someone from the list or type in an email address to invite others to join the conversation.

Starting Word Processing

After you've signed up for a Google account and explored the Docs home page, you're ready to get down to work—writing a report or memo, a term paper, a short story, a holiday letter to friends and family, or any other kind of document. Google Docs' online word processor lets you create, edit, and print documents that look just as sharp as documents created with any other word processor. If you can imagine it, you can write it in Google Docs. This chapter gets you started, covering word-processing basics.

Creating Your First Document

The first time you sign in to Google Docs (at http://docs.google.com), your home page will look something like the one in Figure 2.1. To get started on a new document, click the New button on the upper-left corner of the screen and then select Document. This opens the Google Docs text editor, shown in Figure 2.2, in a new window.

When the text editor opens, a blinking cursor appears inside the text area. Just start typing, and your document is underway.

 If you're already in the text editor working on a document, you can create a new document from there. Click File, New, Document. This opens a new window or a new tab (depending on your browser's settings) with a fresh, new document, ready for you to get typing.

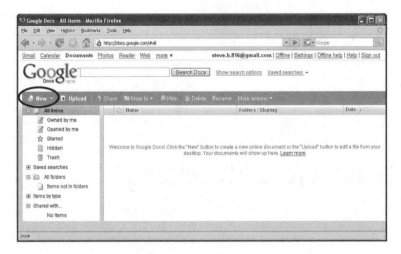

Figure 2.1
To create a new document from the Google Docs home page, click the New button (circled).

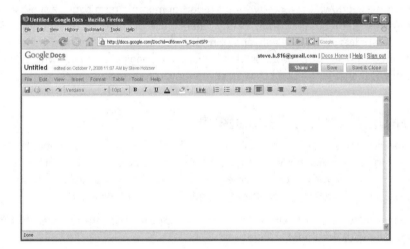

Figure 2.2
The Google Docs text editor.

Naming the Document

As soon as you get to work on a new document, Google gets to work on it, too, saving the document automatically every couple of minutes (see the upcoming section, "Saving the Document," for more about that). Although Google will save a document with the name Untitled, it's not terribly fond of unnamed documents. So if you haven't given your document a name, the first time Google saves the document, it grabs the first few words you've written and uses those as the title.

If you start off a document with a title, such as *Company Leave Policy* or *Trends in Upstate Cabbage Farming,* Google's auto-title feature is a good thing that saves you a step in creating your document. If, on the other hand, you've got a folder full of letters to your mother, each one auto-titled *Dear Mom,* it'll be hard to find a particular letter.

To name an untitled document (or to rename a document that has a title), find the document's title, which appears in the upper-left part of the screen, and click it. A dialog box, like the one shown in Figure 2.3, opens. Type the document's new name inside the text box and then click OK. Google renames your document; you can see the new title in the upper-left part of the page.

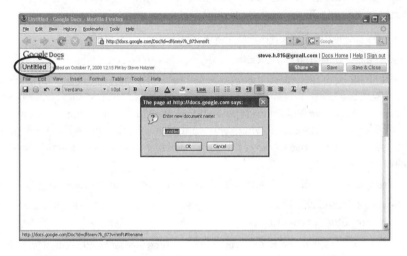

Figure 2.3
Click a document's upper-left title (circled) to open this box and rename it.

 You can also rename a document from the Google Doc's home page. In the Docs list, select the document whose name you want to change (put a check in the checkbox to the left of its current name) and click Rename. The document's name changes to a text box; click inside it and type the new name. Click outside the text box to apply your changes.

Entering Text

When you're using the text editor, entering text is as easy as typing. If you don't see a blinking cursor in the document, click inside the text area to put the cursor there. Then type away.

To move to the next line, press the Enter key. If you notice a mistake as you're typing, use the Backspace key to delete the most recent character you typed. If the mistake is in a different part of the document from where you're typing, use the mouse to position the mouse pointer just before or just after the typo and then click to move the cursor to that position. Press Delete to erase the character immediately to the cursor's right; press Backspace to erase the character immediately to the cursor's left.

 Some people are more comfortable working in page view (which shows the text as it appears on a page, including the sides of the page and margins) than they are in the Docs normal view. To switch to page view, click View, Fixed-width Page View.

Selecting and Deleting Text

Selecting text in a document lets you work with whole words or blocks of text, rather than just one character at a time. To select some text, you've got a couple of options:

- To select a single word, double-click the word you want to select.
- To select a line of text, triple-click the line you want to select.
- To select a block of text, place the mouse pointer at the start of the section you want to select. Hold the left mouse button down (or if you use a Mac, just click) and drag to highlight the text. When you've highlighted the section you want, let go of the mouse button. Alternatively, click to place the cursor where you want your selection to begin. Holding down the Shift key, use your mouse to move the cursor where you want the selection to end and click again.
- Selected text is highlighted; it appears as white characters on a blue background.
- To delete a selected word or block of text, press either the Delete key or the Backspace key on your computer's keyboard.

 If you delete something by mistake, click the Formatting toolbar's Undo button (or press Ctrl+Z on a PC's keyboard, Cmd-Z on a Mac). The Undo button icon is a curved, left-pointing arrow, and it reverses the last action you did in the text editor. The Redo button, a curved, right-pointing arrow, redoes whatever it was you just undid.

Moving Text Sections in a Document

One of the big advantages of using a word processor (as opposed to clacking away on an old-fashioned typewriter or writing things out longhand) is that you can easily move blocks of text around. When you read through a draft of a document and decide to reorganize sentences, steps in a numbered list—even whole paragraphs or sections—you can rearrange them with just a few clicks.

To move text in your document, first select the text you want to move. Next, copy that text to your computer's Clipboard using one of these methods:

- On a Windows computer, press Ctrl+X on the keyboard.
- On a Mac, press Cmd-X on the keyboard.
- Use your mouse—In the text editor's menu bar (above the formatting toolbar), click Edit, Cut.

After you've put the selected text on your computer's Clipboard, you're ready to insert it in its new location. Position your mouse pointer where you want the moved text to begin; click to make the cursor jump to that spot. Then, take one of these actions to move the text from your Clipboard back into your document:

- On a Windows computer, press Ctrl+V on the keyboard.
- On a Mac, press Cmd-V on the keyboard.
- Use your mouse—In the text editor's menu bar (above the formatting buttons), click Edit, Paste.

Presto! The text you cut from one section reappears in its new home.

 When you copy text to your computer's Clipboard, the text stays there until you copy something new over it. So you can paste in the same text multiple times and in different locations.

Finding and Replacing Text

When you realize that John Smith's name is actually John Smythe, and you spelled his name wrong all the way through a personnel report, you don't want to have to hunt through every sentence for the misspelled name. Google doesn't want you to do that either, so there's a Find and Replace function to Google Docs. Currently, Find and Replace finds and replaces *all* instances of your search term—you can't go through and replace your search term one instance at a time. So if you tell Google to find *Smith* and replace it with *Smythe*, it will change Mary Smith's name as well as John's.

To search for and replace all instances of a word or phrase in a document, click Edit, Find and Replace. (Alternatively you can use the keyboard shortcut Ctrl+H on a PC or Cmd-Control-H on a Mac.) This opens the box shown in Figure 2.4. Use the Find/Replace box to provide this info:

- Find what—Type the word or phrase you're searching for in this text box.
- Replace with—To change the search word or phrase, type the replacement text here.
- Match case—Check this box if you want Google to pay attention to upper and lowercase letters in its search.
- Match whole word—To find an exact match of what you typed in the Find What box, check this box. For example, typing *mill* into the Find What box and leaving this checkbox unchecked will highlight words such as *mill, mills, milling, million, millennium,* and so on. If you want to find the word *mill*—and only the word *mill*—check this box.
- Regular expression—Click this checkbox if you want to use wildcards in your search. A *wildcard* is a character than stands in for any character. When this box is checked, you can use an asterisk (*) as a wildcard character. So *mil** will find *mill, milk, mild,* and so on. Then Google replaces *mil* with your replacement term.

After you've set up your search, click Replace All. Google finds all instances of your search term and replaces every single one of them with your replacement term—all in one click.

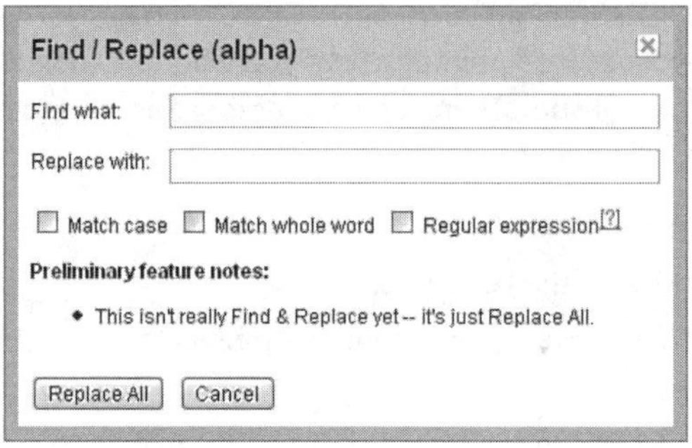

Find / Replace (alpha) ☒

Find what: [   ]

Replace with: [   ]

☐ Match case ☐ Match whole word ☐ Regular expression[?]

Preliminary feature notes:

♦ This isn't really Find & Replace yet -- it's just Replace All.

[Replace All] [Cancel]

Figure 2.4
The Google Docs Find/Replace box.

 You can't use Find and Replace simply to find a word or phrase. If you type a search term into the Find/Replace box's Find What field and then click Replace All, leaving the Replace With field blank, Google deletes all instances of your search term. Basically, it replaces the search term with a blank. To find a word or phrase in your document without replacing or deleting it, use your Web browser. In Firefox 2.x, click Edit, Find in This Page and then search for your term. In Firefox 3.x, click Edit, Find or Edit, Find Again. In Internet Explorer, make sure the menu bar is showing (select View, Toolbars, Menu Bar), then select Edit, Find on This Page and use the Find dialog box to search for a term.

Saving the Document

When you use Google Docs, you may never again have to worry about saving a document. That's because Google does it for you—every couple of minutes as you work on the document. Each saved version of your document gets stored in the document's revision history (Chapter 5, "Sharing and Collaborating on Documents," tells you all about revision histories).

If you want to save the document as it exists at a certain point in time, making sure you've got a snapshot of a particular version, you can do that, too. You've got a wealth of ways to save a document:

- Click the Save button in the upper-left (which looks like a computer diskette).
- Choose File, Save on the menu bar.
- Click the upper-right Save button.
- On your keyboard, press Ctrl+S (Windows) or Cmd-Control-S (Mac).

Whichever method you use, Google saves the document and adds the current version to your revision history. (You'll see the word Saving in a yellow box at the top of the screen as Google does its work.)

Each document in Google Docs has a maximum size of 500 KB, plus up to 2 MB for each inserted image (Chapter 4 tells you how to insert an image). That's a lot of text—the equivalent of 150 to 200 formatted pages in Microsoft Word.

If you're done working on the document at a certain point, click Save & Close. This saves the document and then closes the window in which you've been working.

If you try to close the text editor's window when the document has some changes that haven't been saved, Google warns you that you're about to navigate away from a document with unsaved changes. To save the changes, click Cancel to close the warning box and then click Save & Close. If you don't want to keep the changes, click OK to close the window without saving them.

Saving a Copy of This Document

Sometimes you want to use the current document as the basis for a brand-new document. When that's the case, click File, Save as new copy. Google opens the copy in a new window. It's got the same text, the same formatting, and the same sharing options (see Chapter 5). The only thing that's different is the title, which is how Google identifies the copy. Say you've got a document called *My Great American Novel*. When you select File, Save as Copy, Google names the new document *Copy of My Great American Novel*.

 After you've created a copy of a file, you can rename the copy with any name you like. "Naming the Document," earlier in this chapter, tells you how.

When you save a copy of a document, the copy is a brand new document all its own, separate from the document it originated from. If you make changes to the copy, those changes do not appear in the original document. And the reverse is true, as well: If you make changes to the original, they don't appear in the copy.

Introducing Formatting

Typing usually isn't enough to create a professional-looking document. You want to be able to emphasize certain words and ideas, mark sections and subsections with different styles of headings, or choose a font style that appeals to you. These actions all fall into the category of *formatting* your text—determining how that text appears on the page. This section gets you started with text formatting in the Google Docs word processor.

Using the Formatting Toolbar

Docs' formatting toolbar, shown in Figure 2.5, stretches across the top of the text editor. To apply formatting, either click a formatting button and start typing or select the text you're formatting and click the button you want. Simple.

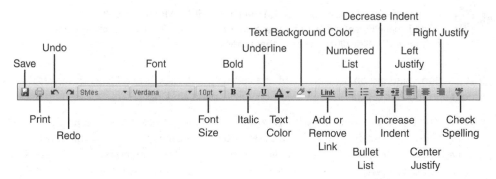

Figure 2.5
The formatting toolbar in the Docs word processor.

From left to right, the Google Docs word processor's formatting toolbar has these buttons:

- Save—Saves the document as it exists right now.

- Print—Starts the process of printing the document (see upcoming section for details on how to print a Google Docs document).

- Undo—Takes your document one step back by reserving your most recent action. If you deleted a word, for example, clicking Undo makes the deleted word reappear.

- Redo—Is for those times when you click Undo and then change your mind. This button redoes whatever it was you just undid. So if you deleted a word then clicked Undo to make the word reappear, clicking Redo deletes the word again.

- Styles—Lets you select Normal (for paragraph text) or different sizes of headings. Heading 1, the largest, works well for a document's title page; Heading 6, the smallest, is good for captions or sub-sections.

- Font—Lets you choose a font style for your text. Google Docs offers about a dozen different font styles. Click Font, and the menu that appears shows each style. Choose a font to apply it to your selected text (or to whatever you type after you've selected the font).

- Font size determines how small or how large the characters are. When you click this button, its menu offers font sizes from 8 points (which might make your readers squint) to 36 points (a good size for screaming headlines).

Tip 4U   For most purposes, a 12-point font is easiest on your readers' eyes.

- Bold—Makes your text stand out with **darker, heavier characters**. Bold text is helpful for emphasizing key points.

- Italic—Create emphasis with *right-slanting characters*. Use italics to identify terms you're defining; to format book, magazine, or movie titles; to set off foreign phrases; and to add a bit of *oomph* to individual words or phrases.

- Underlining—Puts a line <u>under the selected characters</u> as another form of emphasis. If your document will be published on the Web (see Chapter 5), it's best to avoid underlining because readers will probably confuse underlined words and phrases with hyperlinks.

- Text Color—Changes characters' color from basic black to any of a rainbow of options. When you click this button, a menu of colors appears; click the color you want to apply to the text.

- Text Background Color—Highlights text by changing the color that appears behind the characters. It works the same way as the Text Color button; click and choose the color you want for highlighting.

Tip 4U To remove highlighting, choose white for the Text Background Color (it's located in the upper-right portion of the menu of colors).

- Add or remove link—Lets you insert a *hyperlink*, a link to a Web page, into your text or remove an existing link. For details on working with hyperlinks, take a look at Chapter 4, "Taking Your Docs to the Next Level: Lists, Tables, and Insertions."

- Numbered list—Makes each paragraph an item on a numbered list, which is a good format to use when you're describing steps or priorities. As Chapter 4 explains, you can use numbers, letters, or Roman numerals to start off items in this kind of list.

- Bullet list—Makes each paragraph a list items; on this kind of list, each item is marked by a solid dot, called a *bullet*. Chapter 4 tells how to change a list's bullet style.

- Decrease/Increase indent—Moves selected text closer to (decrease) or farther from (increase) the left margin.

- Justify—Determines how your text lines up on the page:

  - Left Justify lines up text along the left margin. This is the alignment style used for most text documents.

  - Center Justify centers the text so that neither margin is straight. Use this alignment style for event announcements and invitations that aren't super-heavy with text.

  - Right Justify lines up text along the right margin, making the right margin straight. This kind of alignment is handy for a column of figures.

Tip 4U If you want your text fully justified—that is, lined up straight along *both* the left margin and the right margin—use this keyboard shortcut: Ctrl+J for Windows or Cmd-Control-J on a Mac.

- Check Spelling—Is a handy feature in any word processor. Even if you're a spelling ace, it doesn't hurt to check for typos before you print, publish, or share a document. For more on using this feature, see "Checking Your Spelling," coming up in this chapter.

Tip 4U If you want to remove formatting you've added, select the text whose formatting you want to get rid of, then click Edit, Remove Formatting. Google scrubs your text clean, removing italics, color, font size—whatever changes you've made to the default formatting.

The formatting toolbar is helpful for formatting individual words, phrases, or sections of text. You can also format entire documents, as Chapter 3, "Formatting Documents," explains.

Using Keyboard Shortcuts

Many people—call them power users—find that they create and edit documents most efficiently when they can enter formatting commands from the keyboard. Think about the time it
takes to move your hand from the keyboard, grope for the mouse, then move your hand back
into position on the keyboard again: a couple of seconds, maybe. But multiply that by dozens or
hundreds of back-and-forth movements in a document, and those seconds add up.

If you prefer to format text without moving a hand away from the keyboard, you'll find Google
Docs' keyboard commands helpful. Table 2.1 lists the keyboard shortcuts that apply to formatting in Google Docs, following the formatting toolbar's buttons from left to right. We even throw
in a few formatting commands that are represented on the formatting toolbar.

Info 4U Not all buttons on the formatting toolbar have keyboard equivalents.

Table 2.1—Keyboard Shortcuts for Formatting Text

Keystroke Combination (Windows)	Keystroke Combination (Mac)	Effect
Ctrl+S	Cmd-Control-S	Save file
Ctrl+P	Cmd-P	Print document
Ctrl+Z	Cmd-Z	Undo
Ctrl+Y	Cmd-Control-Y	Redo
Ctrl+B	Cmd-Control-B	Bold
Ctrl+I	Cmd-Control-I	Italicize
Ctrl+U	Cmd-Control-U	Underline
Ctrl+K	Cmd-Control-K	Add or remove link
Ctrl+7	Cmd-7	Numbered list
Ctrl+8	Cmd-8	Bulleted list
Ctrl+L	Cmd-Control-L	Left justify
Ctrl+E	Cmd-Control-E	Center justify
Ctrl+R	Cmd-Control-R	Right justify
Ctrl+J	Cmd-Control-J	Left–right justify
Ctrl+Space	Cmd-Control-Space	Remove formatting
Ctrl+Shift+K		Check Spelling
Ctrl+1	Cmd-Control-1	Large heading
Ctrl+2	Cmd-Control-2	Medium heading
Ctrl+3	Cmd-Control-3	Small heading

Keyboard shortcuts work best with Windows-based computers using Firefox or Internet Explorer. If you use a Mac, Firefox is the best browser for making these shortcuts work.

Printing a Document

As Chapter 5 explains in detail, you can share documents electronically, publishing them on the Web or working with collaborators you choose. There are times, though, when you want to share a document the old-fashioned way: by printing it out and distributing hard copies. Whether you're printing out a notice to tack up on bulletin boards or copies of an agenda to hand out at a meeting, it's easy to print your Google Docs documents.

Before you send a document to your printer, though, you want to make sure it will look the way you want it to. So this section tells you how to format your documents for printing.

Inserting Headers and Footers

In a printed document, a *header* is text that appears at the top of each page, and a *footer* is text that appears at the bottom of each page. You only have to type the header or footer once—Google takes care of making sure that your text appears at the top or bottom of each printed page.

Whether you're inserting a header or a footer, the process is the same. Open your document and click Insert, Header (or Insert, Footer). For a header, a box opens at the top of the document's first page, as shown in Figure 2.6; for a footer, the box opens at the bottom of the very last page. As Figure 2.6 shows, the header or footer box is outlined by a dashed gray line.

Click inside the box and type your text. When you're done typing, just click outside the box. You can return to the header or footer box at any time to edit what's there.

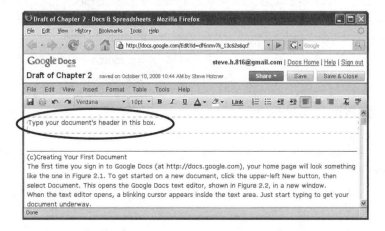

Figure 2.6
The box where you can type a header or footer is surrounded by a dashed gray line.

To delete a header or footer, you can click inside the box and delete the text or click inside the box and then right-click (Control-click on a Mac). From the context menu that pops up, select Delete Header or Delete Footer. This removes the text and the box that contains it.

Inserting Page Breaks

A *page break* tells the printer to print the next line on a new page. Page breaks aren't necessary for documents that appear only on the Web, but if you're printing a document, they're useful for starting a new chapter or a new section on the next page.

To insert a page break, put the cursor just before the line you want to appear on the new page. Click Insert, Insert page break (for printing). Google inserts a row of gray dots to indicate that a new page starts at this point.

To remove a page break, put the cursor at the end of the line that precedes the break and then press the Delete key. The dotted gray line (and the page break it represents) disappears.

Checking Your Spelling

Before you print or publish a document, it's a good idea to check its spelling to help you catch embarrassing typos. Open the document you want to check and on the formatting toolbar, click the far-right Check Spelling button.

When you click Check Spelling, Google finds all the questionably spelled words in the document all at once. Any word that doesn't appear in Google's dictionary gets highlighted in yellow. To see spelling suggestions for a highlighted word, click the word. A menu appears, listing possible spellings. Click the correct spelling to change the misspelled word and remove the highlighting.

If you know a highlighted word is in fact spelled correctly (as often happens with names, foreign words, and technical terms), you can add that word to the dictionary. Click the highlighted word to bring up Google's list of suggestions. At the bottom of that list, click Add to Dictionary. Google adds the word to the dictionary and removes the highlighting. And the next time you run a spell-check, the word you added won't get flagged as a possible mistake.

When you're done with the spell-check, click the formatting toolbar's Check Spelling button again to turn the spellchecker off and remove any highlighting that's still in the document.

Choosing Your Print Settings

Before you print a document, you want to make sure it's set up to print correctly—that it has the right orientation (portrait or landscape), the right margin widths, and so on. The Print Settings dialog box, shown in Figure 2.7, is where you do that.

To open the Print Settings box, select File, Print Settings from the menu bar. Next, choose your settings:

- Orientation—This setting orients your document vertically (Portrait) or horizontally (Landscape). Turn on the radio button of the orientation you want.

- Annotations—You've got two settings to determine here:

    - Include page numbers—Check this box if you want page numbers to show on the printed document. Then choose the location for those numbers from the drop-down (top or bottom and right, center, or left). Page numbers appear in the document's header or footer, so if you have text there, make sure there's room for the page numbers, too.

    - Include comments—If you or your collaborators have commented on a document (see Chapter 5), you can choose to show those comments (check the box) or hide them (uncheck the box) in the printed version of the document.

- Paper size—Tell Google the size of paper you're using. A4 is a standard paper size based on the metric system. U.S. users will probably opt for Letter size (8½" × 11") or Legal size (8½" × 14").

- Margins—Use the drop-downs here to choose the size, in inches, for the top, bottom, left, and right margins of your printed document.

When you've finished setting up the document for printing, click OK to apply your settings. Or if you're ready to print at a given point, click Print—and read the next section of this book.

Figure 2.7
Format a printed document using this box.

Exporting and Printing the Document

You've prepared your document by giving it a header and a footer, inserting appropriate page breaks, checking its spelling, and selecting your print settings. Now you're ready for the main event—printing the document. In Google Docs, printing requires two main steps:

1. Exporting the document as a PDF file.
2. Printing the PDF.

PDF stands for portable document format. It's a format designed to display consistently in Adobe Reader or Adobe Acrobat, no matter which platform was used to create the document. If you don't have Adobe Reader or Adobe Acrobat on your computer, you can download Reader (it's free) at www.adobe.com/reader.

The following sections walk you through both of those main steps.

Step 1: Exporting a Document to Print It

When you want to print a document, Google Docs doesn't send the document directly to your printer. Instead, it exports the document to your computer, so you can print it from there. There are three ways to get the Print process started:

- On the menu bar, click File, Print.
- On the left side of the formatting toolbar, click the Print button.
- Using your keyboard, press Ctrl+P on a PC or Cmd-P on a Mac.

What happens next depends on your Web browser. Some browsers, such as Internet Explorer 7 or higher, export the document as a PDF automatically, opening it in Adobe Reader or Adobe Acrobat.

Other browsers, such as Firefox, open a dialog box that asks how you want to handle the download: open the file in an appropriate program or save it to your computer. Select Adobe Reader or Adobe Acrobat as the program to open the file and then click OK. Firefox opens the file in your Adobe program, ready for you to print.

 If you want to skip the step of telling Firefox what to do with the file, turn on the checkbox labeled *Do this automatically for files like this from now on.* That tells Firefox that whenever you download a PDF file, you want to open it in the Adobe program you've chosen. If you want, you can save the file to your computer from that program.

Step 2: Printing the PDF

When your document opens as a PDF in Adobe Reader or Adobe Acrobat, the Print dialog box shown in Figure 2.8 opens automatically. The Print box has these sections:

- Printer—Here, choose the printer (if your computer is connected to more than one).
- Print Range—The standard option here is to print the entire document, but you can specify the pages you want to print.
- Page Handling—You can set the number of copies to print here, as well as scaling options, such as whether to shrink an oversize document (for example, one with a wide table) to fit within the area that's available for printing.
- Preview—If you make changes in the Print box that will change your document's appearance, this section shows what the document will look like when printed.

All set? Click OK to send the document to your printer for printing.

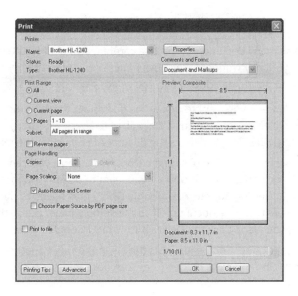

Figure 2.8
Adobe Reader's Print dialog box.

What If My Computer Doesn't Have Adobe Reader?

As a previous note explained, it's easy—and free—to download Adobe Reader and install it on your computer. Occasionally, you may find yourself wanting to print a document, but the computer you're using doesn't have Adobe Reader or Adobe Acrobat installed, and you can't install the Reader for some reason—maybe you're working at a public computer that won't let users download and install files.

Whatever the reason, here's a workaround that lets you bypass converting a file to a PDF and exporting it before you can print it:

1. Open the document you want to print and, on the right side of the screen, click Share, View as Web Page (Preview). This opens the document as a Web page.

2. Use your Web browser to print the page, thereby printing the document. On your browser's menu bar, select File, Print to open a Print dialog box.

3. In the Print box, check the settings and select a page range, number of copies, and so on. Click OK (in Firefox) or Print (in Internet Explorer) to print the page.

When you print a document using this method, the formatting isn't as good as when you export the document as a PDF and then print it, but if you need a paper copy in hand, right now, this method can give it to you.

Deleting a Document

Google Docs holds so many documents—up to a combined total of 5,000 documents, presentations, and images—you may wonder, "Why delete anything—ever?" Well, you may have your reasons. If you do want to get rid of a document, you've got two options:

- From the text editor—If you want to delete the document that's currently open in the text editor, click File, Delete. Google opens a dialog box to check whether you really want to delete the file. Click OK. Google deletes the document and closes the text editing window.

- From the Docs home page—If you're on the Docs home page, you can delete a document right from the Docs list. Find the document you want to delete (you may have to search for it—see Chapter 1, "Getting Started with Google Docs") and select its checkbox to delete it. You can select more than one document if you're doing a major purge of the Docs list—just check the boxes you want. Click the Delete button, and Google moves the files to the Trash.

A deleted file isn't really gone; Google just puts the file in the Trash. That means the file doesn't appear in the All Items list and stays hidden from searches (unless you explicitly tell Google to look in the Trash).

On the Google Docs home page, you can see a list of trashed files by clicking Trash in the left-hand menu. (If you don't see an option called Trash, click the plus sign next to All Items to expand that section.) If you want to delete a particular file from the Trash—deleting it completely from Google Docs—check the box next to that file's name and click Empty Trash. Google doesn't ask for confirmation; it just gets rid of the document. You can delete multiple files from the Trash in this way.

If you want to make a clean sweep, getting rid of all the folders in the Trash, open the Trash and, leaving all checkboxes unchecked, click Empty Trash. Google displays a dialog box warning you that you're about to permanently delete all files in the Trash. If that's OK with you, click OK—and Google deletes all trashed files.

Retrieving a Deleted Document

If you tossed a document in the Trash by mistake—whether you deleted it from the text editor or from the Docs home page—you can easily get it back. On the Google Docs home page, open the Trash (click Trash in the left-hand menu; if you don't see Trash, click the plus sign next to All Items). Find the document you want to restore, turn on its checkbox, and click Undelete. That's all there is to it—Google puts the document back in the All Items list, as well as any folders you'd assigned it to.

Formatting Documents

By now, you've probably created, edited, and saved a document or two. This chapter takes your Google Docs experience to the next level by showing you what you can do with documents:

- Set the formatting for an entire document
- Use templates to create preformatted documents
- Move documents from other word-processing programs into Google Docs
- Save a copy of a document in another format, such as a Word file
- Do research right from a document you're working on
- Edit your documents when you're not connected to the Internet

That's a lot of information to cover, so let's get started.

Formatting a Document

Chapter 2, "Starting Word Processing," gave you the basics for formatting text within a document, and Chapter 4, "Taking Your Docs to the Next Level: Lists, Tables, and Insertions," helps you take your documents to the next level by using the formatting toolbar to insert and format lists, tables, images, and more. Here we look at how to format a document as a whole, setting line spacing, and choosing a consistent font and (if you want) a background color.

You can format the entire document at the start of creating a new document or after you've started writing the document. For example, say you've been typing for a while and Docs' standard single-spacing feels cramped; you'd rather double-space the document. To apply formatting to the entire document—what you've typed already and what you'll type in the future—click Edit, Document Styles. This opens the Document Styles dialog box shown in Figure 3.1.

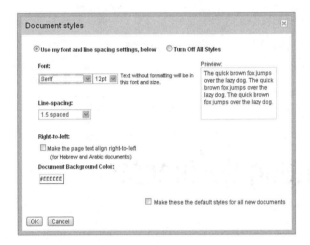

Figure 3.1
The Document Styles box lets you apply formatting to an entire document.

Use Document Styles to set these options for your document:

■ Font—This section offers the same options for font style and size as the drop-downs in the formatting toolbar. Instead of applying to a piece of selected text, though, here they make your selections standard for the whole document.

■ Line-spacing—Choose Normal, Single Spaced, 1.5 Spaced, Double Spaced, or Triple Spaced. Normal spacing has more space between lines than single spacing, but less than 1.5 spacing.

■ Right-to-Left—If you're going to be writing in a language, such as Arabic or Hebrew, which are read from right to left, turn on this checkbox. Otherwise, leave it unchecked, which is the default.

■ Document Background Color—The standard here is white (represented by the hexadecimal code #ffffff). If you want a different background color for your whole document, click this box and select a color from the palette that appears.

■ Make These the Default Styles for All New Documents—If you want the selection you've made in the Document Styles box to be the format for all the documents you create in Google Docs, check this box. If your selections are for this document only, leave it unchecked.

As you make your font and line-spacing selections, the right-hand Preview area shows how they'll look. When you've set up the document's styles the way you want them, click OK to apply them.

 If you played around with document styles and end up wishing you hadn't, you can easily reset the styles to Docs' standards. Click Edit, Document Styles, and then turn on the radio button labeled Turn Off All Styles. This resets the document's styles while saving your settings in the Document Styles box.

Working with Templates

A *template* is a pattern that serves as the basis for creating new items. Cookie cutters, blueprints, and sewing patterns are all examples of templates. In word processing, a template is a pattern for the formatting of a certain kind of document. For example, you'd use one template for the outline format of a résumé, a different template for a cover letter, and a more ornate template for a restaurant menu.

Templates come preloaded with the formatting, colors, and setup you need for different kinds of documents. You can choose a template from Google's library, or you can create your own.

Creating a New Document from a Template

When you need to create a specific kind of document—such as a résumé or report—check out Google's library of templates. Some of these templates were designed by Google; others were designed and added to the library by Google Docs users. To see what's there, you can point your Web browser to http://docs.google.com/templates. Or if you're about to create a specific kind of document, click New, From Template (from the Google Docs home page) or File, New, From Template (from the Docs text editor). Any of these routes gets you to the page shown in Figure 3.2.

The template library shows all templates, or you can choose a specific kind of template (for documents, spreadsheets, or presentations) by clicking a tab at the top of the page. Because we're working with word-processing documents in this chapter, we'll click Documents. Then the next step is to find a template for creating your document.

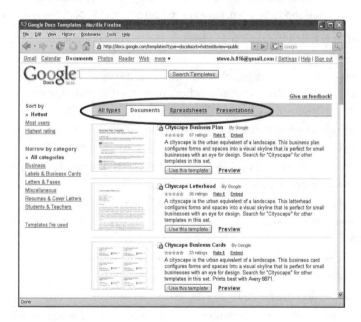

Figure 3.2
The Google Docs template library has templates for documents, spreadsheets, and presentations.

Finding the Template You Want

Google offers several different ways to find a template to use as the basis for your new document.

Search for a Template

You can find a template by typing a keyword or phrase in the search box at the top of the screen. Type in a word or phrase that describes what you're looking for, such as *cover letter* or *report,* and then click the Search Templates button.

Google whizzes through its template collection to find templates whose titles or descriptions match your Search term and then returns them in a list.

Browse Templates

If you've got time to do a bit of window shopping for your template, you can browse the library page by page. This method shows you all templates for the kind of document you chose, in no particular order.

To browse all document templates, click the Next and Previous links at the bottom of each page's templates list. Pages show 20 templates at a time. As more and more templates get added to the library, though, you might not have the patience to find a template this way. You'll probably find it a lot more efficient to browse templates by category, as the next section describes.

Browse Templates by Category

Along the left-hand side of the page, the template library displays categories into which templates are sorted. From top to bottom, here are the categories for document templates:

- Hottest—This is the default when you land on the templates library page. It sorts all templates by their recent popularity.

- Most Users—Looking for the templates adopted most frequently by other Google Docs users? Click this link to sort all templates from most users to fewest users and see what others have found helpful in creating their documents.

- Highest Rating—Users can give the templates they've tried a rating on a scale of one to four stars. To sort all templates from highest rating to lowest, click this link.

- All Categories—This shows all document templates (or the templates for spreadsheets or presentations, depending on the tab you're on.)

- Business—A general category for all business-related templates, including company letterheads, weekly work schedules, meeting minutes, and so on. If it's related to business, you'll find it here.

- Labels & Business Cards—If you're going to print out business cards or mailing labels, see what's available in this category.

- Letters & Faxes—Browse fax cover sheets, letterhead designs, and business letters here.

- Miscellaneous—You'll find everything from lost pet flyers and emergency information for the babysitter to wine-tasting notes and recipes in this catch-all category.

- Resumes & Cover Letters—Looking for a job? Whether you're applying for your first job or looking to climb the corporate ladder, you'll find helpful templates in this category.

- Students & Teachers—This category lists all kinds of education-related templates. Teachers will find templates for setting up a syllabus or lesson plan; students will find templates for writing a report or setting up a bibliography.

All templates show a preview on the left and a title, description, and rating (if any) on the right.

Tip 4U To get a closer look at a template, click its Preview link. This opens a full-sized version of the template in a new window.

Selecting and Using a Template

When you've found a template that looks like it'll suit your purpose, click its Use This Template button. In the template list, you'll find this button under the template's description. If you're previewing the template in a new window, the Use This Template button is above the preview, in the upper-left part of the page.

Google opens the template as a new document in the text editor (Figure 3.3 shows an example). The template has "Copy of *<template name>*" as its title. So the first thing you'll probably want to do is rename the document (Chapter 1 tells you how).

The template has placeholder text that shows its formatting. Just select and delete the placeholder text and type in your own. You can tweak the formatting of a template to work with your own preferences: alter a font style, size, or color, for example. Once you've opened the template in your own Google Docs text editor, you can do what you like with it to make it your own.

Figure 3.3
This example shows a template for a business letter, complete with letterhead.

Google makes it easy for you to find templates you've used in the past. In the Google Docs template library, click the left-hand Templates I've Used link to see a list of only those templates you've used to create a document.

Saving a Document as a Template

Although Google's templates library offers many attractive, well-formatted templates, you're not restricted to using what's available there. Google Docs also allows for do-it-yourself templates.

The first step in creating your own template is setting up and formatting a document that represents the pattern of formatting, fonts, and appearance you want to save as a template. You can do this with placeholder text, like the templates in the template library, or you can create an actual document whose formatting you're likely to reuse.

Next, save the document as a template. If you're creating a template from an actual document, save the document first. Then, select File, Save as New Copy. Google opens the copy in a new window. Rename the copy so its title indicates it's a template, such as *Business Letter Template* or *Company Letterhead*. Thanks to the copy, you've got a template of your very own. The next time you want to use the template, open it and immediately save it as a copy—then rename the copy and use it as the basis of your new document.

 On the Google Docs home page, create a folder called Templates. Store all your templates in that, to make them easy to find whenever you want to use them.

Importing and Exporting Documents

Whether you're starting from scratch (Chapter 1) or using a template (previous section), creating a new document in Google Docs is a snap. But that doesn't mean that you want to create each and every document in Google Docs. In fact, you've probably got documents on your computer, created with a traditional word processor such as Microsoft Word, that you'd *love* to get into Docs.

This section gives you all the details of how to get existing documents into Google Docs (called *importing*) and how to transfer a copy of a Google Docs document into another program (called *exporting*). And whether you're importing or exporting a document, you'll be glad to see how easy it is.

Importing Documents

Say you created a document in Microsoft Word, OpenOffice.org Writer, or a plain-text editor such as Microsoft Notepad, and now you want to work on that document in Google Docs. You can transfer a copy of that file into Google Docs, adding it to your Docs list and treating it like any document you created in Docs itself.

There are three ways to import a document into your Docs account:

- Upload the document from your computer.
- Upload the document from the Web.
- Email the document into your Docs account.

This section explains each method in detail.

Whichever method you choose, start on the Google Docs home page. Above and to the left of the Docs list, click Upload. This opens the page shown in Figure 3.4.

On this page, take a minute to review the restrictions related to uploading a document. Here they are in a nutshell:

- In general, documents must be 500KB—the maximum size for word-processing documents in Google Docs—or smaller.
- You can upload files ending with any of these file extensions:
    - .doc (Microsoft Word, excluding Word 2007 or later)
    - .odt (OpenOffice.org Writer and OpenDocument text)
    - .sxw (StarOffice)
    - .rtf (rich text format)
    - .txt (plain text)
    - .htm or .html (HTML, for display on the Web)
- You can also upload PDF (portable document format) files:
    - Up to 10MB if you upload the PDF from your computer.
    - Up to 2MB if you upload the PDF from the Web.

Uploading a Document from Your Computer

When you want to transfer a copy of a document from your computer to your Google Docs account, start on the Docs home page and click the Upload button. Then in the Upload a File section of the page that opens (Figure 3.4), click the Browse button. A dialog box opens (this might be called File Upload or Choose File, depending on your Web browser), which lets you find the file you want to upload on your computer. Select the file and click Open to put it in the Google textbox labeled Browse Your Computer to Select a File to Upload. Click the Upload File button.

Google uploads the file and then opens the document in the Docs text editor. Once it's there, you can work with it like any document you created in Google Docs.

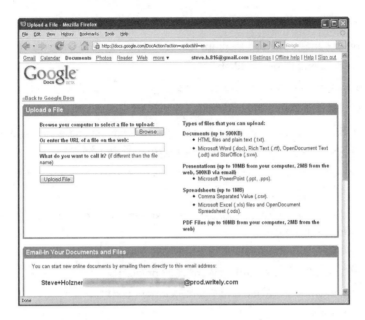

Figure 3.4
Use this page to upload a document or to find the address that lets you email a document into your Docs account.

Uploading a Document from a Web Site

If the document you want to import is on the Web—on your company's Web site or wiki, perhaps—you can upload that document to Google Docs simply by telling Google the document's Web address.

Start by opening the Web page that holds the document you want to import. Copy its Web address (also called its URL, for uniform resource locator) from your browser's address bar.

Next, open the page shown in Figure 3.4 (to get there, click Upload on the Docs home page). Click inside the text box labeled Or Enter the URL of a File on the Web, and then paste in the URL of the document you're importing. Click Upload File.

Google imports the file and opens it in the Docs text editor. There you can rename it (if you want), edit it, and save it to your Docs list.

Emailing a Document into Google Docs

A handy way to get a document into Docs is to email it in. When you click Upload on the Google Docs home page to open the page shown in Figure 3.4, take a look at the lower section of the page. Titled Email-In Your Documents and Files, that section contains an email address that belongs to your Docs account, and *only* your Docs account. You can use this address in two ways:

- Import a document in the body of an email message.
- Attach a document to import into Docs.

Read on to learn the details about these import methods.

 The email address for emailing documents into your account is long and all-but-impossible to remember. Add it to your email program's address book, so that you can easily find the address when you need it.

Importing a Document in the Body of an Email

This method takes an email message and turns it into a document. The subject line of your email becomes the document's title, and the body of the email becomes the document's text. To create a document in this way, follow these steps:

1. If you haven't already added your Google Docs email address to your email program's address book, start on the Docs home page and click Upload.

2. On the page that opens (Figure 3.4), copy the email address that appears in the Email-In Your Documents and Files section of the page. This address starts with your name and ends with *@prod.writely.com.*

3. In your email program, start a new email. Paste your Google Docs email address into the To line, and type the new document's title into the subject line.

4. In the body of the email, type the contents of the new document.

5. Click Send.

When Google receives the email, it uses it to create a new document, adding the document to your Docs list on the home page. At the same time, Google also sends an email to your registered email address, confirming that it received the document. The email tells you that a document as been imported into Google Docs on your behalf and gives a link to the document.

To open the new document, either click the link in the confirmation email or click the document's title in your Docs list.

Importing a Document by Attaching It to an Email

Another way to email a document into your Google Docs account is by attaching an existing document, such as a .doc, .odt, or .rtf file, to an email and sending that email to your Google Docs account. Here's how:

1. If you haven't already added your Google Docs email address to your email program's address book, start on the Docs home page and click Upload.

2. On the page that opens (Figure 3.4), copy the email address that appears in the Email-In Your Documents and Files section of the page. This address starts with your name and ends with *@prod.writely.com.*

3. In your email program, start a new email. Paste your Google Docs email address into the To line. You don't need to worry about a Subject line (unless your email program demands one—if so, type in whatever you like) or typing anything into the body of the email—in fact, it's best to leave these fields blank. (When you use this method, Google ignores anything you type in these fields, anyway.)

4. Attach the file you're importing. The specific steps for this vary depending on your email program. If you're not sure how to attach a file to an email, consult your email program's Help documentation.

5. Click Send. Off whizzes your email—and its attachment—through cyberspace to your Google Docs account.

When Google Docs receives an email that has a file attached, Google ignores the subject line and any message in the body of the email. Instead, it converts the file you attached into a Google Docs document, using the file's name as the document's title and its body as the text.

As when you import a document via the body of an email, Google sends you a confirmation message at your registered email address.

 If you don't receive a confirmation email from Google, it means something went wrong with the import. You may have tried to import a file that exceeds Google's maximum document size (500KB), for example. It can take a few minutes for the confirmation email to appear, so don't panic if you don't see it right away. If you don't get confirmation, fire up your email program and try again.

Exporting a Document

The flip side of importing is exporting—transferring a copy of a file from your Google Docs account into another word-processing program in the correct format for that program. All Google Docs documents are HTML files. HTML (hypertext markup language) allows documents and other files to be read by Web browsers and displayed on the Web. That makes sense given that you use a Web browser to access and work with your Google Docs documents.

When you want to export a Google Docs document to a different program, though—such as Microsoft Word or OpenOffice.org Writer—that document requires conversion into a format that the program can understand. For example, if you're exporting a document into Word, the document has to be converted into a .doc file.

Fortunately, Google takes care of that conversion for you. Your main job is telling Google which format you want to use and what you want to do with the file. And that takes just a few steps:

1. Open the document you're exporting.

2. On the menu bar, select File, Download File As.

3. A submenu appears, as shown in Figure 3.5, listing these file formats: HTML (zipped), OpenOffice, PDF, RTF, Text, and Word. Click the format you want. This opens a dialog box asking what you want to do with the file: open it in the appropriate program or save it to your computer.

4. Choose what you want to do with the file. If you're saving it, specify where you want to save it on your computer.

Once you've opened or saved the file, the export is complete.

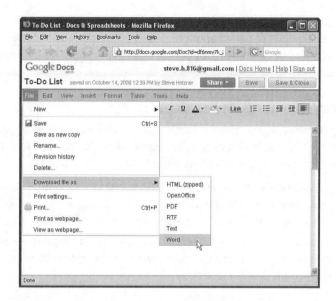

Figure 3.5
Choose a format for the file you're exporting.

 If you open the file in a program such as Adobe Reader, Microsoft Office, or OpenOffice.org Writer, don't forget to save the file in a location on your computer where you can easily find it later.

Doing Research

Students everywhere use Google's search engine to help them with their research. Where else can you type in the name of author William Faulkner, for example, and get 3.5 million results in a quarter of a second?

Now Google brings the power of that search to Docs. You can probably think of lots of times it would be convenient to have a reference library at your fingertips as you work on a document:

- You're writing a book report and need to find a list of Faulkner's novels.
- You're not sure whether you used the word *conundrum* correctly and want a quick definition to check.
- You need demographic information for a new market your company is developing.
- You've already used the word *policy* three times in two sentences and want to find a good synonym.
- You need to find a picture to illustrate a point.

You get the idea. When you're working, it's frustrating and time-consuming to stop what you're doing, open a new window (or get up and walk to the bookshelf), to find information you need. Thanks to new Google Docs tools, you can get that information right inside a document as you work on it.

Using a Dictionary, Thesaurus, or Encyclopedia

To look up a word, name, phrase, place, concept, and so on as you work in Google Docs in a reference resource, highlight what you want to look up. Click Tools, Look up Word. A flyout menu appears, as shown in Figure 3.6, which offers these tools:

- Dictionary—Choose Look up Definition of <*your selection*>. This option looks up your selected word or phrase in an online Merriam-Webster dictionary. The results appear in a dialog box; click its upper-right x to close the box when you're done checking the definition.

- Thesaurus—Choose Look up Synonyms for <*your selection*> to look up the selection in a Merriam-Webster thesaurus. A box opens, showing synonym; to replace your selection, choose a synonym and click Replace.

- Encyclopedia—Choose Look up <*your selection*> in Encyclopedia, and a box (like the one in Figure 3.7) opens, showing a list of related topics from the Encyclopedia Britannica. Click a topic to open an article on that topic in a new window.

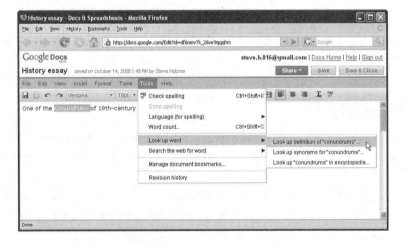

Figure 3.6
The Tools menu lets you look up words and phrases using different sources.

 For full access to Encyclopedia Britannica articles, you must subscribe to the site's Premium Membership plan, which costs $69.95 per year. Before you pay that, though, you can try out Premium Membership with a 30-day free trial. For details, go to www.britannica.com.

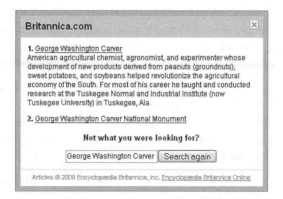

Figure 3.7
This box shows links to articles at Britannica.com.

 Student papers and articles for publication usually have to fall within a word-count range: from 750 to 1,000 words, say. If you need a quick word count, click Tools, Word Count. (Windows users can use this keyboard shortcut: Ctrl+Shift+C.) A dialog box opens, showing the number of words in your document. You also get the number of characters, sentences, paragraphs, and pages, as well as readability statistics.

Searching the Web from Your Document

Besides looking up a word or phrase in reference resources, you can also launch a Web search right from your document. Highlight the word, name, phrase, and so on that you want to look up. Then click Tools, Search the Web for Word. A menu flies out that gives you these options:

- Search the Web for *<your selection>*—Choose this to open a new window that shows Google search results for the term you selected.

- Search the Web for *<your selection>* images—When you click this option, a new window opens, showing the results of a Google Images search for your term.

 When looking for an image to use in your document, be careful not to violate anyone's copyright. If in doubt, email the image's owner (via the Web site where you found the image) and ask for permission to use it.

 To learn how to insert an image into a document, flip ahead to Chapter 4.

Working Offline

A big advantage to Google Docs is accessibility: When your documents are stored online, safe in your Docs account, you can access those documents from anywhere you can connect to the Internet.

But what about those times when you *can't* connect to the Internet? What if you're off in a cabin in the woods, miles from any wireless network, sweating over your novel? What if you're on a plane or in the back of a taxi and you need to go over your presentation notes one more time? All of a sudden, storing your documents on the Web may not seem like such an advantage.

Never fear. Thanks to Gears, software developed by Google that lets Web programs run offline, you can have offline access to your documents. Gears works with your Web browser, so you can work on documents when you're not connected to the Internet; the next time you connect and sign into Google Docs, Gears automatically synchs the offline and online versions, updating the document in your Docs account.

This section explains everything you need to know to work offline with Google Docs: where to get Gears, how to install it, and how to use it.

 Using Google Docs offline does have a few limitations. At this writing, you can use Gears to edit existing documents while you're offline, but not to create new ones. You can view but not edit spreadsheets and presentations.

Downloading and Installing Gears

Before you can work offline, you need to put Gears on your computer—that means downloading and installing the Gears software. With any software, you need to make sure it will work with your computer before you try to install it, and Gears is no exception. Here are the system requirements for installing Gears:

- Windows XP or Vista with Internet Explorer 6 or higher
- Windows XP or Vista with Firefox 1.5 or higher
- Mac OS X 10.4 or higher, with Firefox 1.5 or higher
- Mac OS X 10.4 or higher, Leopard 10.5.3 or higher, or Tiger 10.4.11 or higher, with Safari 3.1.1 or higher
- Linux with Firefox 1.5 or higher
- Windows Mobile 5 or higher with Internet Explorer 4.01 or higher

 If you use Google's Chrome to browse the Web, Gears is already built right in.

If your computer meets any of these requirements, you're good to go. Send your Web browser to http://gears.google.com. Or if you happen to be on the Google Docs home page, just click the upper-right Offline link; a dialog box opens—click Get Gears Now. The main Gears page has a big, blue, can't-miss button labeled Install Gears; click that.

A page opens, displaying Google's Terms of Service and Privacy Policy, as shown in Figure 3.8. As with any download or service, make sure you read and understand these before you continue. If you want, give Google permission to collect information—such as crash reports—about how you use Gears. Google says that any information it collects in this way is anonymous. But if you're

not comfortable sharing that info, you can say, "Thanks t
box on this page. When you're in agreement with Googl
Download.

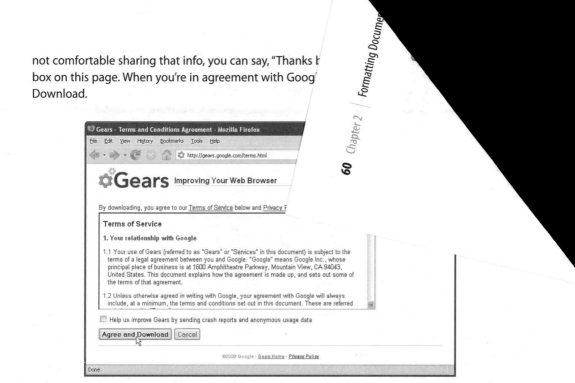

By downloading, you agree to our <u>Terms of Service</u> below and <u>Privacy F</u>

Figure 3.8
Read Google's Terms of Service before you download Gears.

Along with the next page, shown in Figure 3.9, a box opens, asking for your permission to download the file. Click Save File, and the download begins. The file you're downloading is named GearsSetup.exe; when it's been transferred to your computer, simply open it to start the installation. (Your computer may ask for your approval before running the program. If that happens, click OK.) The setup program automatically installs Gears on your computer. When it's finished, you need to close your Web browser and then restart it, as the installation's final step.

That's it! You've installed Gears, and now you're ready to get it working with Google Docs.

 If you regularly work with more than one computer—a desktop at home and a notebook on the road, for example—you need to install Gears on each computer. If you share a computer, though, take care. Installing Gears on a shared computer could give others using that computer access to your documents if they know your Google ID. So if your docs are top-secret, use Gears only on your own, private computer.

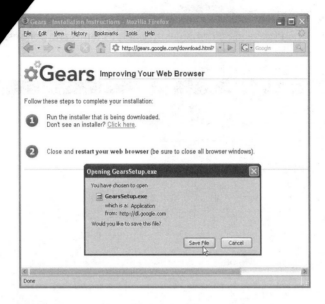

Figure 3.9
Tell your computer it's okay to download Gears.

Activating Gears

Now that you've got Gears on your computer, you're ready to set up Google Docs to work with it. After you've installed Gears and restarted your Web browser, go to the Google Docs home page. Click the Offline link at the top of the page. Google opens the box shown in Figure 3.10. Click Enable Offline Access.

Figure 3.10
Before you can use Docs offline, you have to enable offline access.

Next, a security warning box opens. Don't get alarmed; Gears shows this warning the first time a site attempts to use it. The warning tells you that a Web site (Google Docs) wants to use Gears to store information on your computer. That's exactly what you want, so check the box that says, "I trust this site" and then click Allow.

Another box opens, asking whether you want to create a Google Docs shortcut on your computer. This shortcut gives you one-click access to Google Docs when you're offline. Without the shortcut, you access Google Docs by opening your Web browser (even though you're computer isn't connected to the Internet) and pointing it to docs.google.com. On a Windows computer, for example, you can create a shortcut for any or all of these locations:

- Your computer's Desktop
- The Start menu
- The Quick launch bar to the right of the Taskbar

Check the box for any shortcut location you want and then click Yes. If you'd rather not install a shortcut right now (you can set one up later, as an upcoming section explains), leave the boxes unchecked and click No.

Google gets to work synchronizing the documents between your computer and your Google Docs account. What does that mean? When Google synchronizes documents, it's making sure your Google Docs documents are the same—whether they're stored online in your Docs account or stored on your computer using Gears. Once you're documents are synched, you can open any document and work on it offline.

As Google syncs your documents, a yellow box appears at the top of your screen, with the message *Synchronizing documents now*. At the same time, two white arrows in a green circle turn at the top of the screen, indicating synchronization is in progress. You can see what this looks like in Figure 3.11. The process might take a few minutes, so be patient. When the white arrows in the green circle switch to a white checkmark, also in a green circle, you're ready to work offline.

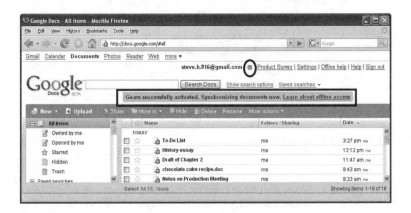

Figure 3.11
A synchronization in process.

Using Gears to Work Offline

You're set up and you're synched. Now comes the main event: using Gears to work offline. As you're about to find out, it's every bit as easy as using Google Docs.

Working on Your Documents While Offline

The next time you find yourself disconnected from the Internet, either click the Google Docs shortcut you installed or open your Web browser and point it to docs.google.com. The Docs sign-in page tells you that you're currently offline (but you already knew that, didn't you?). Type in your Google ID (no password needed for offline access) and click Offline – Sign in.

Like magic, the Google Docs home page opens. It looks very much like the home page you normally see, but with a few differences:

- You can't create or share documents in offline mode, so these options are grayed out.
- In place of the online icon (a white checkmark in a green circle) there's an offline icon, a gray No sign (a circle with a diagonal line through it).

Click the document you want to edit. It opens in a new window, just as it does when you're online. When you've finished working on a document, click Save & Close. Back in the Docs list, any documents you've edited while offline are labeled as such, as Figure 3.12 shows.

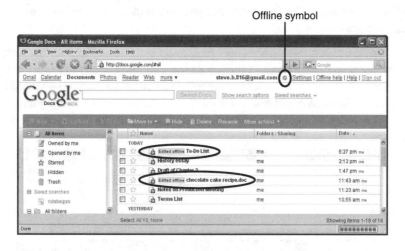

Figure 3.12
When you work offline, the Docs list looks like this.

 Rarely you might see the offline indicator change from a gray No symbol to a red circle with a white exclamation mark inside. This symbol is a warning that your offline edits aren't being saved. Stop working on the document and, if possible, leave your computer on, and the browser window open. (If you shut down either, your changes will be lost.) As soon as you can, reconnect to the Internet so Gears can save your changes in Google Docs.

Synching Your Offline Changes with Your Online Documents

So you've edited some documents offline and saved the changes. Now you want to synch those changed documents with the ones stored online in your Google Docs account. For this to work, you've got to reconnect to the Internet using *both*

- The computer on which you made the changes
- The Web browser you used while working offline

When you next connect to the Internet, go to docs.google.com and sign in. Then just sit back and let Google synch things up for you. The curved green arrows move in a circle to indicate a synch is happening, which means Gears is uploading the edits you made while offline. Once synchronization is complete, Google removes the Edited Offline label from the documents.

 What happens if two people who share a document both edit the same document while offline? Flip ahead to Chapter 5, "Sharing and Collaborating on Documents," to find out.

Tweaking Your Offline Settings

There are a couple of things you can do to customize the way you use Google Docs while you're offline. To tweak offline settings, click the status indicator at the top of the Docs home page. (This indicator is a checkmark in a green circle when you're online or a gray No sign when you're offline.) This opens a small message box that indicates your current status. The box also has a Settings link; click that to open the Offline Access Settings box, shown in Figure 3.13.

The Offline Access Settings box has two options:

- Create Desktop Shortcut—If you didn't create a desktop shortcut when you installed Gears, you can do so now, if you want to get fast, one-click access to Google Docs from your computer's Desktop. The shortcut shows a pencil and some paper; click it to go straight to Google Docs in a new browser window or tab—whether you're online or off.

- Reset and Disable Offline Access—For whatever reason, you might decide you'd rather use Google Docs only when you're online. Or you might want to disable offline access temporarily—if a houseguest is going to be sharing your computer, for example. Click this button to disable the ability to edit your documents while offline. When you do this, the status indicator at the top of the screen changes back to the word Offline.

Change your mind about disabling offline editing? You can turn it back on with just two clicks: Click Offline at the top of the screen. A dialog box opens (the same one you saw in Figure 3.10); click Enable Offline Access. Google synchs your documents, and you're back in business for working offline.

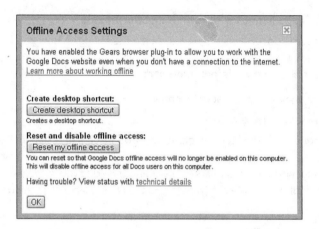

Figure 3.13
Create a shortcut or disable offline editing here.

Taking Your Docs to the Next Level: Lists, Tables, and Insertions

A plain text document is just that—plain. You can snazz up your documents (and get your points across more clearly) with some advanced formatting: insert lists, tables, images, and hyperlinks. Make it easy for readers to find their way around a document with bookmarks and a table of contents. This chapter covers all these topics, so not only can you record your brilliant thoughts in a document, you can use formatting tricks to make that document even more impressive.

Working with Lists

Lists, whether bulleted or numbered, make your documents easier to read. Think of how a page looks when it's made up of nothing but long paragraphs of tightly packed text. Lists give readers' eyes a break, which might mean they pay better attention. And lists can help you communicate more clearly, emphasizing your points by setting them off from the rest of the text.

Some general guidelines can be helpful when you're deciding whether to use a numbered or a bulleted list. Numbered lists suggest a specific order or time sequence, so use a numbered list when you're describing a process or explaining, step by step, how to do something. For example, the instructions on a shampoo bottle would appear like this in a numbered list:

1. Lather.
2. Rinse.
3. Repeat.

Use a bulleted list when you're presenting a series of related items. For example, you might use a bulleted list to list the seasons:

- Spring
- Summer
- Winter
- Fall

Whether you're working with numbers or bullets, this section tells you how to create and edit lists.

Creating a List

Chapter 2, "Starting Word Processing," gave you a guided tour of the text editor's formatting toolbar, and that's what you use to create and edit lists in a document. When you want to put a list in your document, all you need to do is press Enter to put the cursor on a new line and then click either the Numbered List or the Bullet List button on the formatting toolbar, as shown in Figure 4.1.

 If you prefer, use keyboard shortcuts to create your lists. To create a numbered list, press Ctrl+7 (on a PC) or Cmd-7 (on a Mac). To create a bulleted list, use Ctrl+8 (on a PC) or Cmd-8 (on a Mac). Chapter 2 has a lot more keyboard shortcuts you can use in your documents.

When you click one of these formatting toolbar buttons or use the corresponding keyboard shortcut, Google starts your list by inserting a *1.* or a black dot (that's the bullet) where your cursor is and where you type the text for your bullet. When you press Enter, Google starts off the next line with the next number or another bullet.

After you've finished typing the list, press Enter to move to the next line and then click the Numbered List or Bullet List button (or use the appropriate keyboard shortcut) to turn off the list and go back to normal paragraphs.

You can also turn text you've already typed into a list. Make sure that the text has just one list item per paragraph—that is, make sure you've pressed Enter at the end of each list item. Then select the text you want to turn into a list and click the appropriate button or use the appropriate keyboard shortcut. Google applies the selected list style to your text.

 If you change the font color of the text in your list, the color of the bullets or numbers changes to match.

Numbered list ⌐ ⌐ Bullet list

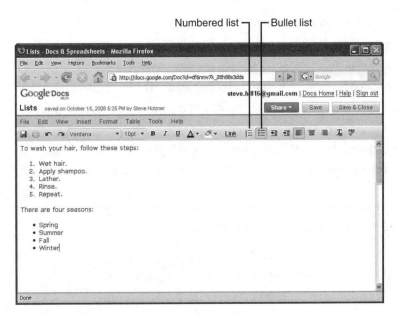

Figure 4.1
The formatting toolbar has buttons for numbered and bulleted lists.

Editing a List

As with any other text in a document, you'll probably find from time to time that you want to make changes to a bulleted or numbered list. This section explains what you can do to edit a list—change the bullet or numbering style, move list items around, and create sub-items—and how to do it.

Changing the Bullet or Numbering Style

You don't have to use Google's standard list styles for your lists. Maybe you prefer the formality of Roman numerals for your numbered lists or don't like solid black dots as bullets.

Google offers these numbering styles for numbered lists:

- Numbers (default)—This is the 1., 2., 3. style of numbering shown in Figure 4.1.
- Capital letters—A., B., C.
- Lowercase letters—a., b., c.
- Large Roman numerals—I., II., III.
- Small Roman numerals—i., ii., iii.

For bulleted lists, you have these options:

- Basic bullets (default)—These are the round dots you can see in Figure 4.1.
- Solid square bullets—These are filled-in squares.
- Hollow round bullets—These are circles that aren't filled in.

For either kind of list, you can change the style of the numbers or bullets by following these steps:

1. Right-click anywhere in the list (Control-click on a Mac). A context menu opens.
2. In the context menu, choose Change List. This opens a Change List dialog box like the one shown in Figure 4.2.
3. From the Appearance drop-down, choose the numbering or bullet style you want.
4. Click Change, and Google applies the new style to your list.

Figure 4.2
The Change List box for a numbered list.

 Tip 4U For a numbered list, you can also change the number that begins the list. In the Change List box (Figure 4.2), type the starting number you want in the Start At text box. If you want, choose a style from the Appearance list. Click Change to apply your changes.

Rearranging List Items

If you're reading through a numbered list and realize that you've got a couple of steps out of order, you can straighten out the steps without redoing the whole list. Here's how:

1. Select (or simply click) the list item you want to move and then right-click (or Control-click on a Mac). A context menu appears, as shown in Figure 4.3.
2. In the context menu, choose Move List Item Up or Move List Item Down.

That's all there is to it. Google moves the list item in the direction you chose. In a numbered list, Google automatically adjusts the numbering. So when you move the current step 3 up a place, for example, that list item becomes step 2, and the previous step 2 becomes step 3.

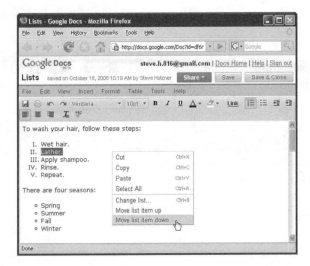

Figure 4.3
Use this menu to move a list item up or down.

 You can use this method to rearrange items in either a numbered or a bulleted list.

Creating Sub-bullets

Sometimes you might find it appropriate for a bulleted list item to introduce its own list of bullets, called *sub-bullets*. Just as bullets are indented under the normal text that introduces them, so are sub-bullets indented under the bulleted list. For example, say you're listing the people in your family.

I have two siblings:

- My brother Joe and his wife Sara have three kids:
    - Molly
    - Justin
    - Caleb
- My sister Kathy and her husband Jeff have two kids:
    - Hannah
    - Zachary

You get the idea. To set up sub-bullets in a Google Docs bulleted list, start by creating a bulleted list, as described earlier in this section. Then select the text you want to be sub-bullets and click the formatting toolbar's Increase Indent button, shown in Figure 4.4. Google indents the bullets and changes the bullets to the hollow round bullet style.

Tip 4U Here's a shortcut for indenting items in a list: Click the list item you want to indent, then press the Tab key.

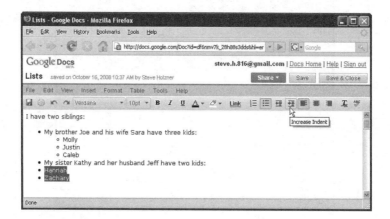

Figure 4.4
The Increase Indent button creates sub-bullets in a list.

You can also use the Increase Indent button with numbered lists. When you do, the indented items do not use standard outlining format (in which, for example, subitems of a 1., 2., 3. numbered list are labeled a., b., c.). In a numbered list, indented items use the same numbering style, so subitems of a 1., 2., 3. numbered list are also labeled 1., 2., 3. Figure 4.5 shows an example, so you can see what this looks like in practice.

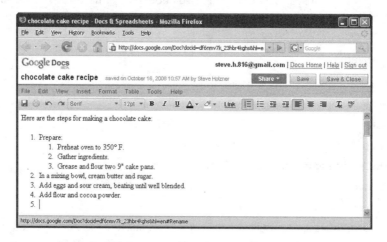

Figure 4.5
In a numbered list, subitems repeat the existing numbering style.

Adding Tables to a Document

With Google Docs, you can add tables to a document, setting up an easy-to-understand comparison using rows and columns to present information. For example, a table might show the sales performance of different sales reps or regions, the indications and side effects of various medications, students' grades, and so on. In Docs, you create a table first and then fill it in with information, as this section explains. You'll also learn how to edit a table after you've created it.

Creating a Table

To create a table, put the cursor where you want the table to appear and then click Table, Insert Table. This opens the aptly named Insert Table dialog box, shown in Figure 4.6. In this dialog box, make your choices regarding these options:

- Size—This section tells Google how big you want your table to be with these settings:
  - Rows/Columns—Specify a number of rows and a number of columns for the new table. (You can always add or delete rows and columns later; see next section.)
  - Width—Here you can specify the table's width. Full width, the default, means the table stretches all the way across the page. You can specify a different width (in pixels or as a percentage of the width of the page) or make table size adjustable by telling Google to size the table's width to the information its cells hold. This creates an initially super-skinny table that expands as you type in each cell.
  - Columns of Equal Width—This box, checked by default, tells Google to keep column widths the same, no matter how much or how little text a column contains. Uncheck the box if you want to size columns to their contents so that, for example, a column containing two-digit numbers is narrower than a column holding sentences.
  - Height—This setting determines the table's overall height; its options are essentially the same as in the Width dropdown.
- Layout—This section contains these settings:
  - Padding—In a table, padding puts some space between the contents of a cell and the cell's boundaries. Padding helps to ensure that the contents of one cell aren't crammed up against the contents of the next, so the table is easier to read. The number in this field tells Google how many pixels to use to pad each cell's contents. Google's default of 3 generally works well, but you can type in a higher number for more padding or a lower number for less padding.
  - Align—This setting lines up a cell's contents along the left or right side or down the center.
  - Spacing—Use this setting to increase the distance between each cell. Standard tables have 0 for spacing, and this is Google's default.
  - Float—Usually, a table interrupts the text so that the text preceding a table is above it and the text following a table is below it. When you *float* a table, however, you can put text to a table's left or right. For this setting, None means that the table has no text on either side of it. Left and Right describe the floated table's position relative to the text.

- Border—If you want lines to appear around the table and between each cell, set that up in this section:
    - Size—Type in the border's width, in pixels.
    - Color—Choose a color for your border by clicking inside this field and then selecting a color from the palette that appears.
- Background—This section has only one field: Color. To select a background color to shade your table's cells, click this field and select from the palette.

After you've set up the table, click Insert. Google creates an empty table and puts it in your document. To enter text into the table, click inside any cell and start typing. Press the Tab key to move to the next cell in the table. Use the up and down arrow keys to move between rows. Of course, you can always click inside the cell you want to move to.

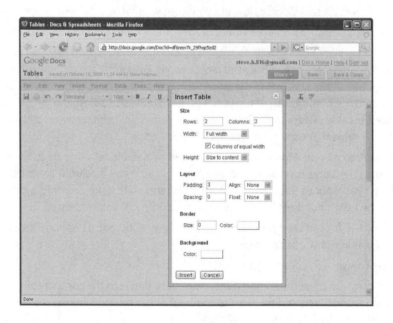

Figure 4.6
The Insert Table dialog box creates a table and puts it in your document.

Editing a Table

As you work on a table, filling its rows and columns with information, you may find you need to make adjustments to the table: add more rows, get rid of a column you don't really use, realign a column of numbers so that they line up on the right, move rows or columns to a different location. This section tells you how to make all those tweaks to your table and more.

Adding or Deleting Columns or Rows

One of the most common reasons to make adjustments to a table is that you've run out of rows and need to add some more. Or maybe you're done adding information and you've got some left over rows that you want to delete. Or you might think of a new category of information that needs a column of its own. Whether you're working with rows or columns, the process is the same, as the following sections explain in detail.

Adding a New Row or Column

When you want to add a new row or column, click inside a cell that's next to the location where you want to insert the row or column. Click Table and then choose one of these options:

- Insert Row Above
- Insert Row Below
- Insert Column on the Left
- Insert Column on the Right

When you select one of these options, Google inserts a blank row or column in the location you specified.

 Here's a shortcut: Right-click (Control-click on a Mac) the table. A context menu appears (Figure 4.7); choose what you want to insert from that menu.

Deleting a Row or Column

To remove a row or column from a table, click inside a cell in the row or column you want to delete and then select Table, Delete Row or Table, Delete Column. (Alternatively, you can right-click [Control-click on a Mac] the cell and make your choice from the context menu shown in Figure 4.7.)

Google deletes the row or column immediately, with no dialog box to confirm the deletion. If you accidentally deleted the wrong row or column, click the Undo button to bring it back.

Moving a Row

Say you've created a table that lists students alphabetically, but then you notice that a name or two are out of order. You can move rows up or down in the table, one row at a time.

Select the row you want to move. Then click Table, Move Row Up or Table, Move Row Down. Figure 4.7 shows the alternative method: Right-click or Control-click the table and then select Move Row Up or Move Row Down from the context menu.

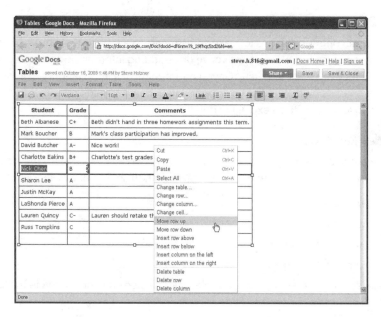

Figure 4.7
Use the context menu to move a row up or down.

Changing Properties

There's more you can do to adjust a table than change the number of rows or columns. In fact, just about any decision you made when you created the table can be changed. This is called editing the table's properties, the essential qualities that make up the table's structure. As this section explains, you can adjust the properties of an entire table, a row or column, or a single cell.

Changing Table Properties

When you want to change the properties of an entire table, click somewhere inside the table and then select Table, Modify Table Properties. Or you can right-click (Control-click if you use a Mac) and select Change Table from the context menu.

Either method opens the Change Table dialog box, shown in Figure 4.8. In this box, which looks a lot like the box you used to create the table, you can adjust the following properties:

- Size—Here you can tweak the width and/or height of the entire table.

- Layout—If you want to try a different padding, alignment, spacing, or float setting, apply the changes here.

- Border—To adjust the border that surrounds the table and separates cells, type in the width (in pixels) in the size field and choose a color in the Color field. If you want to remove the table's border, set the size to 0.

■ Background—To change cells' background color, click and select here. To remove background shading, select white.

After you've set the new properties, click Change to apply them to the table.

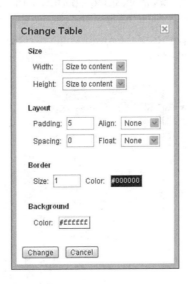

Figure 4.8
The Change Table dialog box is where you adjust the setting for a whole table.

Changing Row or Column Properties

There are several properties you can change for a row or a column. To get started, use one of these methods:

■ Click inside a cell in the row or column whose properties you want to change. Select Table, Modify Row Properties or Table, Modify Column Properties.

■ Right-click (on a PC) or Control-click (on a Mac) in the appropriate row or column. From the context menu (Figure 4.7), choose Change Row or Change Column.

If you're altering a row's properties, the Change Row dialog box, shown in Figure 4.9, opens. If you're altering a column's properties, you get the Change Column dialog box. The contents of these boxes are essentially the same; the main difference is whether your settings are applied to a row or to a column.

Here's what you can change in the properties of a row or column:

■ Size—As in the Create Table box, this section lets you adjust the height (for a row) or the width (for a column). The difference here is that your changes apply to the single row or column you selected—not to the whole table.

- Alignment—Within the row or column, you can align the cells' contents horizontally (Left, Center, Right), vertically (Top, Middle, Bottom), or both. For example, to line up a column of dollar amounts, you'd select Right from the Horizontal drop-down.

- Background—This is handy for emphasizing a particular row or column within the table, such as a row showing totals. Click the field and choose the shading you want.

After you've adjusted the properties of the row or column, click Change to save the new properties and apply them to your table.

Figure 4.9
This box lets you change the properties of a particular row.

Changing Cell Properties

You can also change the properties of one particular cell in the table—great for calling attention to important information that otherwise might get swallowed up by a large table. Find the cell whose properties you want to change; click inside the cell to select it, then choose Table, Modify Cell Properties. Or right-click inside the cell (Control-click on a Mac) and pick Change Cell from the context menu.

Either method opens the Change Cell dialog box. This box looks just like the Change Row box shown in Figure 4.9, with this difference: the Size section lets you adjust the width *and* the height of the cell. Make your selections and then click Change to apply them.

Deleting a Table

You can't delete a table from a document by hitting the Delete key. Instead, use one of these methods to remove a table:

- Click anywhere inside the table and then select Table, Delete Table.
- Right-click (Control-click on a Mac) the table and then select Delete Table from the context menu.

However you delete the table, it disappears immediately—no confirmation box to make sure. If you deleted the whole table by mistake (maybe you meant to delete just a row or column), click the Undo button as soon as the table has vanished to bring it right back.

Table-Editing Shortcuts for Firefox Users

If you use Firefox as your Web browser, you've got an advantage in editing your tables. In Firefox, you've got a built-in set of table-editing tools at your fingertips, as Figure 4.10 shows.

When you click the table, a set of editing tools appears:

- Eight small squares, called handles, appear around the table's border—four at the corners and four more at the half-way points between corners.
- A circle with an x inside, surrounded by two arrows, appears at the top and the left border of the selected cell.

Here's how to use these editing tools:

- To resize a table—Click and drag any handle. As you move your mouse, the table stretches or shrinks. When the resized table looks good, let go of the mouse button to apply the new size.
- To delete a row—Click the circle holding an x at the left edge of the cell.
- To delete a column—Click the circle holding an x at the top edge of the cell.
- To add a row—Click either of the triangular arrows at the left edge of the cell. The up arrow inserts a row above this one; the down arrow inserts a row below this one.
- To add a column—Click either of the triangular arrows at the top edge of the cell. The left-pointing arrow inserts a row to the left of this one; the right-pointing arrow inserts a row to the right of this one.

Resizing handles

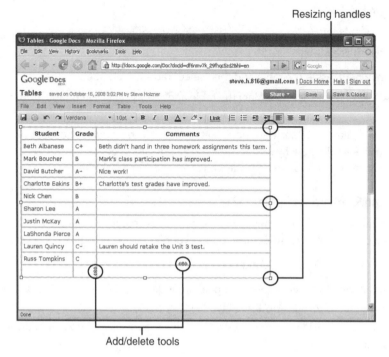

Add/delete tools

Figure 4.10
This box lets you change the properties of a particular row.

Inserting and Editing Images

If it's true, as they say, that a picture is worth a thousand words, you can see the benefit of putting images into a document. Like the figures in this book, images illustrate what's discussed in the text, making your points clearer and easier to understand.

This section is all about working with images in Google Docs documents: how to get them into a document and how to make them look great once they're there.

Getting an Image into Your Document

Before you can insert an image into a document, you need to have that image in a place where Google can find it to insert. That means the image has to be stored in one of these places:

■ On your computer—This means that the image file is stored on your computer's hard drive or on a portable drive (such as a memory stick) that can be accessed through your computer.

■ On the Web—This means the file has a URL (uniform resource locator) that you can give Google so it can find the file. For example, if you use an online photo-sharing site, such as

Photobucket or Google's own Picasa Web albums, each image has its own URL that allows the image to be displayed on another Web page.

This section covers both locations.

 Many of the images you'll find on Web pages are protected by copyright laws. So before you insert an image into a document, make sure that you're legally allowed to use it. If you're not sure, contact the Webmaster of the site where you found the picture.

Uploading an Image from Your Computer

To move a copy of an image from your computer into a document, follow these steps:

1. In the document, position the cursor where you want to insert the image.

2. Click Insert, Picture to open the Insert Image box shown in Figure 4.11.

3. In the Insert Image box, click the Browse button to open a window where you can search for the image file.

4. Browse to the image you want and click it to select it. Click Open to put the image's filepath into the Insert Image box.

5. Back in the Insert Image box, click Insert.

That's all there is to it! Google inserts the image in your document.

Figure 4.11
Inserting an image from your computer.

Inserting an Image from a Web Page

When the image you want lives on a Web page, you can get that image into your document simply by clicking and dragging. With your document open in one window, open another window and surf to the Web site that holds the image you want. Resize the image's window so that you can see both that window and your document at the same time. Then just click the image and drag it into your document. Let go of the mouse button to drop it into place.

If this method doesn't work (some images can't be dragged into an Internet Explorer window), you can also insert an image from the Web via the Insert Image box shown in Figure 4.11. If you use this method, the first step is to copy the Web address (known as its URL, for *uniform resource locator*) of the image you want. To copy the URL, right-click it (Control-click on a Mac), then select Copy.

Then back in your document, position the cursor where you want the image to appear and click Insert, Picture. This opens the Insert Image box. Click the From the Web (URL) radio button. The Insert Image box changes to look like the one shown in Figure 4.12.

Paste the image's URL into the Enter Image Web Address box. When you've done that, a preview of the image displays below the Web address. If the preview shows the right image, click Insert to put the image in your document.

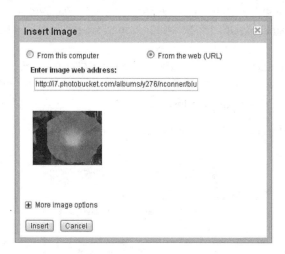

Figure 4.12
Inserting an image from the Web.

Advanced Options for Inserting an Image

As the previous sections describe, all you need to do to get an image into a document is tell Google where to find the file and then click Insert. The Insert Image dialog box has a few other settings you might want to use when you insert a document. To see them, open the Insert Image box (Insert, Picture) and then click the plus sign (+) next to More Image Options. The Insert Image box expands to look like the one in Figure 4.13.

These are the additional options you can set:

- Size—Select from the three options in this drop-down to tell Google what size to make the file you're inserting:
    - Original Image Size—This option, the default, uploads the image in the size at which it's stored, even if the image is much bigger than a standard document page.
    - Custom Size, Enter Maximum Width—When you choose this option, a field appears for you to enter the maximum width of the image (in pixels) as it appears in your document.
    - Fit Page Width—This option tells Google to adjust the image to fit the width of the page. Fit Page Width makes a small image bigger and a large image smaller.
    - Thumbnail—The image will be no wider than 160 pixels.
    - Small—The maximum width using this option is 320 pixels.
    - Medium—Choose this option if you want the image to be no more than 640 pixels wide.
    - Large—The image's maximum width will be 1024 pixels.
    - Extra large—Google will make the image up to 1600 pixels wide.
- Position—Your choices here are Left-aligned, Centered, and Right-aligned.
- Wrap Text Around Image—Standard practice when you're inserting an image is not to allow text on either side of the image. If you want text to appear next to the image, check this box.
- Link to Original File—This option makes the image a clickable link when you publish the document on the Web. It's useful, for example, when you want a thumbnail of the image in your document that readers can click to open the full-sized image in its Web page. If you want to make the image a link to its source, check the box labeled Clicking This Image Links to the Original Image File.

After you've made your choices, click Insert to put the image in your document using these settings.

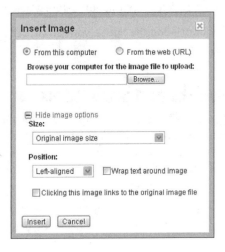

Figure 4.13
Advanced options for inserting an image.

Editing Images

If the image you've inserted doesn't look quite right—perhaps it's bigger than you thought it would be or you want to try centering it instead of having it on the left side of the page—you can change how the image looks in your document. In Docs, editing an image means resizing it or changing where the image appears in the document.

 In this context, editing the image *doesn't* mean cropping or sharpening the image. To make those kinds of changes, open the file in an image editor such as Photoshop or Paint. Make your changes there and then (re)upload the edited file into your document.

To edit the image, right-click it (on a PC) or Control-click (on a Mac). From the context menu that pops up, select Change Image to open the Change Image dialog box.

The Change Image box offers the same options listed in the previous section. You can change the image's size, its alignment, whether or not text can wrap around the image, and whether or not the image links back to its source. Tweak these settings however you like and then click Change to apply the changes.

 Instead of guessing at how many pixels across the image should be, you can resize a picture by eye, right in the document. Click the image, and eight small, square handles appear around its border: four in the corners and four more halfway between corners. Click a handle and drag it to resize the image. Corner handles work best for resizing because dragging a corner handle keeps the picture's horizontal and vertical dimensions in proportion.

Deleting an Image

If you tried out an image and decided it isn't worth a thousand words after all, you can remove it by clicking the image to select it and then pressing either Delete or Backspace on your keyboard. That's all it takes. Google doesn't ask for confirmation before it deletes the image.

If you change your mind about deleting the image, you can click the Undo button (immediately after deletion) or insert the image again.

Working with Hyperlinks and Bookmarks

A great advantage of using Google Docs is that because your documents are stored on the Web (and can be published there, as Chapter 5 explains), you can put links to all kinds of information right into your documents: A sales letter can link to an online order form, for example, a specification to a vision-and-scope document, or a report to an online article that supports your point. If it's on the Web, your document can link to it.

Google Docs also let you insert bookmarks, internal links to another place in your document. Instead of just referring to a figure or section of the document, you can make the reference into a bookmark. That way, readers don't have to hunt for the reference; one click, and they can jump right to it.

This section gets you up to speed on working with hyperlinks and bookmarks in Google Docs.

Inserting a Hyperlink

A *hyperlink* (*link* for short) lets you jump from the document to a new Web page. You can choose to have the linked-to Web page open in a new window, so your readers don't lose their place in the current document.

To insert a hyperlink, first select the text that will hold the link. That means the text will be underlined and the cursor will change to a pointing hand when readers move the cursor over that text. When a reader clicks the link, the page you've linked to opens.

Then click the Link button on the formatting toolbar. (If you prefer, you can select Insert, Link from the menu bar.) This opens the Insert Link dialog box, shown in Figure 4.14. This box contains these options:

- Link To—In this section, choose what you're linking to:
  - URL—As Figure 4.14 shows, when you choose this option, Google asks for the URL (Web address) of the Web page you're linking to. Type or paste it into the URL box.
  - Document—You can link to another document in your Google Docs account. When you choose this option, a drop-down list appears, preloaded with all your documents, so you can pick the one you want.
  - Bookmark—As the upcoming "Creating Bookmarks" section explains, you can create an internal link to a section within the current document. If you've created some bookmarks, they appear in a drop-down list; choose the one you want. A bookmark must already exist before you can link to it.
  - Email Address—Make it easy for your readers to contact you (or another relevant person) by inserting a *mail-to* link. When a reader clicks a mail-to link, a new message opens in his or her email program with the email address already filled in. To make the link a mail-to link, select E-mail Address, then enter an address in the E-mail To field.
  - Link Display—If you've already selected text to hold the link, that text appears in this field, as shown in Figure 4.14. If you didn't select any text when you click the Link button, type in the text that will hold the link here, and Google will insert both text and link into the document.
  - Flyover—A *flyover* is text that appears when a reader hovers the cursor over a link. Flyovers are optional but can be helpful when you need to provide a little extra explanation about the link. If you want a flyover, type it into this field.
  - Open Link in New Window—This checkbox, available for URL and Document links, does just what it says: When a reader clicks the link, the linked-to Web page or document opens in a new window, leaving your document open in the current window. If that's what you want, check this box.

Once your settings are all set, click Insert to put the link into your document.

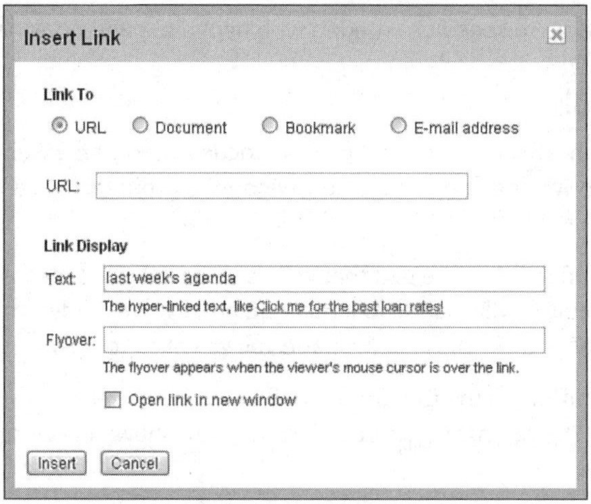

Insert Link

Link To
○ URL   ○ Document   ○ Bookmark   ○ E-mail address

URL: [   ]

Link Display

Text: [last week's agenda   ]
         The hyper-linked text, like Click me for the best loan rates!

Flyover: [   ]
         The flyover appears when the viewer's mouse cursor is over the link.

☐ Open link in new window

[Insert] [Cancel]

Figure 4.14
You can insert four different kinds of links into a document.

To check that the link works, click Share, View as Web Page (Preview). This opens the document as it will appear after you've published it. In this preview, the link is now clickable. Click it to test its behavior.

Editing a Hyperlink

You may need to make changes to a link after you've inserted it. If so, open the document in the text editor and click the link. As Figure 4.15 shows, a box appears beneath the link, containing these three elements:

- The link's target—Click this to open a new window that displays the linked-to Web page, document, or bookmark. If you've created a mail-to link, the box displays the email address (but it's not clickable).
- Change—Click Change to open the Change Link dialog box, which has the same fields and options as the Insert Link dialog box (Figure 4.14).
- Remove—To remove the hyperlink from the text (while leaving the text in place), click Remove.

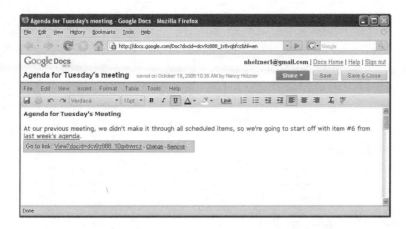

Figure 4.15
Click hyperlinked text to edit or remove the link. This example shows a link to another document.

Inserting a Bookmark

As mentioned earlier, a bookmark links to another part of the current document, so you can link, for example, to a referenced section or the bibliography. Bookmarks are also helpful for creating a table of contents (see next section) or an index.

There are two steps to inserting a bookmark:

1. Create the bookmark.
2. Link to it.

Read on to learn more.

Creating Bookmarks

To create a bookmark—that is the target of a link—select the text that you want to use as a bookmark. Click Insert, Bookmark to open the Insert Bookmark box shown in Figure 4.16.

In the Insert Bookmark box, the text you select appears in the New Bookmark field. You can change this text if you want—if you do, be sure to give the bookmark a descriptive name so you can find it in a list of bookmarks later.

Any existing bookmarks in the document appear in the Other Bookmarks field.

Once you've named the bookmark, click Insert to save it. Now you can link to the bookmark. If you want to insert more bookmarks before you create links to any of them, just repeat the process.

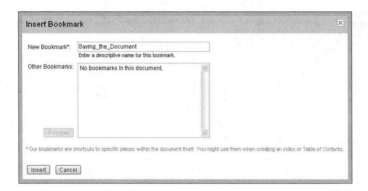

Figure 4.16
To create a bookmark, give it a descriptive name.

 Besides text, you can also link to an image, such as a figure or chart in the document. When you create a bookmark for an image, the New Bookmark field is blank. Just type in the name you want for the bookmark, such as Figure 1.1 or Jimmy's School Play Photo, and then click Insert.

Linking to a Bookmark

After you've inserted at least one bookmark into a document, you can link to the bookmark from other parts of the document. The process is the same as for inserting a hyperlink (see earlier section).

In the Insert Link dialog box (click Link on the formatting toolbar), when you select Bookmark in the Link To section, the dialog box changes to look like the one in Figure 4.17. Use the Bookmark drop-down list to choose the part of the document you're linking to. (Now you can see why it's good to give each bookmark a descriptive name—in a long document with lots of bookmarks, you want to be able to find the bookmark you're looking for.)

Finish filling out the Insert Link box and then click Insert. Your text is now linked to the bookmark.

Editing Bookmarks

You edit a link to a bookmark in the same way you edit hyperlinks (see previous section). You click the linked text, and a box appears beneath the link (Figure 4.15). In that box, click Change to open the Change Link box and make your changes. Click Remove to remove the link to the bookmark from this text.

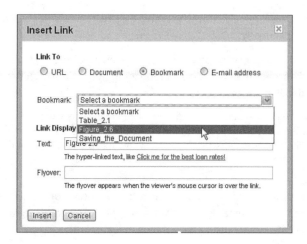

Figure 4.17
Choose a bookmark from the list to link to it.

Removing a Bookmark

To remove the bookmark itself, select Insert, Bookmark to open the Insert Bookmark dialog box (Figure 4.16). Existing bookmarks appear in the Other Bookmarks field. Click the bookmark you want to delete and then click the Remove button. Google removes the bookmark from the text or image that held it and closes the Insert Bookmark box.

Creating a Table of Contents

In a printed book or other document, a table of contents lets readers see at a glance what topics the document covers and how it's organized. If the table of contents reveals that the first couple of chapters cover introductory material, for example, a reader can start with that chapter or flip right to Chapter 3.

In Google Docs, a table of contents has the same purpose: to show your readers what your document covers and how it's organized. Instead of flipping pages, however, your readers have the advantage of clicking a link in the table of contents and going straight to the section they want.

You can build a table of contents by hand, inserting bookmarks into section and subsection headings and then typing up a list of those sections and subsections and linking to the appropriate bookmarks. But that's a lot of work. And one of the reasons you use Google Docs is because you're smart enough to avoid extra work when you can.

Let Google do the work for you. Follow these steps to create a table of contents for a document—quickly and painlessly:

1. As you create your document, use the heading levels available in Docs: Heading (suitable for the title of a chapter or major section), Subheading (for main subsections), or Minor heading (for minor or detailed subsections).

 To format text with a heading level, click Format and then choose the level you want. You can also use these keyboard shortcuts: Ctrl+1 (Heading), Ctrl+2 (Subheading), Ctrl+3 (Minor heading). For Mac users, those shortcuts are Cmd-1, Cmd-2, and Cmd-3, respectively.

2. After you've got your headings set up, click at the beginning of the document, putting the cursor where you want the table of contents to appear. Select Insert, Table of Contents to open the Table of Contents dialog box, shown in Figure 4.18.

3. In the Table of Contents box, select the numbering style you want for your table of contents. For example, you can choose to assign a number to each heading but none for subheadings and minor headings. As you click options in the Numbering Style drop-down list, the Preview boxes show you how this numbering style will look in both the onscreen and printed versions of the document.

4. Click Insert Table of Contents.

Google creates and inserts the table of contents at the point you specified in the document. Figure 4.19 gives you an idea of what the results look like.

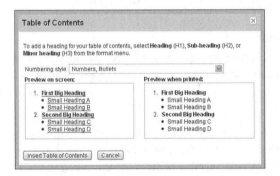

Figure 4.18
Choose a numbering style for your table of contents.

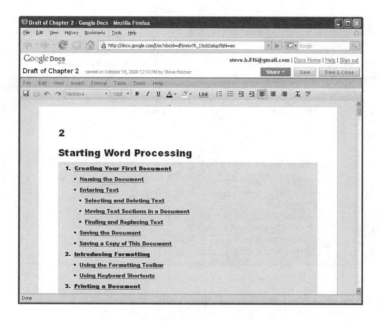

Figure 4.19
Google created this table of contents and inserted it into the document.

Editing a Table of Contents

As you edit and work on a document (on your own or with collaborators), headings might change; as new sections are added, a section gets broken down into subsections, or typos get found. And the table of contents can change right along with the changes you make to a document's headings.

When you change headings, change them in the body of the document—*not* in the table of contents. After you've made some edits, go to the table of contents and right-click it (Control-click it if you're using a Mac) .

As Figure 4.20 shows, a box appears above and to the right of the table of contents. Here's what you can do in that box:

- Update—When you click this link, the table of contents updates to reflect whatever changes you've made to the headers in the body of the document.

- Properties—Click Properties to open the Table of Contents dialog box (Figure 4.18) and choose a different numbering style.

- Remove—Don't need a table of contents after all? Click this link to delete it. Google doesn't ask for confirmation before it axes the table of contents, but if you remove the table of contents by mistake, you can click the Undo button to bring it right back (or simply reinsert it by following the steps in the previous section).

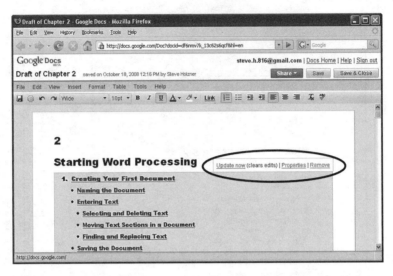

Figure 4.20
Use the circled box to update, edit, or delete a table of contents.

Sharing and Collaborating on Documents

The preceding chapters have shown that the Google Docs word processor is convenient, flexible, powerful, and easy to use. This chapter shows what makes Google Docs revolutionary, going to the heart of how Google has changed the landscape of word processing: the ability to share a document with others, collaborating on it simultaneously in real time.

Whether you're planning the itinerary for a family reunion, working on a group report for class, or putting together a project specification for work, collaborating on a shared document means that everyone who shares the document always has the latest version right at their fingertips. And you can work more efficiently because several people can edit the document at the same time—no more waiting for a document to be checked back in before you can work on it or wondering who's going to merge the changes three different editors made.

This chapter tells you all about sharing and collaborating on a Google Docs document, focusing on these topics:

- How to share a document
- Viewers versus collaborators
- How to publish a document as a Web page or blog post
- Collaborating in real time
- Commenting on a document
- Finding and comparing past versions of a document

Sharing a Document

In Google Docs, *sharing* a document means giving someone else access to that document. The level of access is up to you: Viewers can read the document but not edit it, whereas collaborators can both read and edit the document. You can change a person's access level or remove sharing privileges at any time.

When you're ready to share a document with someone else (or a whole group of others), click the upper-right Share button from within the Google Docs text editor and then select Share with Others. The Share This Document page, shown in Figure 5.1, opens. The left side of this page is where you invite others to share the document; once you've shared a document, the right side lists those whom you've given permission to view or edit the document.

 To view or edit a document you've shared, the person you've invited must have a Google account. Those without an account can create one from the Docs sign-in page by clicking the big, blue Get Started button.

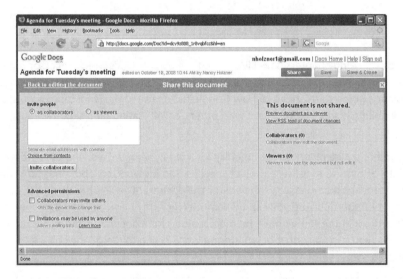

Figure 5.1
Use this page to invite others to view or edit a document.

 You can share a document with up to 200 other people. But only a maximum of 10 people can read or work on a document at the same time.

Step 1: Choose Sharers and Set Permissions

To invite people to share your document, start by choosing how you want to share this document with the people you're inviting:

- As collaborators—Collaborators can both view and edit the document. They can also export the document to store it on their own computers. If you, as the owner (that is, the creator) of a document give them permission, collaborators can also invite others to view or edit the document.

- As viewers—Viewers can read the document, but they can't make changes to it in Google Docs. They can, however, save a copy of the document to their own Google Docs account (by selecting File, Save as New Copy) or download it to their computer.

 You can't mix viewers and collaborators in your invitation. If you want to invite some people to collaborate on the document and others only to view it, you need to go through the invitation process twice: once for the collaborators and once for the viewers.

Type or paste in the email addresses of the people you're inviting, separating multiple addresses with commas. Before you invite them, take a look at the Advanced Permissions section to see whether you want to grant or deny these permissions:

- Collaborators May Invite Others—This permission is on by default, and it means that anyone you invite as a collaborator on a document may invite others to collaborate on or view the document as well. If you don't want collaborators to have this ability, uncheck the box.

- Invitations May Be Used by Anyone—This permission, on by default, lets you invite a whole bunch of collaborators or viewers all at once, using a single email address. For example, say you've created a mailing list called projectteam@mycompany.com. That one mailing list address covers many people; when you send an email to that address, it lands in the inbox of each person on your project team—each person can then respond to the invitation separately. You can use the mailing list address as a single email address to invite everyone on the list—as long as this checkbox is turned on.

 Gmail users have an easy way to find and invite viewers and collaborators. Click the Choose from Contacts link just above the Invite Collaborators button. A new window opens, showing your ten most recent Gmail *contacts*—people you've received email from or sent email to. (You can also find contacts via Search.) Click a contact's name to add that contact to your list of invitees. When you've added all the contacts you want, click Done to insert those contacts into the Invite People box.

When your list of addresses and permissions are all set, click Invite Collaborators or Invite Viewers, depending on which privilege level you're assigning your invitees

Step 2: Send an Optional Email Invitation

After you click the Invite Collaborators (or Invite Viewers) button, Google opens the dialog box shown in Figure 5.2. This dialog box lets you send an email to the people you're inviting.

Sending an invitation email is optional. If everyone you're inviting knows that you're going to share the document—because you made an announcement to expect it in a meeting, for example—just click Skip Sending Invitation. When you do, Google adds the new viewers or collaborators to the list of people who have access to the document. At the same time, Google adds your document to the Docs list of each sharer's Google Docs home page. No email involved. But if sharers don't know that you're sharing the document—or if you're not sure whether they have Google accounts—it's a good idea to send the notification email.

The title of the document appears as the email's subject line, and you can type in a message giving a little context about the document. (Google's standard email, sent with every notification, tells recipients that you've shared a document and includes a link to it.)

If you want to paste a copy of the document into the notification email, check the box for that option. If you want to receive a copy of the email Google sends out to your invitees, check the CC Me box.

To send out the notification emails inviting others to share your document, click Send.

Figure 5.2
You can send viewers and collaborators an email telling them about the document you're sharing.

Receiving a Document-Sharing Notification

Google's invitation email, which notifies the recipient that someone has shared a document with him or her, looks like the one shown in Figure 5.3. As the previous section explained, you can send this email when you invite someone to share a document.

Of course, you might also receive this kind of notification email. When you do, click the link to check out the document. If you're already signed in to your Google account, the document opens in a new window. If you're not signed in to Google, clicking the link lands you on the Google Docs sign-in page; type in your Google ID and password. When you're signed in, Google opens the document automatically.

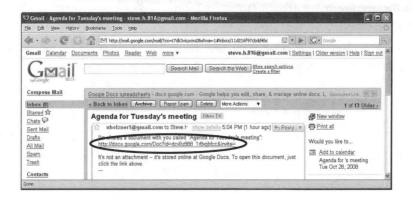

Figure 5.3
Click the link (circled) in Google's notification email to see the shared document.

Changing a Document's Ownership

When you create a document, you're that document's owner. When you own a document, you have control over a couple of issues related to sharing:

- As owner, you can give—or deny—collaborators to share the document with others.
- When you delete a shared document that you own, Google deletes it from all collaborators' Docs accounts as well.

There are numerous reasons why you might want to transfer ownership of a document to someone else. For example, maybe you're leaving your project team or company, and someone else needs to take over the work-related documents you own. Or perhaps you don't need a document any longer, but some of your collaborators want to keep working on it; if you transfer ownership to one of those collaborators, you can delete the document without making it suddenly disappear from everyone else's Docs list. When you transfer ownership of a document to someone else, you become a collaborator on the document with viewing and editing privileges.

To give someone else ownership of a document you own, go to the Google Docs home page and find the document whose ownership you're transferring. Click the box to the left of the document's title to put a checkmark in it. If you're transferring ownership of several documents, check their boxes, too.

Click the More Actions button (above the Docs list), and then select Change Owner. This opens the Choose New Owner dialog box, shown in Figure 5.4. This box shows the name of the document (or a list of names, if you chose more than one document)—check to make sure any documents that appear here are the ones you want because if you make a mistake, the only way to get ownership back is to ask for it (nicely).

If the document title (or titles) are correct, type in the email address of the person who will become the new owner. If you want, customize the notification email's message in the Message to the New Owner box. When everything in the dialog box looks good, click Change Owner.

Google sends the notification email to the new owner. The new owner can't refuse ownership, but of course he or she can transfer ownership to someone else.

Figure 5.4
Transferring ownership of a document.

 You can transfer ownership of documents and presentations (Chapters 9 and 10). At this writing, though, Google doesn't yet support changing the ownership of spreadsheets.

Emailing All Viewers/Collaborators

When you need to send an email about a document to all (or even just some) of the people with whom you shared it, you can do so from the Share this Document page (Share, Share with Others). After you've shared a document, this page looks something like the one in Figure 5.5, with collaborators and viewers listed on the right-hand side. (Because they have different levels of access, collaborators and viewers are listed separately, each in their own section.)

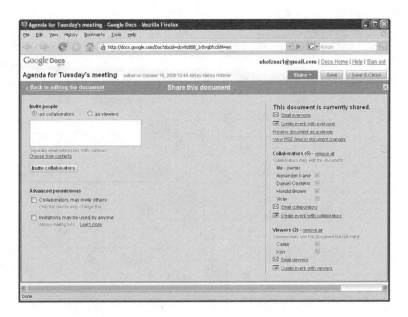

Figure 5.5
After you've shared a document, collaborators and viewers appear on the right-hand side of this page.

To send an email to all sharers, click any of these links: Email Everyone, Email Collaborators, or Email Viewers (as you'll see in a moment, it doesn't matter which link you click). The Email Document box, shown in Figure 5.6, opens. In this box, the To section shows the names of everyone with whom you've shared the document: collaborators in one section and viewers in another. Beside each name is a checkbox; initially, these boxes are all checked. If you want to email only some of these people, uncheck the box for each person to whom you *don't* want to send the email.

Google has already filled in the Subject line with the document's title (you can change the subject if you like). Click inside the Message box and then type your message there. (Google includes a link to the document in the message it sends.) If you want the document included in the email, check the box labeled Paste the Document Itself into the Email Message. If you want to receive a copy of the email yourself, check the CC Me box.

When you're ready, click Send to email sharers *en masse*.

 To send a group email to collaborators only (some or all of them), click Share, Send message to collaborators. When the Email Document box opens, it lists collaborators only.

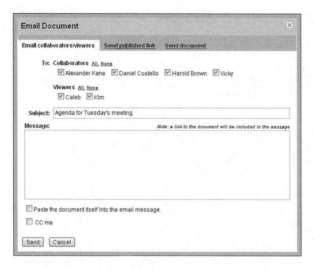

Figure 5.6
Select recipients and email a message, along with a link to the document.

Removing Sharing

They say it's nice to share—and usually, that's true. But once in a while you may get someone working on a document who's more hindrance than help. Or maybe a collaborator leaves your company for a new job, and there's no point in giving that person continued access to work-related documents. It might even just be that you're sick of hearing everyone's criticisms of your Great American Novel.

Whatever the reason, you can stop sharing a document, whether with one person or with everyone. When you stop sharing with someone, Google removes that person's name from the Share This Document page and also removes the document from his or her Docs list. The person may have saved a copy of the document, but he or she will no longer have access to the original version in your Docs account.

To stop sharing a document, go to the document's Share This Document page (shown in Figure 5.5) and look at the lists of collaborators and viewers. If you're just removing one person, find the person you want and click the x to the right of his or her name, removing the x from the box. Google immediately stops that person from sharing the document.

To remove all collaborators or all viewers in one fell swoop, click the Remove All link next to the kind of sharers you want to remove: Collaborators or Viewers. A dialog box appears, asking whether you're sure that you really want to stop sharing with all those people. Click OK to stop sharing the document.

Other Ways to Share a Document

Besides adding others as viewers or collaborators, there are a couple of other ways you can share a Google Docs document. You can email it—either in the body of the email or as an attachment. Or you can publish it on the Web: on its own Web page or as a post on your blog.

Emailing a Document

Share your document the old-fashioned way: email it! Email may not have been around when the Pony Express was delivering mail, but it's still the most traditional option for quickly sharing a document with someone else. You can send the document as part of the email message, or you can send the document as an attached file. You might want to email a document to someone who doesn't have a Google Docs account, to someone who wants a copy for their own records, or to someone who wants to print a copy.

To email a document, click Share, Email as Attachment to open the Email Document dialog box. You saw this dialog box in Figure 5.6, but now it opens with the Send Document tab selected, as shown in Figure 5.7.

On the Send Document tab, type or paste in the email address of each recipient (use commas to separate multiple addresses). If you use Gmail, you can select recipients from your Gmail contacts by clicking the Choose from Contacts link.

Next, select how you want to send the document by turning on one of these radio buttons:

- Paste the Document Itself into the Email Message—This puts a copy of the document into the body of the email.
- Attach Document As—Choices here are Microsoft Word Document (.doc), Open Document Format (.odt), Portable Document Format (.pdf), and Rich Text Format (.rtf).

The Subject line is the same as your document's title, although you can change this if you want. Type your email message into the Message box. (There's no standard Google message when you send a document using this method, so if you leave this box blank, the email has no message, just the pasted-in document or the attached file.) Check CC Me if you want Google to send a copy of the email to your registered email account.

When your email is ready to go, click the Send button—and your document is on its way.

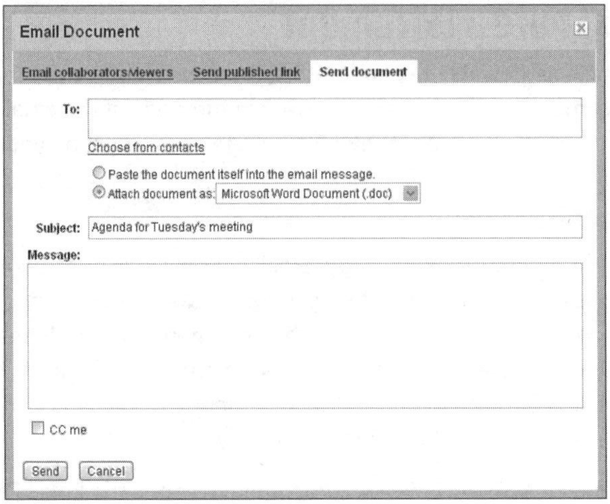

Figure 5.7
You can email your document in the body of the email or as an attachment.

Publishing a Document on the Web

So far, the methods this section has discussed for sharing a document are great for when you want to share a document with one person, a few people, or a couple of target groups. But what about when you've got a document you want to share with the whole world?

You can—or at least with that part of the world that's connected to the Internet—by publishing your document online. When you publish a document in this way, Google gives the document its own Web page, which anyone with Internet access can find. Then you can send out the published document's Web address, link to it from your Web site, or post it to your blog.

To make your document public, open the document you want to publish and click Share, Publish as Web page to open the Publish This Document page shown in Figure 5.8. That's the starting point, whether you're publishing the document as a Web page or posting it to your blog.

 To make sure your document looks just right before you publish it, click Share, View as Web Page (Preview). Google opens the document to show exactly how it will look when you publish it on the Web.

Publishing a Document as a Web Page

To make your document a public Web page, open the Publish This Document page. The top section of this page tells you that "This document is not yet published" and explains what publishing a Google Docs document means: The document gets a public Web address (called URL, for uniform resource locator), where anyone can view the document.

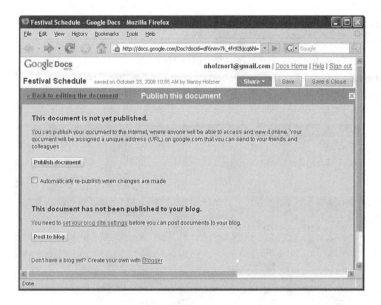

Figure 5.8
The Publish This Document page is your starting point for publishing a document as a Web page or a blog post.

This section also has a checkbox labeled Automatically Re-Publish When Changes Are Made. When you check this checkbox, it means that any changes you make to the document in Google Docs automatically update the public version—in other words, Google displays the changes as you make them, each time it saves the document. If you'd prefer not to publish changes until you've had a chance to go over your edits and maybe run a spell-check, leave this box unchecked. (You can change this setting later if you want.)

Click Publish document, and the page changes to look like the one in Figure 5.9. Here's what's on the Publish This Document page when you've made a document public:

- The notification at the top of the page says, "This document is published on the web."

- The document's URL—Google tells you "Your document is publicly viewable at" and gives a Web address that looks something like this—http://docs.google.com/Doc?id=df6jmv7k_4fr81hjcq. Use this URL to send to others or to link to the document from a Web page.

- Re-publish Document—Click this button to update the document's published version with its current version. When you've left the Automatically Re-publish When Changes Are Made box unchecked, click this button to publish edits you've made to the document.

- Stop Publishing—This button cancels publication of the document. When you've stopped publishing a document, people who try to visit the page get an error message: "Sorry, the page (or document) you have requested does not exist."

- Automatically Re-publish When Changes Are Made—As mentioned earlier, checking this box means that Google updates the public version of the document whenever it saves your edits.
- Track Visitor Stats for Your Published Documents—You can use Google Analytics to see how many people are visiting this published document. See the "Tracking Visitors" section that follows for more information about this feature.

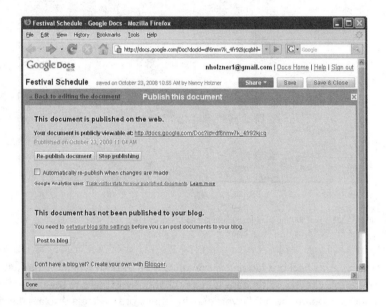

Figure 5.9
This is what the Publish This Document page looks like after you've published the document.

Tracking Visitors

Google offers a program called Google Analytics, which lets you track information about who visits your Web page. Before you can track visitors to your published Google Docs document, you need a Google Analytics account. (If you don't already have one, you can sign up at www.google.com/analytics.)

To track traffic to your published Google Docs documents, go to the Docs home page and click the upper-right Settings link to open to the Settings page's General tab, shown in Figure 5.10. Find the Track Published Documents section (circled in the figure) and turn on the checkbox labeled Track Visits to My Documents Using Google Analytics. Next, type or paste your Analytics tracking code, which looks something like UA-7654321-1, into the Google Analytics Tracking Code text box. (You can find and copy this code on the Analytics Settings page of your Google Analytics account.) Click Save.

Now you're set up to track the documents you publish. To check tracking statistics, sign in to your Google Analytics account and click View Reports. The page that opens shows visitor statistics for your published Google Docs documents.

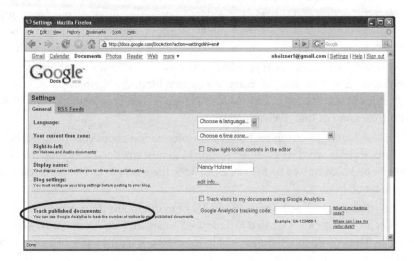

Figure 5.10
The Track Published Documents section of the Settings Page is where you set up Google Docs to work with your Google Analytics account.

Publishing a Document as a Blog Post

A blog, short for Web log, is an online journal where you can post your thoughts on any topic under the sun. Many blogs have themes, such as politics, recipes, or movie reviews; others chronicle the blogger's daily life, and still others are just random musings. A blog's articles, called *posts*, usually appear with the most recent at the top of the page.

If you have a blog, you can write a post in Google Docs and then publish it straight to your blog. First, set up Docs to work with your blog. When you've done that, you can publish any document you create as a blog post.

 Don't have a blog? Head over to www.blogger.com to start one. Blogger is a Google service, so it's easy to integrate with Docs.

Step 1: Setting up Docs to Work with Your Blog

To make Docs work directly with your blog, go to the Docs home page and click the upper-right Settings link. This opens the General tab of the Settings page (shown in Figure 5.10). In the Blog Settings section, click the Edit Info link. The Blog Site Settings box, shown in Figure 5.11, opens.

In the Blog Site Settings box, fill out this info:

- Existing Blog Service—You have two choices here:
  - Hosted Provider (like Blogger, etc.)—If you use one of the following blogging services, select this option and choose your service from the list: Blogger.com, BlogHarbor.com, BlogWare.com, LiveJournal.com, SquareSpace.com, WordPress.com. Most bloggers use one of these services.
  - My Own Server/Custom—If your blog is part of your Web site (not hosted by one of the providers just mentioned) or you use a custom blog, choose this option. The dialog box changes so you can tell Google which API (application programming interface) your blog uses and its URL (Web address).
- Existing Blog Settings—In this section type in information about your blog settings: your user name and password (so Google can sign in to post the document) and if you've got more than one blog hosted by the same provider, the blog's ID or title (so Google can post to the right blog).
- Options—If you want the title of your document to do double duty as the title of your blog post, turn on the checkbox labeled Include the Document Title When Posting. Not all blog services will let you do this, though. So if it doesn't work, it's probably because of the way your service is set up.

To see whether you've set things up correctly, click the Test button. Google tries to sign in to your blog, using the information you gave it and then opens a dialog box letting you know the results. If Google was able to sign in successfully, you get this message: "Test completed. Your settings appear to be correct." If Google can't sign in, adjust the settings in the Blog Site Settings box and click Test again.

When everything's all set up, click OK to save these settings.

Step 2: Post a Document to Your Blog

Writing your blog post is the time-consuming part—posting a document to your blog is a snap. Just follow these steps:

1. Open the document you want to post to your blog and click Share, Publish as Web Page. This opens the Publish This Document page you saw back in Figure 5.8.
2. In the bottom part of the page, click the Post to Blog button. Google opens a box that asks you to confirm that you want to post the document to your blog now.
3. Click OK.

That's it! Google posts the document to your blog.

After you've posted a document to your blog, you can update or remove that post, just as you can a document you've published on the Web. If you've edited the document and want to update the associated blog post, come back to the Publish This Document page and click the Republish Post button. If you want to take the document off your blog, click Remove from Blog. In either case, you'll need to click OK to confirm.

Blog Site Settings

Existing Blog Service

◉ Hosted provider (like Blogger, etc.)   ○ My own server / custom

Provider: [Select which blog provider to use   ▾]

Existing Blog Settings

User Name: [   ]   Password: [   ]

Blog ID/Title: [   ]

Optional. If you don't specify one, we'll use the first blog we find, and you can change it later

Options

☑ Include the document title when posting (if supported)

To automatically categorize your blog posts, just tag your documents with a category name you already use on your blog site.

[OK]   [Cancel]   [Test]

Figure 5.11
Before you can post a document to your blog, you need to give Google access to your blog.

Collaborating on a Document

Earlier in this chapter, you learned how to share a document. This section tells you what happens next, as you and your collaborators work on a document together.

In Google Docs, collaboration happens in real time—that means that several people (up to 10) can work on the document simultaneously. If you're at the office, Bill is working from home today, and Margaret is at a coffee shop across town, as collaborators you can all work on the same copy of the document, all at the same time. When Google saves the document, all the edits from all the collaborators are saved together. No more emailing a blizzard of attachments, hoping the document you've got is the current version.

After you've invited some people to collaborate on your document (see earlier section), those people can open and work on the document right away. The document you've shared appears on their Docs list (at the top of the All Items list and also under your name in the Shared With section). As with any other document, one click opens it in a new window.

As you work on a document, Google lets you know if someone else is editing it at the same time: A box appears in the lower-right part of the screen, showing the name of the other person who's editing the document now. (A similar notification appears on the other person's screen, giving your name.)

When Google saves the document, it merges all the changes the different collaborators have made since the last save. For this reason, it's a good idea to give each collaborator a clear idea of which part of the document he or she is responsible for: You're writing the Introduction, for example, as Margaret proofreads the first two sections, and Bill types up the Bibliography. Occasionally, you might find that a sentence paragraph you're working on changes in a way you don't expect. For example, perhaps you're typing a heading for a new section, *Policies and Procedures,* and at the same moment, Margaret across town is typing *Company Policies* on the same line. When Google attempts to merge the changes to the document, you're likely to get something like *Policies and Procedures Company Policies* on that line. When that happens, call or email your collaborator and hash out who's editing what.

 If a collaborator messes up your document, you can always roll back changes to an earlier version. See the section "Working with a Document's Revision History."

After you (or any of your collaborators) have edited a document and saved the changes, the most up-to-date version is the one on everyone's Docs list. So you never have to worry about someone working on an obsolete version of the document.

Collaboration and Offline Editing

When several people work on the document at once, Google saves and merges all their edits. What happens, though, when you (or one of your collaborators) work on a shared document while offline? As Chapter 3 explains, thanks to Google Gears, you can edit documents even when you're not connected to the Internet. When you reconnect to the Internet and sign into Docs, Google automatically updates the online document with the changes you made while offline.

But what if the online document has changed in the meantime? While you were working offline, perhaps Margaret and Bill were both editing the document online. How does Google synch your changes with the changes your collaborators have made in the meantime?

In that case, when you sign back in, Google displays a message box telling you that your offline editing conflicts with changes collaborators have made in the meantime—and that Google is discarding your text. As part of the message, Google shows you the text it's about to discard. If you want, you can copy that text, click OK to discard your changes, and then paste the text you copied into the document.

 Google uploads the edits you made and saves them as a version before checking to see whether there's a conflict with the document's online version. That means you can find the version you edited while offline in the document's revision history. See "Working with a Document's Revision History" to learn how to find a previous version, compare it with other versions, and revert to the version you want.

Using Color-Coded Comments

Simultaneous, real-time collaborating can do a lot to speed up the process of creating and editing a document. Another helpful Docs feature for collaboration is the ability to insert comments into a document. Comments are highlighted text that stand out from the text of the document, so you can ask questions and make suggestions without directly altering the text itself. Each comment is "stamped" with the name of the person who made the comment and the date and time it was made.

Inserting a Comment

To put a comment into a document, click to put the cursor where you want the comment to appear. Next, click Insert, Comment. As Figure 5.12 shows, Google inserts the comment, with your name and the current date and time. Sample text, *type here,* is already selected by Google, so all you have to do to replace that sample text is start typing. When you're done commenting, simply click outside the comment.

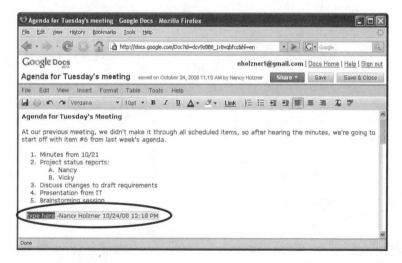

Figure 5.12
Inserting a comment into a document.

 When you publish a document on the Web, the document's comments do not appear in it. Comments may or may not appear when you export the document: They're visible in a PDF file, for example, but not if you export as a Word or OpenOffice document.

Choosing a Comment Color

The default color to highlight comments is yellow, but there are other highlighting colors to choose from. When you've got several collaborators on a document, it's a good idea to assign each commenter a particular color to highlight their comments. That way, you can see at a glance who made which comment.

To assign a color to a comment, click the comment. The context menu shown in Figure 5.13 appears. In the menu's Comment Color section, select one of these options:

- Yellow
- Orange
- Pink
- Green
- Blue
- Purple

When you click a color, Google closes the context menu and applies the color you chose to the comment's background.

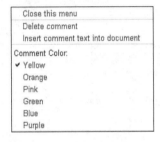

Figure 5.13
Click a comment to make this context menu appear.

 When you assign a new color to your own comments, subsequent comments you insert also have that color. You can change the color of a collaborator's comment as well, but doing so has no effect on that person's future comments.

Editing a Comment

To change the text of a comment, double-click the comment and start typing. You can edit your own comment or anyone else's. In fact, any collaborator can edit any comment in the document. If you want to respond to someone's comment, the best idea is to insert a comment of your own next to or below it. That makes it clear who made which comment.

Making a Comment Part of the Document

Although you can see a document's comments when you edit the document in the Google Docs text editor, those comments aren't visible when you publish the document on the Web. If someone's made a good comment, added relevant information to a report, for example, you may want to convert that comment into part of the document's text.

To make a comment part of the document, click the comment to bring up the context menu shown in Figure 5.13. From that menu, choose Insert Comment Text into Document. Google removes the highlighting from the comment, making the comment part of the document's text.

 When you convert a comment into document text, you've got a little editing to do. Google converts the comment itself but also the name, date, and time stamps. Be sure to delete that extra info from the document.

Deleting a Comment

When a comment has been addressed or is simply no longer needed, you can delete it from the document. To delete a comment (your own or someone else's—any collaborator can delete any comment), click the comment; from the context menu, choose Delete Comment. Google immediately deletes the comment from the document.

Working with a Document's Revision History

As Chapter 2 explained, when you work on a document, Google saves your changes every few minutes, so your work is always backed up. What's more, those backups are always accessible to you, in case you ever need to roll back a document to a previous version. So if you or one of your collaborators takes a document down the wrong track, you can easily find an earlier version and make it the current one.

Viewing Revisions

To see a document's revision history, open the document and select File, Revision History. This opens a page that looks like the one in Figure 5.14. This page shows a list of versions of the document; each version is basically a snapshot that Google took of the document at a particular point in time. Google tells you the revision number, when that version was saved, and a brief overview of the changes in that version.

When you look at a document's revision history, you may be surprised to see how many versions of the document Google has recorded. This is because of all those frequent saves. It may look as though Google has skipped some versions—for example, in Figure 5.14, it looks as though the versions jump from Revision 59 to Revision 74. If you look at the right side of the list, however, you'll see a link: Revisions 59–74. If you think the revision you're looking for is in that range, click the link to show those revisions.

To see a previous version of the document, click its revision number. When you open a previous version of the document, what you see on the screen is a read-only version of the document. There's no formatting toolbar above the document, just these actions:

- Back to Revision History—Click this link to return to the list of revisions.
- Older/Newer—If you're hunting for a particular version of a document and you're sure the version you're looking at now isn't the one you want, use these buttons to look backward and forward through other versions.

Figure 5.14
A document's revision history shows a list of previous versions of the document.

■ Revert to This One—Found the version you want? Great! Click this button to make it the current version. Google asks for confirmation; click OK, and Google makes this version the current one, opening it in the text editor.

 When you revert to a previous version, the version of the document that *was* the current one (that is, before you reverted) itself becomes a version in the document's revision history. Even so, if you're not sure whether you really want to replace the current version with a previous one, it's a good idea to make a copy of the document before you revert.

Comparing Versions

When a document has gone through a lot of revisions, you may find that you want to compare versions to see which is the one you want. Google lets you compare two versions of a document, highlighting differences between the versions and letting you know who made which change.

To compare two versions, open the document and select File, Revision History. When the revision history list opens, find the two versions you wish to compare and check the checkboxes to the left of their revision numbers. Then at the top of the screen, click the Compare Checked button.

Figure 5.15 shows an example comparison page. The top of the page identifies which versions you're comparing. To the right, the Authors section lists the collaborators who've worked on this document, assigning each a color. The main part of the page uses these colors to show who's made which changes to the more recent of the two versions, striking through deleted text and highlighting added text. For example, Figure 5.15 shows that Steve deleted *Prioritizing* and added *Happy hour*.

You can't revert to a version from the comparison page. To revert to one of these versions, make a note of the version you want and then go back to the revision list, click that version to view it, and then click Revert to This One.

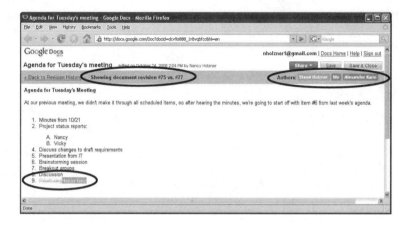

Figure 5.15
Comparing versions 75 and 77 to show changes collaborator's have made.

Introducing Spreadsheets

How did people ever keep track of things before there were spreadsheets? A spreadsheet is an unbelievably useful tool for organizing data. Your money, the kids' chores, your rare book collection, your holiday card list, your company's products or customers, your project team's tasks and due dates—anything that you can put in a list would probably work in a spreadsheet.

Of course, spreadsheets aren't just for storing information—they're for working with it. Sort data (to group customers by town, for example, or your rare books by value). Format data to emphasize deadlines or totals and set up rules that apply formatting automatically when certain conditions apply.

This chapter presents an introduction to spreadsheets: what they are and how to design a good spreadsheet and start working on it. Along the way, you'll also learn how to format your spreadsheet, create multiple sheets, work with rows and columns, and enter data more efficiently.

Spreadsheet Basics

Before you start creating spreadsheets in Google Docs, it's a good idea to get the basics down for what a spreadsheet is and how best to design one. Of course, if you're already a spreadsheet power-user, feel free to skip this section and dive into the specifics about getting started with Docs spreadsheets.

What Is a Spreadsheet?

A spreadsheet stores, organizes, and performs calculations on data. Its layout is a grid made up of horizontal rows and vertical columns, like a big table. Where a row and column intersect is a rectangular box, called a *cell*. Cells hold individual pieces of information, such as a number, date, currency amount, name, or other text. A cell can also be empty or hold a *formula*, a mathematical equation that calculates a value (more on formulas in Chapter 7, "Spreadsheets: Formulas and Charts").

A spreadsheet can hold an enormous amount of data. In Google Docs, each spreadsheet you create can have up to 256 columns, 200,000 cells, or 100 sheets—whichever comes first. Your spreadsheet can have as many rows as it needs (within those limits).

Spreadsheets are often used for working with financial data, such as a family budget, business expenses, or investment portfolio information. You can use a spreadsheet, though, to hold and organize other kinds of information as well—your CD collection, a newsletter mailing list, employee information, a weekly work schedule, and so on. Spreadsheets' flexibility is what makes them so popular.

What Can a Cell Contain?

Earlier, we said that cells contain data, that is, pieces of information. You can put just about any kind of data you desire into a spreadsheet, using one of these datatypes:

- Text—In a spreadsheet, text can be letters and words, numbers, or a combination of both. The text you put in a spreadsheet might be labels, descriptions, names, addresses, notes, phone numbers, employee IDs—whatever you want.

- Numbers—You could easily argue that numbers are the raison d'être for spreadsheets because a spreadsheet is such a powerful tool for performing calculations. You can format numbers to represent a particular kind of data, such as currency amounts, percentages, dates, and times.

- Formulas—As Chapter 7 explains, a formula performs calculations on the data in your spreadsheet. Formulas range from simple operations, such as adding or averaging a column of numbers, to complex statistical or engineering calculations. When you insert a formula into a cell, what the cell displays is the result of that formula.

What Makes a Good Spreadsheet Design?

Anyone who works with spreadsheets will tell you that a spreadsheet needs two things to be effective: good design and good data. And these two qualities go hand in hand. A well designed spreadsheet calls for the best data. In addition, good spreadsheet design facilitates the main goals of working with spreadsheets:

- To understand the purpose of the spreadsheet
- To read the spreadsheet's data
- To use that data for analysis
- To notice important aspects of the data
- To update the spreadsheet easily

Let's look at a quick, simple example to illustrate spreadsheet design. Say you want to set up a spreadsheet to track your progress on a project: a book or report you're writing. This spreadsheet will hold several kinds of information: segments of the project (these could be sections or chapters; we'll call them chapters in the example), milestones, and the dates those milestones are reached. Knowing the kinds of information your spreadsheet will track, you can start to design it.

Give the Spreadsheet a Title

A title makes the spreadsheet's purpose clear. For the example, you'd probably choose a title such as *Track Project* or *Book Progress*.

Define Columns

Column headings are important in a spreadsheet because they tell you the kind of information the column holds. Without clear headings, a spreadsheet can look like little more than a vast sea of numbers. With good headings, you know exactly what those numbers represent.

In the Book Progress spreadsheet, you might identify these points as the major milestones:

- First Draft Finished
- Second Draft Finished
- Edits Reviewed
- Revision Completed

Each of these columns will contain a particular type of data. In this case, all of the columns we've defined so far will contain dates so that we can track exactly when we achieved each milestone.

 To make column headings stand out, you might want to make them bold. Similarly, an especially important column, such as Revision complete, can be made to stand out by using a background color to highlight its contents. "Formatting a Spreadsheet" later in this chapter tells you how to emphasize parts of your spreadsheet using formatting tools.

Besides the date columns that show when you've reached each milestone, you can give your spreadsheet a little extra oomph with a different kind of column. Say you wanted a column to keep track of the number of pages in your book. This column—we'll call it Page Count—holds numbers. After you've used this column to hold the number of pages for a couple of chapters, you can create a formula to add up the numbers in the column and display a running total. (Chapter 7 tells you how to write a spreadsheet formula.)

 If you want a quick total of just some of the numbers in the column, simply select the numbers you want to add in that column. Google sums the selected numbers and displays the total in the bottom-right corner of your spreadsheet.

Define Rows

As we look at the milestones we've used to define our column headings, another question arises. What, exactly, are we tracking? We can't determine when we've reached a milestone until we know the answer to that question.

For a book, it makes sense to track the progress of each chapter. That breaks the information down into discrete, manageable units. So for Chapter 1, you can read across the row and track the dates that each milestone was met.

Defining the spreadsheet's rows as chapters means we need to add one more column heading: Chapters. Although it might seem obvious, as you read down the leftmost column, that it contains chapters, it's always a good idea to label columns so there's no doubt what the column holds. Also unlike the milestone columns, which hold dates, the Chapters column will hold plain old numbers. We won't use these numbers to perform any kind of calculation (the column could also be a text column), but formatting the data as numbers here automatically makes those numbers right-aligned, so the digits line up correctly as you read down the column.

Another benefit to defining the rows as chapters is that it's easy to update the spreadsheet if the book changes. For example, if we decide to add an appendix, all we need to do is start a new row called Appendix.

Ask Yourself Whether Your Spreadsheet's Design Serves Its Purpose

Use the list of goals for a spreadsheet defined at the beginning of this section as a checklist to see whether your spreadsheet is well designed:

- Is the spreadsheet's purpose clear?
- Is it clear what each piece of data represents?
- Are columns and rows clearly labeled?
- Is it easy to spot important information?
- Can the spreadsheet be updated easily? (If new information would force a drastic redesign of the spreadsheet, it's better to redesign it now rather than later when it's filled with data.)

Figure 6.1 shows the sample spreadsheet we've designed.

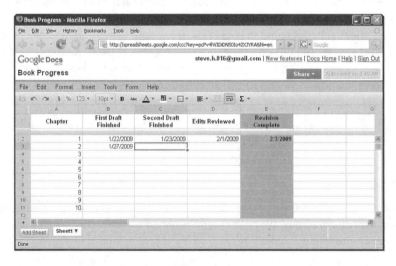

Figure 6.1
In this example columns and rows are clearly labeled, and highlighting makes important information easy to find.

One way to ensure ease of updating is to use formulas that automatically recalculate certain kinds of information when new information is added. The Page Count column mentioned earlier is an example: Whenever you add a new number to the Page Count column or change an existing number, the total updates automatically. As another example, a spreadsheet tracking customer purchases can automatically figure sales tax and recalculate the total when an order is changed. Chapter 7 covers spreadsheet formulas in detail.

Creating Your First Google Docs Spreadsheet

Ready to get started with your first Google Docs spreadsheet? Go to the Docs home page and click New, Spreadsheet to open a new, blank spreadsheet in the Docs spreadsheet editor, as shown in Figure 6.2.

 If you're already in the spreadsheet editor, you can create a new spreadsheet by selecting File, New, Spreadsheet.

The main area of the spreadsheet editor is the spreadsheet itself, the grid of rows and columns that will contain your data. Letters across the top of the spreadsheet and numbers along the left side identify the columns and rows that make up the spreadsheet. At the bottom left of the spreadsheet is a tab that names the sheet you're currently looking at. A brand-new spreadsheet has just one tab, with the generic name Sheet 1, but you can add more sheets, as "Working with Multiple Sheets" explains later in this chapter.

Above the spreadsheet are two bars for working with the spreadsheet: a menu bar and a formatting toolbar. You'll learn how to use these as we go through the specific actions you can take when working with a spreadsheet.

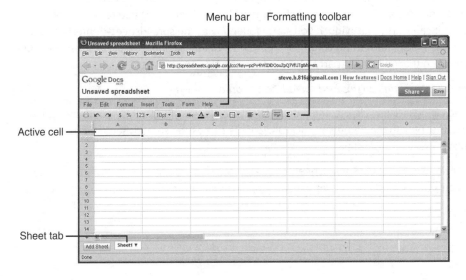

Figure 6.2
When you create a new spreadsheet, it opens in the spreadsheet editor.

Selecting Cells and Entering Data

To select a cell, click the cell you want, and a thick blue line appears around the cell to mark it as active. (As Figure 6.2 shows, when you create a new spreadsheet, the top left cell is the active cell.) When you've selected a cell, start typing to enter some data in it. To move to the next cell, press Tab or use your keyboard's arrow keys.

Besides selecting an individual cell, you can also select a group of adjacent cells, called a *cell range*. To select a range, click the top-left cell of the range. When you select the cell, a small square appears in its lower-right corner; this square is called a handle. Place your mouse pointer over the handle so that the cursor becomes a crosshairs. When it does, click and drag horizontally or vertically to select the group of cells you want. As you move the mouse, the cells you're selecting are shaded so you can see the extent of the range. When you've selected the range you want, let go of the mouse button.

 Another way to select a range of cells is to hold down the Shift key as you use the arrow keys to expand or contract the range.

You can also select entire rows or columns. To select an entire row, click the number at the row's far left. To select a column, click the letter above the column. Clicking a number or letter in this manner, then dragging the mouse selects multiple rows or columns, respectively.

 To select the entire spreadsheet, click the blue square in the upper-left corner, which is above row 1 and to the left of column A.

Saving a Spreadsheet

As with its word processor, Google automatically saves your spreadsheet every few minutes. Unlike the word processor, though, Google's spreadsheet editor needs you to save a spreadsheet first before it can start autosaving. If you start working with the spreadsheet—entering data, selecting cell ranges, formatting columns, and so on—before saving the spreadsheet, a warning box pops up in the lower-right part of the screen, with this message:

Careful. You're editing an unsaved spreadsheet. Start autosaving.

Start Autosaving is a link; click it, and a dialog box opens asking you to give your new spreadsheet a name. Type in the name and click OK. Google names the spreadsheet and from now on autosaves it every few minutes.

You can also save your new spreadsheet by clicking the upper-right Save button. This button appears only on a brand-new, never-yet-save spreadsheet. After you've saved the spreadsheet for the first time, Google replaces the Save button with a notice that tells you when it last saved the document for you.

When you're done working with the spreadsheet for now, click File, Save & Close. Google saves the spreadsheet and closes the spreadsheet editor's window.

Creating a New Spreadsheet from a Template

Although you can custom-design your own spreadsheet from scratch, Google also gives you the option of using a *template* as a basis for a new spreadsheet. A template is a sample spreadsheet already set up for a particular purpose. For example, if you want to create a spreadsheet to plan and track your family's monthly budget, you don't have to start from square one: Choose a budget planner from Google's available template to create your own budget-planning spreadsheet. You can use the template as it is or tweak it to suit your own needs.

Using a template as the basis for a new spreadsheet can save you a lot of work, so let's see just how easy it can be. When you create a new spreadsheet from a template, you take one of these routes, depending on your starting point:

- From the Google Docs home page—Click New, From Template to open Google's Template Gallery. There, click the Spreadsheets tab.
- From the spreadsheet editor—Click File, New, From Template. The Template Gallery opens with the Spreadsheets tab already selected.

Figure 6.3 shows the Spreadsheets tab of Google's Template Gallery, which has tons of templates, ranging from amortization schedules and teacher grade books to invoices and a checklist for planning your wedding. You find and select a spreadsheet from this library in the same way you'd use a template to create a new word-processing document (described in Chapter 3, "Formatting Documents"). To find a template, use the search box at the top of the page or browse a category from the list on the left. To find a family budget template, for example, you might search for *budget* or browse the Personal Finance category.

To get a close-up look of a template before you use it, click the Preview link; the template opens in a new window. To create your own spreadsheet from the template, click its Use This Template button, either from the list of templates or from the preview page of the template you want. Google opens the template in your spreadsheet editor—ready for you to start entering data—and adds it to your Docs list.

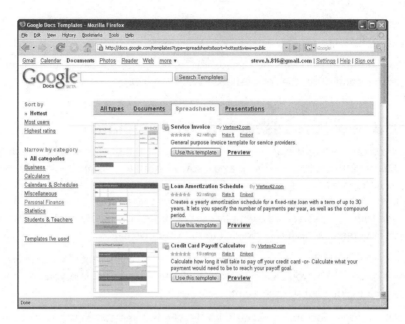

Figure 6.3
Google's Templates Gallery may have just the spreadsheet design you're looking for.

Formatting a Spreadsheet

As you've seen, a blank spreadsheet is a huge grid of rows, columns, and cells. In addition, that blank spreadsheet treats all cell content in the same way, using the Normal format. Normal format can be fine for numbers (it treats them as everyday, run-of-the-mill numbers), but sometimes you're using numbers in a more specialized sense, and you want your spreadsheet to reflect that. If you're planning the family budget, for example, you're going to want to treat expenditures as dollar amounts. And that means you have to apply formatting to certain parts of the budget spreadsheet so that Google will know those parts refer to money, not to (for example) quantity.

So as you work with a spreadsheet, you'll want to apply different kinds of formatting. Besides formatting different kinds of numbers in different ways (currency, percentage, and so on), you can choose a standard format for dates and times. You might want to call attention to a particular row, column, or cell through formatting or highlighting. This section tells you how to do all that and then goes on to explain how you can set up formatting rules to look for certain criteria and, when these are met, to apply formatting automatically, such as displaying a date in red to get viewers' attention.

Formatting Numbers

Spreadsheets hold many different kinds of numbers—dates, dollar amounts, percentages, and so on—and you want to distinguish among these different kinds. Doing so makes your spreadsheet much easier to read and understand at a glance. In addition, using the right numeric format makes sure that your formulas (Chapter 7) are accurate.

When you format a column's numbers, you're telling Google how to treat those numbers—whether to add a dollar or a percent sign, for example, and whether to use a decimal point or round numbers up or down. Table 6.1 shows the different number formats you can use in Google Docs spreadsheets, along with an example of how each format looks in practice.

Table 6.1   Number Formats for Google Docs Spreadsheets

Format	Example
Rounded	2,500
2 Decimals	2,500.00
Financial rounded	(2,500)
Financial	(2,500.00)
Scientific (for large numbers)	1.25E+12 (This number is equivalent to 1,250,000,000,000.)
Currency rounded	$2,500
Currency	$2,500.00
Percent rounded	25%
Percent	25.00%

Choose the cell or range of cells you want to format. For example, to apply a format to all the cells in a column, click the letter above the column you want (this selects the entire column). If you want to quick-format the column as a rounded currency amount or a percentage, click the Format as Currency or Format as Percentage button, respectively, on the toolbar above the spreadsheet (see Figure 6.4).

Otherwise, click the More Formats button on the toolbar: 123 with a down arrow next to it. From the menu that appears, select the format you want. Google immediately applies it to the column you chose.

 Tip 4U If you work in a currency besides dollars or in multiple currencies you'll be glad to know that Google offers a range of currencies to format money-related numbers. To choose a currency, select the cells you want to format and then click More Formats, More Currencies and then choose the currency you want. Don't see that currency on the list? Click Custom Currencies, designate a symbol and position (to the left or right of the number) for the currency you're adding, and click OK.

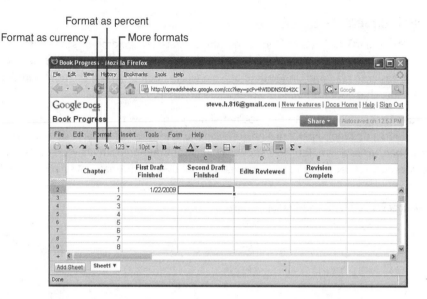

Figure 6.4
Use these buttons to format numbers in your spreadsheet.

Formatting Dates and Times

If your spreadsheet will contain dates, times, or both, you'll want to standardize their formats to avoid confusion. For example, maybe you format a date as 3/31/09, but folks in the London office use 31-Mar-2009. And while you're used to thinking in terms of AM and PM, your London counterparts use a 24-hour clock—for you, quitting time is 5:00 PM, but for them it's 17:00. It's much easier for everyone if you choose a standard format for dates and for times and use them consistently.

To choose and apply a format for dates or times, select the cell or cell range to which you're applying the format and then click the More Formats button. You can choose a format from the menu's date and time section or click More Formats to see the options shown in Figure 6.5. For each date or time format style, Google shows an example, so you know what the format will look like in the spreadsheet. Click the format you want, and Google applies it.

Formatting Appearance

In a sea of numbers and other data, it can be easy for important information to get lost. You can make sure that doesn't happen by formatting that important info in a way that makes it stand out.

Figure 6.5
Google offers many styles for formatting dates and times.

As Figure 6.6 shows, the spreadsheet editor has a toolbar above the spreadsheet itself. This toolbar has these formatting buttons:

- Font Size—When you click this button, your options range from 6 to 36 points. Google's standard of 10 points is good for most cell data. Smaller can work well for notes and larger for emphasis.

- Bold—Make a cell or cell range stand out by formatting it in bold.

- Strikethrough—This formatting puts a horizontal line through the text or numbers in the cells you've selected. You might want to use this, for example, to emphasize that a deadline has changed, striking through the old deadline and highlighting the new one in bold or with color.

- Text Color—Click this button and then choose from a palette of colors to change the text in the cell(s) from black to the color you select.

- Background Color—Define cell ranges or highlight important information by clicking this button and selecting the background color you want.

- Borders—This is another good way to set off a cell or range of cells by outlining them with a border. Click this button and then choose from eight border styles.

- Align—This button gives you options for aligning a cell's contents horizontally (left, center, or right alignment) or vertically (top, middle, or bottom alignment) .

- Merge Across/Break Apart—It can be helpful to identify sections of a spreadsheet by merging several cells and then typing in a title for that section. When you merge cells across, a single cell stretches across several columns, instead of a being the intersection of one row and one column. If you select a merged cell, this button changes to Break Across; clicking it will break the merged cell into individual cells again.

- Wrap Text—If a cell holds a lot of text, some of that text may not display. When you tell Google to wrap the text, it means that the cell lengthens to display all the text it holds. So instead of being tall enough to display a single line of text, the cell (and its row) expands so that it's tall enough to display two or more rows of text. This button toggles text wrapping on and off.

To apply any of these kinds of formatting, choose the cell or cell range you want to format and then click the appropriate toolbar button. If you make a mistake, click the toolbar's Undo button.

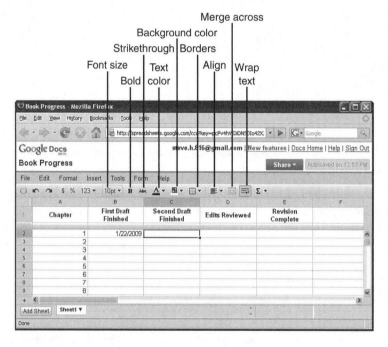

Figure 6.6
Use the toolbar to format cells in your spreadsheet.

The menu bar's Format button repeats some of the formats in the toolbar and offers a few others. Select a cell or range, click Format, and then choose from one of these options: Font (six font styles), Bold, Italic, Underline, Strikethrough.

To remove all the formatting from a section of your spreadsheet, choose the cell or range you want and then click Format, Clear Styles.

Creating Formatting Rules

Formatting rules let you set up criteria that determine when to apply color to certain cells—automatically. For example, you might want to highlight in red due dates that have passed or expenses that go over budget. Sure, you can hunt down data and highlight it yourself, but why spend the time when you can tell Google to do that for you?

Setting up a formatting rule tells Google to apply specific formatting—text or background color—to a cell or a range of cells under certain conditions. To write a formatting rule, follow these steps:

1. In the spreadsheet for which you're creating the rule, select the cell or cell range to which the rule will apply.

2. Select Format, Change Colors with Rules. This opens the dialog box shown in Figure 6.7.

3. Set the condition for applying the color change. In the first drop-down, choose a condition for text, dates, or numbers, such as Text Contains, Text Does Not Contain, Date Is After, Is Equal To, Is Between, and so on. You can also apply a color change when a cell is empty.

4. Set the specifics for applying the color change. These depend on what you choose for the first drop-down list. For example, if you choose Is Between from the first drop-down, the dialog box presents two text boxes, where you can enter two numbers or dates that define the range. Or if you select Date Is After, the dialog box presents a drop-down list from which you can choose a date such as Today, Tomorrow, In the Past Week, or an exact date that you specify.

5. Select the color change you want to apply. When you check the Text or the Background box, Google displays its color palette. Click a color to select it. You can change the text color, the background color, or both.

6. If you want to create another rule for the same cell or cell range, click Add Another Rule, and the dialog box expands. Repeat steps 3 through 5. When you're done, click the Save Rules button to apply the rule or rules you've created.

Figure 6.7
When a cell or cell range meets conditions you set, Google applies the color formatting you specify here.

As you create formatting rules, Google adds them to the Change Colors Based on Rules dialog box. To edit a rule, select Format, Change Colors with Rules. When the dialog box opens, find the rule you want and change its criteria or colors.

If you don't need a particular rule anymore—for example, a deadline has been met and no longer needs highlighting—you can remove that rule. Open the spreadsheet and select Format, Change Colors with Rules. In the Change Colors Based on Rules dialog box, find the rule you want to delete and click the x to its right. Google deletes the rule immediately. Click Save Rules to close the dialog box.

Working with Multiple Sheets

When you create a new Google Docs spreadsheet, you start off with a single sheet. As you work on a spreadsheet, however, you may find that you need more than one sheet to collect separate but related data. If you use a spreadsheet to schedule employees, for example, you may want to use one sheet per month to make the schedule easy to read.

You can tell how many individual sheets a spreadsheet has by looking in the lower-left part of the screen. As Figure 6.8 shows, the current sheet appears as a tab; other sheets appear as links. Click a link to select that sheet. To add a new sheet, click the Add Sheet button. Google adds the new sheet to the right of the currently selected one.

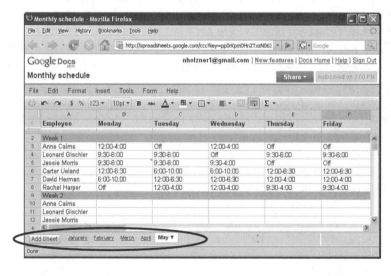

Figure 6.8
Work with multiple sheets in the lower-left part of the screen.

When you double-click an individual sheet's name (or click the selected sheet's tab), you can choose one of these actions from the context menu that appears:

- Delete—When you choose Delete, a dialog box appears, asking whether you're sure you want to delete the sheet and all its data. If you are, click OK. (If you delete the sheet by mistake, immediately click the toolbar's Undo button to bring it back.)

- Duplicate—This makes an exact copy of the current sheet, including its data, and inserts it to the right of the current sheet. Google names the new sheet *Copy of <sheet name>*, so if you're copying a sheet called *Quarter 1 Grades,* for example, the new sheet's name is *Copy of Quarter 1 Grades.* Copying a sheet is useful when you want to use the existing sheet's setup; make a duplicate and then clear its data (see upcoming section), leaving just the existing structure, ready for new information.

- Rename—When you choose this option, a dialog box appears. Type in the sheet's new name and click OK. This option is handy when you discover a typo or you want to give a duplicate sheet its own name, rather than *Copy of <sheet name>*.

- Move Left/Move Right—Choose one of these options to move the sheet in the direction you specify. If the sheet you're moving is first or last among the sheets, you'll see only one direction (because the sheet can't move any farther in the other direction).

Working with Data

Earlier in this chapter, you saw how easy it is to get some data into your spreadsheet: simply click inside a cell and type. And while that gets you started with Google Docs spreadsheets, this section takes you to the next level. Learn how to import existing spreadsheet data into Google Docs, get up to speed with data-entry tips and tricks, work with rows and columns, sort data, and move data from Google Docs to another spreadsheet program. It's all covered here.

Importing Data into Google Docs

If you've been working with spreadsheets for a while, you've probably got data that you'd like to move into Google Docs—and you definitely want to do that as quickly and painlessly as possible. When you have spreadsheet data that lives outside of Google Docs, you can create a new spreadsheet from that data by importing the info into Docs.

Before you import a spreadsheet, keep in mind that imported spreadsheets must be 1MB or smaller and in one of these formats:

- Microsoft Excel (.xls)—If you have spreadsheets in Excel, you can import them directly into Docs.

 If you use Excel 2007, be sure to save your spreadsheet in .xls format before you import it. (To do that, click the Office Button, then select Save As, Excel 97-2003 Workbook.) At this writing, you can't import .xlsx files into Google Docs.

- OpenDocument Spreadsheet (.ods)—This is the format used by the spreadsheet programs of OpenOffice.org and StarOffice, among others.

- Comma-separated values (.csv)—This format contains pieces of data separated by commas. Most spreadsheet programs let you export or import data using this format.

- Tab-separated values (.tsv)—This is like a CSV file except that the pieces of data are separated by tabs rather than commas.

- Text file (.txt)—As its name suggests, this kind of file holds text: unformatted letters and numbers. If you've got a text file set up like a table (one record per row with tabs between each record's individual pieces of information), you use the text file to create a new spreadsheet. If you want to import a text file, start the import from the spreadsheet editor; otherwise, Google will interpret the file as a word-processed document, not a spreadsheet.

 If your spreadsheet file is password-protected, Google can't import it.

The steps for importing a file depend on your starting point:

- From the Google Docs home page—Click the Upload button. On the page that opens, click the Browse button. This opens a new window; find and select the file you're importing and then click Open. Back in Google Docs, click Upload File.

- From the spreadsheet editor—Click File, Import. This opens the Import File dialog box. Click Browse and in the window that opens, select the file you want and click Open.

Whichever method you use, Google imports the data, using it to create a new spreadsheet. The Docs spreadsheet has the same title as the file you imported.

Exporting Data from Google Docs

Just as you can import data from other programs into a Google Docs spreadsheet, you can also transfer data from a Docs spreadsheet into another program. This is called *exporting,* and it's useful when you want to download the spreadsheet to your computer and then work on it offline, using a program such as Microsoft Excel or OpenOffice.org Calc.

 As Chapter 3 explains, you can work on Google Docs word-processing documents offline if you have Google installed. Not so with spreadsheets. Currently, Gears lets you view but not edit or create your Docs spreadsheets when you're not connected to the Internet.

When you export spreadsheet data from Google Docs, you can save it in one of these formats:

- Microsoft Excel (.xls)
- OpenDocument Spreadsheet (.ods)
- Comma-separated values (.csv)
- Text file (.txt)
- Hypertext markup language (.html)
- Portable document format (.pdf)

The exporting process varies, depending on the format you choose to export the file. The next three sections explain.

Exporting as an XLS or ODS File

If you want to export the spreadsheet's data into Excel, OpenOffice.org Calc, or StarOffice Calc, open the spreadsheet you want and click File, Export. From the menu that appears, select .xls (for Excel) or .ods (for Calc).

Your Web browser opens a dialog box asking how you want to handle the file. There, choose to save the file to your computer (in the format you chose) or to open it in the appropriate program. Your computer downloads the file and then, depending on what you chose, either saves it or opens it.

 If you exported data from a Docs spreadsheet, worked on it in another program, and now want to update your Docs spreadsheet with the new info, you can. Open the spreadsheet that will receive the new data and then click File, Upload New Version. In the dialog box that opens, click Browse to find and select the updated file on your computer and then click OK. Google automatically imports the new data and uses it to update your Docs spreadsheet.

Exporting as a CSV, HTML, or TXT File

When you export spreadsheet data in one of these formats, Google converts the file to the format you choose and opens it in a new browser window. (For this reason, you can export just one sheet at a time when you choose one of these formats).

Open the spreadsheet you want (if the spreadsheet has multiple sheets, select the sheet whose data you're exporting). Click File, Export and then choose one of these options:

- .csv Sheet Only
- .html Sheet Only
- .txt Sheet Only

Your Web browser opens the spreadsheet data in a new window. How it looks depends on the format you chose:

- CSV shows one record per line with commas separating pieces of information. This kind of file does not preserve your spreadsheet's formatting, just its data.
- HTML looks like a table and shows your spreadsheet's formatting.
- TXT shows one record per line with tabs separating pieces of information.

After the exported file has opened in a new window, use your Web browser's File menu to save the file. Then you can reopen it in the program you want.

 Just about all spreadsheet programs understand CSV format, so if you use a spreadsheet program other than Excel or Calc, exporting data as a CSV file will most likely get the data into your spreadsheet program.

Exporting as a PDF

PDF stands for *portable document format,* and what it means in practice is that your document's formatting gets preserved no matter what platform you use to create it or to view it (such as Windows XP or Vista, Mac, or Linux). Simply open the document in a PDF reader such as Adobe Reader, Adobe Acrobat, or Foxit, and you can read it as it was formatted. And as you'll see in "Printing a Spreadsheet" later in this chapter, the first step in printing a spreadsheet is exporting it in this format.

When you want to export spreadsheet data as a PDF, open the spreadsheet and choose File, Export, .pdf. This opens the Export to PDF dialog box shown in Figure 6.9.

The dialog box has four sections for you to fill out:

- What Parts? Choose whether you're exporting just the current sheet or all sheets.
- How Big? Choose Fit to Width (which shrinks or expands the text to suit the size of the page) or Actual Size (which, for large spreadsheets, may overrun the page). Also in this section is a checkbox labeled Repeat Row Headers on Each Page, which is checked by default. If your spreadsheet will run to multiple pages, it's a good idea to leave it checked.
- Which Way? Select Landscape (horizontally oriented) or Portrait (vertically oriented).
- What Paper Size? You've got three choices:
    - Letter (8.5 inches ? 11 inches)
    - Legal (8.5 inches ? 14 inches)
    - A4 (210 mm ? 297 mm)—If you're not up on the metric system, that's about 8.25" ? 11.7."

After you've made your selections, click Export. Your Web browser opens a dialog box asking whether you want to save the file or open it in an appropriate program. Make your selection, and your computer downloads the PDF file.

Entering Data

Anyone who's ever worked with spreadsheets knows that entering data can get awfully repetitive. You can speed up your work and lower the boredom factor by using the techniques in this section to enter data more efficiently.

Using Auto-Fill

Auto-Fill is a helpful feature when you're repeating a set of data and you don't want to have to type the same thing over and over (and over) again. For example, imagine you have a spreadsheet that tracks, on a weekly basis, when your organization's meetings rooms are in use. At the start of a new week, you don't want to have to type in all the meeting rooms' names all over again. When you use Auto-Fill, you don't have to. Just choose a range of cells and use Auto-Fill to copy their contents into an adjacent group of cells.

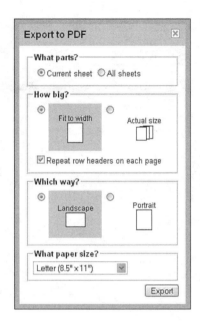

Figure 6.9
When you export spreadsheet data as a PDF, choose the data you want to export and how you want it displayed.

Here's how to use Auto-Fill:

1. Select the range of cells you're copying. Notice the small blue box (called a handle) that appears in the lower-right corner of the range.

2. Put your mouse pointer right on top of the handle. When the cursor becomes a cross hairs, click and drag in the direction you want to Auto-Fill.

3. As you drag, a dashed gray line shows the Auto-Fill area—the cells to which Google will copy your original selection. Figure 6.10 shows what this looks like.

4. When the dashed gray line surrounds the cells you want to fill, let go of the mouse button.

Like magic, Google pastes the contents of the cells you originally selected into the Auto-Fill area in order and repeated as many times as necessary to fill in the Auto-Fill area.

Auto-Fill can do better than just copying what you've already typed. It can also recognize common patterns—as long as you give it enough information to recognize the pattern. Say you're typing the names of the months of the year across your spreadsheet, one month per column. If you type January in column A, February in column B, and March in column C, you can stop typing right there. Select the three months you've typed so far, and use the lower-right handle to drag the Auto-Fill area nine columns to the right. When you let go of the mouse button, Google fills in the other months of the year across the spreadsheet.

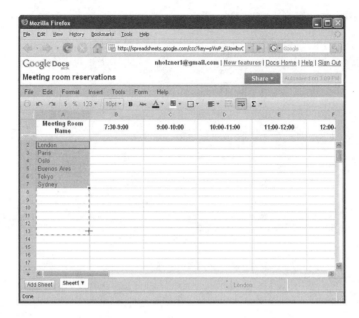

Figure 6.10
Auto-Fill in action: the contents of the first six cells will be pasted into the six cells below them.

Copying Data

Auto-Fill is fast and easy when you're copying data to next-door-neighbor cells, but you might want to copy cells' content to other places, as well, such as another part of the spreadsheet or a different sheet.

To copy the contents of a cell or range of cells, select what you want to copy and then use one of these methods:

- Right-click (Control-click on a Mac) to open a context menu. Select Copy.
- Select Edit, Copy.
- On the keyboard, press Ctrl+C (Cmd-C on a Mac).

Tip 4U If you want to cut the data, rather than copying it, you can. Instead of the options just listed, right-click (Control-click) and choose Cut, select Edit, Cut, or press Ctrl+X (Cmd-X).

Next, go to where you want to paste in the cell contents you copied. You can select a range of cells or just click inside the first cell in the range. Use one of these methods to paste what you copied into the new location:

- Right-click (Control-click on a Mac) and select Paste from the context menu.
- Select Edit, Paste.
- On the keyboard, press Ctrl+V (Cmd-V on a Mac).

Google pastes the data into its new home. Note that what you paste into a cell overwrites the cell's current contents (if any).

 You can also paste just the values or just the format of what you copied. Click Edit and then select Paste Values Only or Paste Format Only.

Copying Down or Right

When you copy down or copy right, it means that you copy the contents of a single cell to a range of cells. To do this, select the cell whose contents you want to copy. With that cell selected, expand the range to include the cells you want to copy to. You can expand the range in any of these ways:

- By dragging the mouse.
- By holding down the Shift key as you use the down or right arrow key.
- By holding down the Shift key as you click the last cell in the range.

When you've selected the cell you're copying and the range of cells you're copying to, press Ctrl+D (Cmd-D on a Mac) to copy down or press Ctrl+R (Cmd-R) to copy right. Google pastes the contents of the cell into the range you selected.

Clearing Data

You can easily clear the data from a single cell or an entire spreadsheet. The ability to clear data is useful when, for example, you've made a duplicate of a spreadsheet and want to keep its formatting but not its contents.

To clear data from a cell or a range of cells, select the cell or range you want to clear. Use any of these methods to clear the contents from your selection:

- Right-click (Control-click on a Mac) and choose Clear Selection from the context menu.
- Select Edit, Clear selection.
- On the keyboard, press Delete.

 Those methods clear the contents of the cell or range you chose but leave the formatting intact. If you want to remove formatting, select a cell or range and then choose Format, Clear styles.

Working with Rows and Columns

As you work on a spreadsheet, you'll probably find that you need to adjust its columns and rows. Maybe you need to insert a new column between two existing ones, or perhaps you want to hide some rows or columns to give a more focused view of the data. This section explains your options for working with rows, columns, and their data.

Adding a Row or Column

When you want to insert a row or column into a spreadsheet, select a row or column next to the spot where you want to insert the new one. (To select a row, click the number on its left; to select a column, select the letter at its top.) Then take one of these actions:

- Right-click (Control-click on a Mac). From the context menu shown in Figure 6.11, choose Insert 1 above or Insert 1 below (when you've selected a row) or choose Insert 1 left or Insert 1 right (when you've selected a column).

- Click Insert. From the Insert menu, choose Row Above or Row Below (when you've selected a row) or choose Column Left or Column Right (when you've selected a column).

Google inserts a row or column according to what you chose.

 If you need to insert multiple rows or columns, select the same number of rows or columns as you want to insert. When you right-click (on a PC), Control-click (on a Mac), or choose Insert, you can insert the same number of rows or columns that you selected.

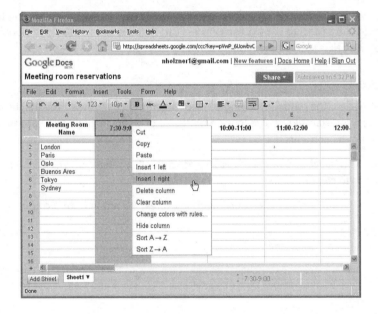

Figure 6.11
Select a column and then right-click it to get this menu of options.

Deleting a Row or Column

To delete a row or column, select the row or column you want to remove from the spreadsheet. Then choose a deletion method:

- Right-click (Control-click on a Mac). The control menu shown in Figure 6.11 appears; choose Delete Row or Delete Column.
- On the menu bar, click Edit. From the Edit menu, select the row, column, or range you want to delete.

Whichever method you choose, Google doesn't ask for confirmation before it deletes the row or column (and all its data), so watch what you're doing. If you make a mistake, click the Undo button immediately.

Moving a Row or Column

You can move a row or column by cutting it from its present location and pasting it elsewhere, but that's not the quickest way.

First, make sure that you've got room to move the row or column to: Insert a row or column (see earlier section) at the location where you're moving the data.

Warning If you try to move a column, for example on top, of an existing column, you'll overwrite that column's data.

Next, select the row or column you want to move. Hover the mouse pointer over the selection's border. When the cursor changes to a pointing hand, click and drag the selection to its new location. Let go of the mouse button to drop the row or column into place.

Tip 4U You can move multiple rows or columns—or any range of cells—using the method described here.

Hiding a Row or Column

Sometimes you want a narrower view of the data. You might have a spreadsheet listing customer contacts, for example, that lists name, job title, address, phone number, email address, product interest, and notes. But right now, you're making phone calls, so all you need to see are names and phone numbers. You can hide everything except the information you need to see.

To hide a row or column, select what you want to hide. Right-click (Control-click on a Mac) to see the context menu shown back in Figure 6.11. From the menu, select Hide Row or Hide Column. Google hides the row or column you chose, putting in a marker to indicate that a hidden row or column occupies that spot of the spreadsheet. The column and its data are still part of your spreadsheet; they're just not displayed in the current view. (To display the row or column again, click the marker.) Figure 6.12 gives you an idea of what a spreadsheet looks like with some rows and columns hidden.

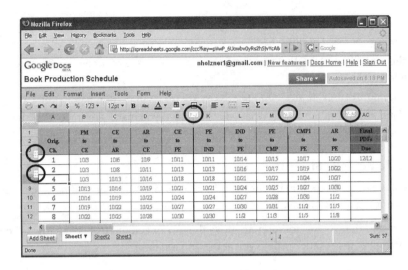

Figure 6.12
When a row or column is hidden, Google puts in a marker (circled).

Sorting Data

You enter data as it comes to you: Three new employees join your company, so you add them to the employee register. Or you got five new DVDs for your birthday, so enter them in the spreadsheet that tracks your movie collection. As the data in your spreadsheet grows, however, it can be hard to find a particular employee or DVD title in all that information. And that's where sorting comes in handy. Sorting lets you organize the information in your spreadsheet so you can answer questions about the data (do you have all the Hitchcock movies yet?) or find a particular piece of information.

When you *sort* data, you simply arrange the data in your spreadsheet in a particular order, either ascending (from A to Z or from the lowest number to the highest) or descending (from Z to A or from the highest number to the lowest). For example, say you're looking for information about an employee named Mary Zimmerman. Because Zimmerman begins with the letter *Z*, it'd be easiest to find Mary if you start at the end of the alphabet—that is, if you sort employees by last names in descending order so that names starting with Z appear at the top of the spreadsheet.

The example uses last name as the basis for sorting, but you can sort the data in your spreadsheet by any column. For example, you might sort employees by department, job title, or employee ID.

To sort a spreadsheet's data, select the column you're sorting by and then use one of these methods:

- Right-click (Control-click) the column. From the context menu that appears, select Sort A, Z (for ascending order) or Sort Z, A (for descending order).

■ On the menu bar, click Tools. From the Tools menu, select Sort by column *x* A, Z (for ascending order) or Sort by column *x* Z, A (for descending order). In the Tools menu, x will be replaced by the letter of the column you chose.

Google rearranges your spreadsheet's records according to the kind of sort you selected.

Sorting Data by Using the Sort Bar

Google offers a super-quick shortcut for sorting the data in your spreadsheet. It's called the *Sort Bar*, and you can see it at the top of a spreadsheet between rows 1 and 2, as shown in Figure 6.13. (You can also move the Sort Bar, as the next section explains, but for now, we'll just work with the Sort Bar where it is.)

When you want to sort by a particular column, hover the mouse pointer over the Sort Bar in that column—and you'll see why it's called the Sort Bar. The color of that segment of the bar changes to orange, and the word *Sort* appears, along with a downward-pointing arrow. Click the arrow and choose either A, Z or Z, A to select ascending or descending order for your sort.

But sorting isn't all the Sort Bar can do. As the next section explains, you can also use the Sort Bar to freeze rows, keeping them out of any sorts of the data.

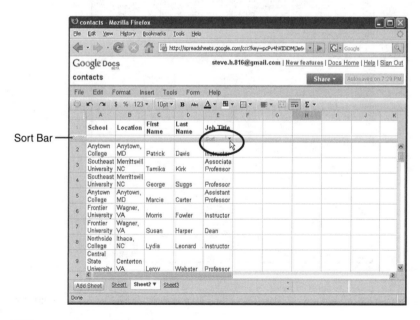

Figure 6.13
Use the Sort Bar to quick-sort your data. Here, the data will be sorted on Job Title.

Freezing Rows and Columns

You're probably wondering already: What if I don't want to include everything in the sort? A good example of something you don't want to sort is column headings: you need those at the top of your spreadsheet to make it clear what kind of data each column holds. And when you do a sort, you find that Google doesn't sort the headings. That's because in any new Docs spreadsheet, row 1 (the row that holds column headings) is *frozen* by default. Frozen simply means that the row (or column) doesn't participate in a sort; it stays right where it is while the sort rearranges the spreadsheet's data.

You can freeze up to ten rows and up to five columns in a spreadsheet. This can be helpful when, for example, you have column subheadings that you want to stay in place. Figure 6.14 shows an example of a frozen row and a frozen column.

To freeze a row or column, click Tools in the menu bar. From the Tools menu, select the number of rows or columns you want to freeze. Google freezes that number: for rows, it freezes the top x number of rows; for columns, it freezes the leftmost x number of columns.

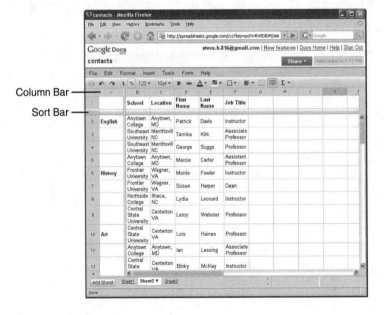

Figure 6.14
Drag the Sort Bar and the Column Bar to freeze rows and columns, respectively. In this example, Column A and Row 1 are both frozen.

Freezing Rows by Using the Sort Bar

To freeze a row using this method, place your mouse pointer on the far-left end of the Sort Bar so that the cursor changes to a four-way arrow. Click and drag the Sort Bar downward, positioning it just below the row you want to freeze. When you let go of the mouse button, the Sort Bar jumps to its new location, freezing any and all rows above it.

To unfreeze a row, simply move the Sort Bar above that row.

Freezing Columns by Using the Column Bar

As Figure 6.14 shows, a narrow gray bar separates frozen columns from the rest of the spreadsheet. Google calls this the Column Bar, and it freezes columns in the same way that the Sort Bar freezes rows.

To freeze a column, place your mouse pointer over the highest part of the Sort Bar. When the pointer becomes a four-way arrow, click and drag the Column Bar to the right. Let go of the mouse button to drop the column bar into place and freeze all columns to its left. If you want to unfreeze a column, drag the Column Bar to the left side of that column.

 You can't delete frozen rows or columns. If you want to delete one of these rows or columns, unfreeze it first and then delete it.

Printing and Deleting Spreadsheets

To finish up this chapter on the basics of using spreadsheets, we cover printing and deleting spreadsheets. Both of these common activities are straightforward in Docs, as you'll soon see.

Printing a Spreadsheet

Sometimes, only a hard copy of a spreadsheet will do. In Google Docs, printing out a spreadsheet is really a matter of exporting the spreadsheet as a PDF file, opening the file in a PDF reader, and then printing the file from there.

So when you want to print a copy of your spreadsheet, the first step is to convert the spreadsheet into a PDF. "Exporting as a PDF," earlier in this chapter, gave you detailed instructions on how to do that. The only difference here is that you tell Google to convert the current spreadsheet to a PDF file by selecting File, Print. (Alternatively, you can click the toolbar's Print button or press Ctrl+P [Cmd-P] on your keyboard.) This opens the Print Settings dialog box, whose options are exactly the same as in the Export to PDF dialog box shown in Figure 6.9. If you want, flip back to that figure to take a look.

When you've chosen the options you want for your printed spreadsheet in the Print Settings box, click Print. Your Web browser opens a window asking how you want to download the file: Save it to your computer or open it with an appropriate program, such as Adobe Reader (the suggested program depends on what's installed on your computer). Because you're going to print the file, you want to open it, so select that option.

The PDF opens in the program you chose. From there, print the file as you normally would from that program.

Deleting a Spreadsheet

If you no longer need a spreadsheet, you can delete it from the Docs home page. In the Docs list, find the spreadsheet you want to delete and check the box to the left of its name. Click Delete, and Google moves the spreadsheet to the Trash.

 Having trouble finding the spreadsheet you want to delete among all the documents and presentations in your Docs list? In the home page's left pane, look for Items by Type. If this section isn't expanded, click its plus sign. Then click Spreadsheets to show just spreadsheets in the Docs list.

Putting a spreadsheet in the Trash doesn't mean it's gone. If you really want to get rid of the spreadsheet for good, click Trash in the pane on the left (it's under All Items). When the list of trashed files displays, check the box to the left of the spreadsheet's name. Click Empty Trash to remove that spreadsheet from your Google Docs account.

Spreadsheets: Formulas and Charts

Spreadsheets can do more than simply store and sort data. In fact, what makes spreadsheets so useful—and so popular—is their ability to perform calculations on data and report on the data by creating easy-to-understand charts.

This chapter takes your spreadsheet skills to the next level with these topics:

- Defining a spreadsheet formula
- Creating a formula
- Using functions
- Naming cell ranges
- Creating charts from spreadsheet data
- Putting images into a spreadsheet
- Working with spreadsheet gadgets

Working with Spreadsheet Formulas

In Chapter 6, "Introducing Spreadsheets," you learned how to set up and format a spreadsheet, as well as a few tricks for entering data. But tracking and organizing data isn't all spreadsheets can do. What makes a spreadsheet such a powerful tool is its ability to perform calculations, from the simple to the complex. When you write a formula, you tell the spreadsheet what data to look at, what calculation to perform on that data, and where to display the results. The spreadsheet takes care of everything else. And as the numbers in your spreadsheet change, the results of the calculation automatically update.

This section shows you how to use spreadsheet formulas, starting with the basics and moving on to using functions to create more complex formulas. You also learn how to use formulas to calculate with date and time data.

What Is a Formula?

A *formula* is a calculation that a spreadsheet performs on your data. This can be as simple as adding up or averaging a column of numbers. It can also be quite complex for making advanced financial, engineering, or scientific calculations. This section gets you started with spreadsheet formulas, explaining what they are and what goes into them.

Creating Formulas: The Basics

Before you can write a formula, you need to be able to tell the spreadsheet which cells to act on. You do this with *cell references*. A cell reference is like a street address, indicating the location of the data you want. In other words, it tells the spreadsheet where to find a particular piece of data and can identify a single cell or a range of cells.

For a single cell, the reference is a combination of its column letter and row number. The upper-left cell in a spreadsheet, at the intersection of column A and row 1, is A1. A cell reference always shows the column letter first and then the row number: B2, C47, AB4, Q563. In each case, the reference specifies the cell at the intersection of a particular column and a particular row.

The formula itself lives inside a cell in your spreadsheet. After you insert the formula into the cell, the formula goes to work, performing its calculation and displaying the result in the cell.

The Anatomy of a Formula

When you create a formula, you're giving the spreadsheet a set of directions: Take this data and perform this calculation. To work properly, each formula needs these elements:

- An equals sign (=) at the beginning—This marks what follows as a formula, rather than just regular data.
- Cell references—This tells the spreadsheet where to look to find the data.
- An operator—This tells the spreadsheet what to do with the data—add it, average it, find a percentage, and so on.

Let's put those parts together to create a simple formula. Say you want to add the contents of the first two cells in column C. Assuming that row 1 is reserved for column headings, your formula would look like this:

```
=C2+C3
```

This formula has all the elements just mentioned: It begins with an equals sign (=), identifies the cells you want (C2 and C3), and uses an operator to indicate the calculation you want: a plus sign (+) for addition.

If the contents of C2 and C3 are 5 and 10, respectively, the formula returns 15. But if the cells' contents change, the formula's result changes, as well. No need to get out your calculator or rewrite your formula to update results: They're updated automatically whenever the relevant data changes.

Tip To edit a formula, double-click the cell that holds the formula and then edit away.

Of course, addition isn't the only operator you can use in the formulas you write. Table 7.1 lists operators that work in Google Docs spreadsheets formulas. For example, if you changed the example formula to

    =C2*C3

the spreadsheet would multiply the contents of C2 by the contents of C3.

Besides cell references, you can also use regular numbers in a formula. For example, this formula tells the spreadsheet to divide the contents of cell C2 by two:

    =C2/2

Table 7.1   Common Operators in Google Docs Spreadsheet Formulas

Operator	What it does
+	Addition
-	Subtraction
*	Multiplication
/	Division
=	Equals
<	Less than
<=	Less than or equal to
>	Greater than
>=	Greater than or equal to
<>	Not equal to
^	Raises to the power of
%	Percentage

Inserting a Formula into Your Spreadsheet

As mentioned earlier, you insert a formula into a cell, which then displays the formula's results. To insert a formula, click the cell you want and type = to begin your formula. After the equals sign, type the rest of your formula, making sure you include cell references and at least one operator. (This is true of just about all the formulas you'll write. However, an operator isn't necessary if all you're doing is referencing another cell's value, such as =C2.) Figure 7.1 shows an example of inserting a formula into a cell.

When you're done typing the formula, press the Enter key. (If you want to cancel the formula, press Esc.) The spreadsheet goes right to work, displaying the formula's result.

If you're squinting at the screen trying to figure out a cell reference, use your mouse to select the cells for your formula. Start in the cell where you're inserting the formula by typing =. When you need to put a cell reference in the formula, click the cell you want. Google automatically inserts the cell reference for that cell into your formula. The cursor stays in the cell where you're writing the formula, so you can type in operators. When you've finished the formula, press Enter.

When you click a cell that holds a formula, you can see the formula in the lower-right part of the screen, as shown in Figure 7.1. This lets you read the formula at a glance.

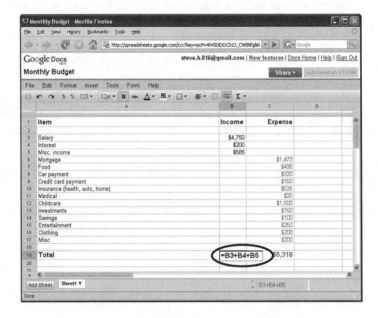

Figure 7.1
Click a cell and enter your formula. This example adds the contents of three cells (B3, B4, and B5) and displays the result in cell B19.

Relative vs. Absolute Cell References

You can use Auto-Fill to copy a formula, just as you can use it to copy the data a cell holds. (Chapter 6 gives you the lowdown on using Auto-Fill.) What happens to the cell references when you Auto-Fill a formula into a new location on the spreadsheet?

The answer depends on how you've written the cell reference:

Relative cell reference—The examples we've given so far show relative cell references. And that means that when you Auto-Fill a formula, the cell references change to reflect the formula's new location. For example, say you have a formula that adds the contents of B5 and B6, displaying the results in B10. If you Auto-Fill the formula down one row, to B11, Google

assumes that you want to move each of the cell references down as well. So the Auto-Filled formula that appears in B11 becomes =B6+B7.

Absolute cell reference—If you want one or more of the cell references to stay exactly as it is in the formula, even if you Auto-Fill the formula to a new cell, you need to let the spreadsheet know that it's *not* okay to change the reference to that cell. So you use an absolute cell reference, which says, in effect, "No matter where this formula appears in the spreadsheet, the reference is to this particular cell." Use a dollar sign ($) to show an absolute cell reference. You can fix the column ($B5), the row (B$5), or the cell (B5).

An example of when you'd use a absolute cell reference would be in a spreadsheet where you have a formula that calculates sales tax. When the sales tax rate appears in a particular cell, you want the reference to that cell to remain constant when you Auto-Fill the formula.

Referring to a Range of Cells

The example of cell references we've seen so far have been to individual cells. If you want to refer to a range of cells, though, you don't have to type them one by one; you can use a bit of shorthand to refer to the whole range.

To refer to a range of cells, start with the first cell of the range, insert a colon (:), and then end with the last cell in the range. So if you want to refer to the first ten cells below the column heading in column A, you'd write the reference as A2:A11. (As you saw in Chapter 6, the first row of a spreadsheet usually contains headings that identify what's in that column.)

 You refer to cell ranges in this way when you're working with functions. See "Supercharging Your Formulas with Functions," coming up in this chapter, for more information.

Naming a Range of Cells

Although you can refer to a cell range in the way just described, you can also name a cell range and then refer to that range by name in your formulas. So instead of trying to remember exactly which cells make up the range you want, you can simply include the name that specifies that range.

To name a cell range, start by selecting the range you want. Then choose Edit, Named Ranges, Define New Range to open the Range Names box, shown in Figure 7.2.

In the Range Names box, give the range a name in the Nickname field. Pick a descriptive name that's easy to remember, such as *expenses* or *prices* or *grades*. In the field to the right of the Nickname field is the cell range field, showing the range you selected. Check to make sure the range is correct; edit if necessary. (If you didn't select a cell range before you started creating the range name, you can type a range into this field now.) When everything looks the way you want it, click Save.

If you're naming several cell ranges, click Add Another (at the bottom of the Range Names box) to open new Nickname and Cell Range fields to fill in and save. When you're completely finished, click Done.

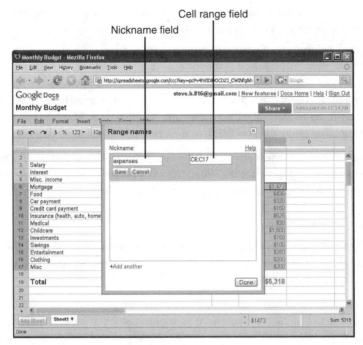

Figure 7.2
Use the Nickname field and the Cell Range field to create a named cell range.

To edit or delete a named cell range, select Edit, Named Ranges, Manage Ranges. This opens the Range Names box, displaying a list of all existing named ranges in that spreadsheet. Double-click a name to edit its cell range; click Save to apply the edit. If you want to delete a named range, click the x to the right of its name. A confirmation box asks whether you're sure; click OK to delete the named range. (Deleting a named range simply removes the name from that range; it doesn't affect the actual cells or their contents.)

Now that you've got some named cell ranges, you can use those names in your formulas, as you'll see later in this chapter. First, though, we'll see how to use functions to make your formulas easier to write—and also more complex and powerful.

Referring to a Cell or Range on a Specific Sheet

As Chapter 6 explains, a Google Docs spreadsheet may consist of more than a single sheet. When you're creating cell references, you may want to specify that a cell is on a particular sheet within the spreadsheet. That way, if you copy a formula and paste it elsewhere, there's no confusion about exactly which cell or range you want.

To link a cell or cell range reference to a particular sheet, put the name of the sheet, followed by an exclamation mark (!) in front of the cell or range. For example, say you're working with a household budget spreadsheet and each sheet is named after a different month. You want to refer to cell C3 on the sheet named January. Here's how you'd write that reference:

`January!C3`

If you want to refer to cells C3:C10 on the January sheet, write the reference like this:

`January!C3:C10`

Supercharging Your Formulas with Functions

A *function* is an advanced formula that's already built in to your Google Docs spreadsheet. (And that means you get to benefit from someone else's hard work.) The function tells the spreadsheet what to do—you simply supply the values to work on. For example, the Sum function adds a range of numbers and looks like this:

`=SUM(C6:C17)`

You can use a single function to create a quick formula, as just shown, to add a range of numbers, or you can string functions together to perform more complex calculations.

But the really good news about functions is that Google has made it easy for you to insert a function into your formula. You don't have to type out the function name—just click a button, choose the function you want, and Google gets you started. Here's how:

1. Click the cell where you want to insert the formula.
2. On the toolbar, click the Formulas button. This button, on the right side of the toolbar, looks like the Greek letter sigma (Σ).
3. From the Formulas menu (shown in Figure 7.3), which lists the most common functions, choose the function you want. Google inserts that function into your formula. For example, if you choose Average from the list, Google inserts this into your formula cell:

    =AVERAGE(

4. Complete the formula by providing cell references and closing the parentheses. For example, if the range of cells you're averaging is C6 through C17, the completed formula would look like this:

    =AVERAGE(C6:C17)

5. Press Enter to complete your formula and get the results.

The Formulas menu has these commonly used functions:

- Sum—Adds a range of numbers.
- Average—Finds the average of a range of numbers.
- Count—Tells you how many values are in the range.
- Max—Finds the maximum value in the range.
- Min—Finds the minimum value in the range.

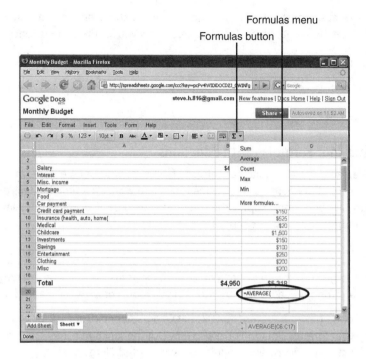

Figure 7.3
Select a function from the Formulas menu to insert it into a cell.

Info 4U Besides ranges of continuous cells, you can also list cells that aren't contiguous in these functions. In that case, use commas to separate the cells in your list.

Tip 4U Need to quickly add a range of numbers without writing an actual formula? Select the range you want to add, and then check the lower-right corner of the screen. Google's already added the numbers for you and presents the sum there—no formula required.

If you want a function that's not listed on the Formulas menu (or you just want to see what other functions are available), follow steps 1 and 2 just listed for creating a formula using a function. In step 3, click More Formulas to open the Insert a Formula box, shown in Figure 7.4.

This dialog box lists categories on the left: Math, Financial, Logical, and so on. When you click a category, the right side of the box displays functions related to that category. Scroll through the list to find the function you want; click a function to select it.

When you click a function, it appears in a field at the bottom of the dialog box. To help you out, Google tells you what kinds of values the function can accept or what kind of syntax the formula requires. If the formula looks like what you want, double-click it to insert it into your spreadsheet where you can finish writing it.

Figure 7.4
Select a function and then write your formula in the field at the bottom of the box.

 If you want to know more about a function, what it does, and how to use it in a formula, select the function in the Insert a Formula dialog box and then click the More link in the lower-right corner. A new window opens, giving detailed information about that function.

 A Google Docs spreadsheet can contain a maximum of 50 functions.

Using Named Ranges in Your Formulas

If you've got some named ranges that you want to use in the formulas you're writing, doing so is easy. For example, take a look at the monthly budget in Figure 7.5. Say you want to know the average amount of the household's expenditures each month. You've already selected a range of cells (C6:C17) and named it *expenses*. (See "Naming a Range of Cells," earlier in this chapter, to find out how to do that.)

When you write your formula, you can use the name of that cell range, rather than the actual cell references. First, you click the cell where you want to insert the formula. Then click the Formulas button and select Average. Google inserts this into the cell:

    =AVERAGE (

All pretty familiar so far, right? But now, instead of typing in cell references or clicking individual cells to complete the formula, type in the name of the cell range instead, so the formula looks like this:

```
=AVERAGE(expenses)
```

Press Enter, and Google calculates the average using the range of cells linked with the *expenses* range name.

Info 4U If you edit the cells in a named range (see "Naming a Range of Cells"), the formula automatically takes the edited range into account.

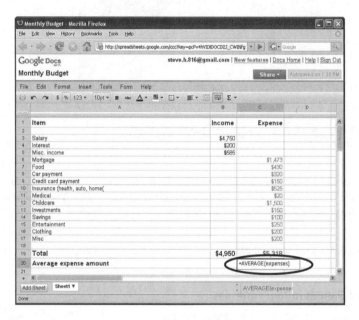

Figure 7.5
Use a range name to simplify formula writing.

Getting the Big Picture with Charts, Graphics, and Gadgets

With up to 200,000 cells to contain data, a Google Docs spreadsheet can hold a lot of information. But looking at all those cells and all those numbers, it's easy to become overwhelmed. You need a way to make sense of the data: show how parts of the spreadsheet relate to other parts, identify trends, and find patterns. And that's where charts come in.

A *chart* is a graphical representation of your data (or some part of it). You might use a chart, for example, when you want to see how much of the household budget is going for different expenses or when you want to compare how sales reps are doing in a particular region. As your data changes, the chart changes, too.

Google Docs offers several different chart styles, so you can present the data in the most effective way. With just a few clicks, you'll have a clear and sharp-looking chart ready to use in a report or presentation.

Kinds of Charts

All charts are not created equal. The style of chart you should choose depends on the kind of information you want to show. In Docs, you can create these kinds of charts:

- Columnar chart—This kind of chart, shown in Figure 7.6, shows the data in vertical columns. Each column represents a piece of data, and columns vary in heights so you can make comparisons. And comparisons are precisely what this kind of chart illustrates well—for example, you could use a bar chart to compare the performance of different sales reps or the popularity of different products.

- Bar chart—A bar chart is like a columnar chart turned on its side. Instead of vertical columns, horizontal bars represent the data, as shown in Figure 7.7. Like columnar charts, use bar charts to show comparisons.

- Pie chart—In a pie chart, the data is represented by a circle carved up into pieces of different sizes and colors. Each piece of the "pie" is proportional to the data it represents. Figure 7.8 shows an example of a pie chart. Use this chart to show how different parts contribute to the whole—for example, to show how different expenses add up to the total money budgeted for a month.

 You can click a column, bar, or pie piece in a Google Docs chart to get more information about what it represents (see Figure 7.8 for an example).

- Line chart—This kind of chart, shown in Figure 7.9, displays data as a series of points, usually connected by lines. Use a line chart to show trends over time: how sales have increased or decreased, for example, or how student grades have improved or declined.

- Area chart—An area chart adds an extra dimension to a line chart by filling in the area below each line with transparent color, as shown in Figure 7.10. This style of chart emphasizes how values change over time.

- Scatter chart—This kind of chart shows data as a set of individual points, as shown in Figure 7.11. In a scatter chart, each axis represents a set of numbers and a dot represents a single data point. This gives you a visual distribution of the data and can show trends. Scatter charts are useful for plotting statistical data.

Docs' chart offerings let you present your data in the clearest, most effective way; take a look at the examples to get a sense of which chart style works best for different kinds of data. The next section tells you how to create a chart.

Tip 4U   Other kinds of charts, such as timelines, motion charts, pivot tables, and more, are available as Google gadgets. See the section "Google Docs Spreadsheets and Google Gadgets," near the end of this chapter, to learn about inserting a gadget to display your data.

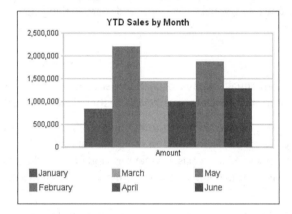

Figure 7.6
A columnar chart shows the data as vertical columns.

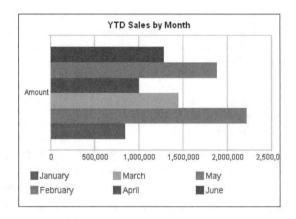

Figure 7.7
A bar chart shows the data as horizontal bars.

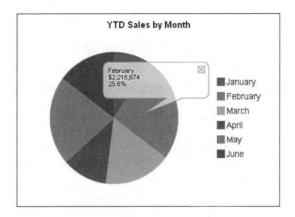

Figure 7.8
Use a pie chart to slice up the data into proportionate "pieces." Click any piece to get more information about what it represents.

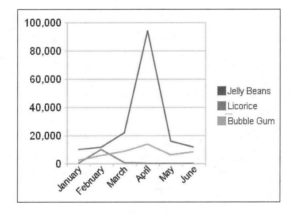

Figure 7.9
This line chart compares sales of three products over a six-month period.

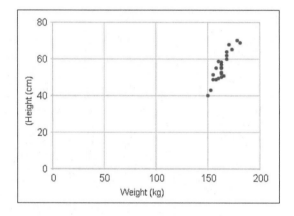

Figure 7.10
An area chart is a line chart with shading below each line.

Figure 7.11
This scatter chart shows how weight relates to height in a group of subjects.

Creating a Chart

To create a chart, begin by selecting the data you want to graph—that is, the data Google will use to create the chart. This might be all the data in a spreadsheet, or it might be just a particular range of cells. When you've selected the data you want, follow these steps:

1. Click Insert, Chart. This opens the Create Chart box shown in Figure 7.12.

2. In the What Type? section, select the kind of chart you want. When you click a chart type, subtype for that kind of chart appear. (In Figure 7.12, for example, the subtypes for a columnar chart are columns, stacked columns, 3D columns, and stacked 3D columns.) If you want, click a subtype to select it.

When you select a type or a subtype, take a look at the Create Chart box's lower-right Preview section to see how that style of chart will look using your data.

3. In the What Data? section, check the cell range for your chart. If the cell range isn't what you want (or if you started creating the chart without selecting a cell range), enter the range in this section's text box. Choose whether you want to group the data by rows or by columns (the Preview changes to show how each grouping method looks). Check or uncheck the boxes here to indicate your preferences about labeling the data. Labels link the information in a chart with the data, showing what columns in a columnar chart or segments of a pie chart represent.

 You can select a cell range while you're creating a chart. Click any cell in the spreadsheet. Google temporarily hides the Create Chart box and opens the What Data? box instead. Select the cell range you want, and that range appears in the What Data? box. Click OK. Google closes the What Data? box and reopens the Create Chart box, with the cell range you selected in place.

4. If you want to create additional labels for your chart, do so in the Labels section. Here you can type in a title for the chart; label the horizontal and/or vertical axis; tell Google where to place the chart's legend, which shows what the different colors in the chart mean (or not to display a legend at all); or reverse the categories in the chart (so that left to right goes from June to January instead of from January to June, for example). Everything in the Labels section is optional.

5. When your chart is all set—you like the way it looks in the Preview section—click Save Chart.

Google creates the chart and inserts it into your spreadsheet.

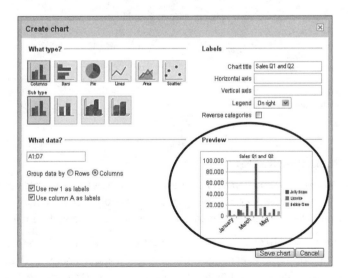

Figure 7.12
As you set up a chart, Google shows you a preview of how the chart will look.

Editing a Chart

After you've created a chart and inserted it into your spreadsheet, you may want to edit that chart, whether to tweak its settings, add a label or title, or add or remove data from the chart's display. This section describes how to edit or otherwise work with a chart you've created.

Changing a Chart's Settings or Labels

To make adjustments to an existing chart, click the chart. A gray frame appears around the chart. Click Chart in the upper-left part of the frame. From the menu that appears (shown in Figure 7.13), choose Edit Chart.

The Edit Chart dialog box opens. Edit Chart looks just like the Create Chart box you saw in Figure 7.12, but it has your settings and selections for this chart already filled in. Make the adjustments you want (watching the Preview section to see how those adjustments affect the chart). Click Save Chart to apply your changes.

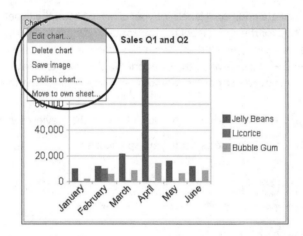

Figure 7.13
A chart's Chart menu offers the options shown here.

Putting a Chart on Its Own Sheet

When you create a chart, Google inserts the new chart in the sheet whose data the chart displays. If the chart covers up your data, the spreadsheet becomes hard to read. You can move the chart to its own sheet in your spreadsheet, keeping the original spreadsheet legible.

To put a chart on its own sheet, click the chart and then select Chart, Move to Own Sheet. Google creates a brand-new sheet in your spreadsheet, giving it a name such as *Chart1* (or, if *Chart1* already exists, *Chart2* or *Chart3* and so on). Click the chart's tab to see an enlarged version of the chart, such as the example shown in Figure 7.14. The new sheet is for the chart only; you can't enter data on this sheet.

When you display a chart on its own sheet, use the upper-right buttons to work with that chart. (The buttons are the same as the Chart menu options—except for Move to Own Sheet—because you've already done that.)

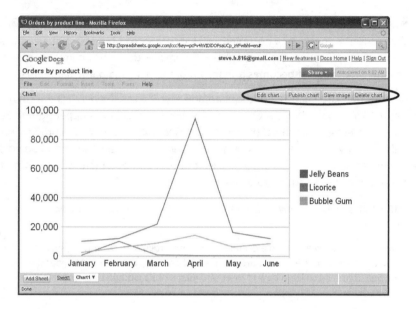

Figure 7.14
You can put a chart on its own sheet and then use the upper-right buttons to work with that chart.

Moving a Chart

If you want to keep a chart on the same sheet as its data but you still need to keep the chart from obscuring the data, you can move the chart to a different part of the sheet.

Click the chart. In the gray frame that appears, move your mouse pointer to the top part of the frame. When the cursor changes to a pointing hand, click and drag the chart to a new location. Let go of the mouse button to leave the chart at that location.

Resizing a Chart

Is the new chart you've created making you squint trying to read its labels? You can make the chart larger to make it easier to read. Or you can make a chart smaller so it takes up less space in a data-packed spreadsheet. This resizing method applies to charts that appear in a sheet that also contains data.

Click the chart to make its frame appear. Next, place your mouse pointer on the frame so that the cursor changes to a two-headed arrow. Click and drag to resize the chart. To keep the chart in proportion, click and drag either bottom corner—this adjusts the chart's size both horizontally and vertically as you drag.

The only way to resize a chart that's displayed on its own sheet is to resize the window that contains the chart.

Saving a Chart as an Image

If you want to insert a chart into a document, save it to your computer, or print it, you can save the chart as an image. Because the saved chart is an image, the chart no longer changes with changes to the data; rather, it becomes a snapshot of the data at a particular moment in time.

When you want to take a snapshot of the chart and save it as an image, click the chart and then choose Chart, Save Image. (Or if the chart is on its own sheet, click the upper-right Save Image button.) Google creates an image of the chart in PNG format, and your Web browser opens a dialog box asking how you want to handle the image's download. Select whether you want to open the image with an appropriate program or save it to your computer (and where). After the download, you've got an image of your chart.

 PNG, which stands for *portable network graphic,* is a format for digital images.

 If you want to display a chart in a Google Docs word-processing document, such as a quarterly report, save the chart as an image and then insert the image into your document. See Chapter 4 to learn how to insert an image into a Google Docs document.

Publishing a Chart in a Web Page or Blog

Your chart doesn't have to be restricted to your Google Docs account. Maybe your company wants to trumpet the success of its new product line on its home page. Or maybe you've created a chart about pollution in your region that you want to use to illustrate a blog post calling for more environmental regulation. With a little bit of HTML code, you can display a chart on a Web page or blog (and you don't need to know HTML to do it).

When you've got a chart you want to publish on your Web site or blog, click the chart and then select Chart, Publish Chart. (If the chart is on its own sheet, open that sheet and click the upper-right Publish Chart button.) Google asks you to save your spreadsheet (if you haven't already) and opens the Publish Chart dialog box, shown in Figure 7.15.

The Publish Chart box contains the HTML you need to embed the chart in another page on the Web. Select the HTML and copy it (press Ctrl+C on a PC or Cmd-C on a Mac). Click Done to close the box.

Next, paste the HTML into an HTML document and upload that document to your Web site. If you use a popular blogging program such as Blogger or WordPress, you can paste the HTML right into your post and then save the post to your blog. Your chart appears on the page or post where you pasted it.

Figure 7.15
Google generates the HTML you need to display a chart in your own Web page or blog—just copy and paste.

Deleting a Chart

If you've made your point and no longer need a chart to illustrate it, you can delete the chart:

- If the chart appears on a sheet with data—Click the chart and select Chart, Delete Chart. Google immediately deletes the chart.

- If the chart appears on its own sheet—Open that sheet and click the upper-right Delete Chart button. Google opens a confirmation box, asking whether you're sure that you want to delete the sheet that holds the chart (deleting the chart along with it). Click OK, and both the chart and the sheet that holds it disappear.

In either case, if you deleted the chart by mistake, you can get it back by immediately clicking the Undo button.

Putting an Image into Your Spreadsheet

Google Docs lets you insert images into a spreadsheet. Many situations exist where you might want to show an image as part of a spreadsheet. For example, if you're tracking requirements for an IT project, you might want to insert images of your business process flows. Or a spreadsheet that holds information about properties in your real estate portfolio could show an image of each building on the sheet that holds its data.

Before you can insert a graphic into a spreadsheet, that image must exist on the Web. So upload any images you want to display to a Web site—this can be a page in your own site, or it could be a photo-sharing service such as Picasa Web albums or Photobucket. You'll need the image's Web address (URL), so open the image and copy its URL.

Back in Google Docs, open the sheet where you want to insert the image. Select Insert, Image. The Insert Image dialog box opens. This box has only one field: Image URL. Paste the URL of your image in this box and then click OK. Google inserts the image into your spreadsheet.

Editing an Image

After you've inserted an image into a spreadsheet, you can tweak the image in various ways. Click the image, and a gray frame appears around the image. The gray frame means that the image is ready to edit, move, or resize.

Reinserting an Image

Other than changing an image's size (see "Resizing an Image," coming up in the next section), Google currently doesn't offer any way to edit an image that's part of a spreadsheet. So if you find you need to make changes to a spreadsheet's image (such as sharpening or cropping the image), you must make those changes to the original image in an image editor such as Paint or Photoshop.

Open your image editor of choice and edit your image there. Next, upload the edited image so that Google can find it on the Web.

Back in Docs, open the sheet that holds the image you want to replace with the new, improved edited image. Click the image so its frame appears. In the upper-left corner, click Image to open the menu shown in Figure 7.16. From the menu, select Edit Image. This opens the same dialog box you used to insert the image. Paste in the edited image's URL and then click OK. Google replaces the original image with the edited one.

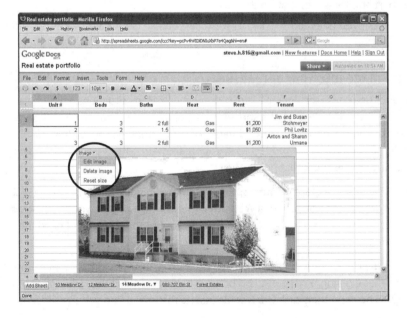

Figure 7.16
The Images menu offers these options for working with an image you've inserted into a spreadsheet: Edit Image, Delete Image, Reset Size.

Resizing an Image

If the image is too big or too small as it appears on your sheet, you can adjust its size. Click the image so that its frame appears. Hover your mouse pointer over the frame's bottom, left, or right border. When the cursor becomes a two-way arrow, click and drag to resize the image. Let go of the mouse button to make the image its new size.

If you've resized an image and decided that the new size doesn't work, click Undo. Alternatively, click the image. When its frame appears, click Image, Reset Size, and Google returns the image to its original size.

Moving an Image

To move an image to another part of the spreadsheet it's on, click the image to bring up its frame. Place your mouse pointer at the top of the frame so that the cursor becomes a pointing hand. Click and then drag the image to its new location, releasing the mouse button to drop it into place.

Deleting an Image

Decided you don't want that image in your sheet, after all? Click the image. In the upper-left part of its frame, click Image, Delete Image. Immediately, the image disappears. (If you want it back, click Undo.)

Google Docs Spreadsheets and Google Gadgets

Chapter 1, "Getting Started with Google Docs," explained that a gadget is a self-contained mini-program that you can put on a Web page, and it also discussed filling up your iGoogle page with useful or fun gadgets—but you can also put gadgets into your spreadsheets. A gadget expands your options for displaying your data beyond Google's built-in chart types. For example, there's a pivot table gadget for cross-tabulating data, a timeline gadget, and an organization chart gadget. Gadgets also let you display your data in whimsical or attention-getting ways: compare dollar amounts, for example, using stacks of hundred-dollar bills, rather than boring old columns.

 Some gadgets are developed by Google, others by third parties. But third-party developers must submit their gadgets to Google for approval before Google will make them available for use with your spreadsheets.

Inserting a Gadget Into a Spreadsheet

Ready to try a gadget? Start by selecting the cell range you want the gadget to display. Then click Insert, Gadget to open the Add a Gadget dialog box, shown in Figure 7.17.

The left side of the box contains categories of gadgets; click any category to browse it. Gadgets in the selected category appear in the right side of the box. Each gadget has information about who created it, along with a brief description and an image to give you an idea of what the gadget looks like in practice. When you see the gadget you want, click Add to Spreadsheet.

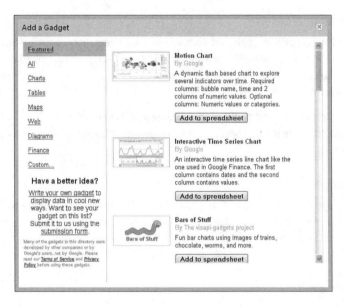

Figure 7.17
This dialog box shows the gadgets available for spreadsheets.

After you've selected a gadget, Google inserts the gadget into your spreadsheet. Before you can see your new gadget in action, however, you've got to set it up, as Figure 7.18 shows. The settings for your gadget depend on the kind of gadget you've chosen. In Figure 7.18, the gadget creates a columnar chart whose columns appear as piles of money—so the settings required are similar to the settings you'd choose in creating a columnar chart.

After you've filled out the fields to set up the gadget, click Apply. The box expands to show a preview of your gadget. If necessary, adjust the settings and click Apply again to see their effects. When your gadget looks good, click Apply and Close; Google inserts the gadget into your spreadsheet, as shown in Figure 7.19.

Editing a Gadget

As with any charts you create from a spreadsheet, you can edit the gadgets that display your data, as this section explains.

Changing a Gadget's Settings or Labels

If you need to tweak a gadget you've created, click the gadget so that a gray title bar appears at its top. On the left side of the gadget's title bar, click Edit. The gadget expands to show its current settings (similar to what's shown in Figure 7.18). Use this form to make any edits you require. As you did when you created the gadget, click Apply to see how the settings affect the gadget, and then click Apply and Close when you're done.

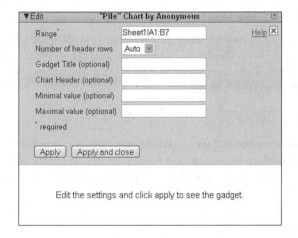

Figure 7.18
After you've selected a gadget, you need to set it up to work with your data.

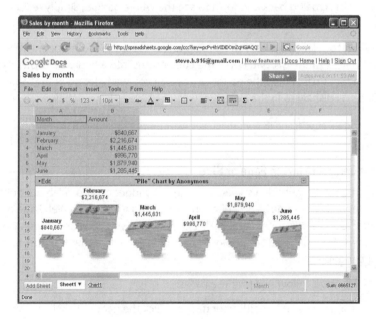

Figure 7.19
This gadget shows financial data as piles of money.

Putting a Gadget on Its Own Sheet

To display a full-sized version of the gadget on its own sheet, click the gadget and then click downward-pointing arrow on the title bar's right side (you can see this arrow in Figure 7.19). A menu appears; select Move to Own Sheet. Google creates a new sheet (with a name such as *Gadget1*) and moves the gadget there.

Moving a Gadget

If you don't want to move the gadget to a whole new sheet—just to a different part of the sheet it's currently on—click the gadget and then hover your mouse pointer over the gadget's title bar (the gray bar at the top of the gadget). Click and drag the gadget to where you want it and then drop it into place.

Resizing a Gadget

You can make a gadget larger or smaller. You might want to resize a gadget when, for example, the default size of the gadget you created is too small to show all the data, making a scrollbar appear. Instead of scrolling back and forth to see the whole gadget, simply resize so you can see all its data.

Click the gadget to select it (its gray title bar appears). Place the mouse pointer on the left, bottom, or right border of the gadget. When the cursor turns into a two-way arrow, click and drag to change the gadget's size. When the gadget is the size you want, let go of the mouse button. The gadget adjusts its display to fit the new size.

 If the gadget appears on its own sheet, you can't resize the gadget; it's already full size.

Publishing a Gadget in a Web Page or Blog

As with a chart, you can publish a spreadsheet-linked gadget on your Web site or blog. The process is essentially the same as described in "Publishing a Chart in a Web Page or Blog," earlier in this chapter: Google generates some HTML code, which you copy and then paste into an HTML document, Web page editor, or blog post. Upload the document or post to your site, and there's your gadget.

To get the HTML code, follow one of these paths:

- Open the spreadsheet that holds your gadget. Click the gadget to select it and then click the downward-pointing arrow on the right side of the gadget's title bar. The Publish Gadget dialog box opens, displaying the HTML you need. Select and copy the HTML and then click Done to close the dialog box.

- If your gadget is displayed on its own sheet, open that sheet and then click Publish. Google displays a message box telling you that the gadget refers to data that's on a different sheet—so publishing the gadget means that both sheets will be published. If that's what you want, click OK. The Publish Gadget dialog box opens; copy its HTML code; click Done.

Putting a Spreadsheet's Gadget on Your iGoogle Page

Chapter 1 introduced iGoogle, your personalized Google start page, and explained some ways to make iGoogle work with Google Docs. Here's another way to supercharge your spreadsheet use: After you've created a gadget based on spreadsheet data, put that gadget on your iGoogle page. The gadget shows the most up-to-date data, whether or not you've got Google Docs open. If you're working on a spreadsheet with collaborators (Chapter 8, "Sharing and Collaborating on Spreadsheets," tells you all about that), your iGoogle page shows changes to the data as they happen.

When you want to display a spreadsheet gadget on your iGoogle page, open the spreadsheet you want and click the gadget to select it. In the gadget's title bar, click the downward-pointing arrow on the right side and then select Add Gadget to iGoogle. (If the gadget is on its own sheet, open that sheet and click its upper-right Add Gadget to iGoogle button.)

A new window opens, asking for your permission to add the gadget to iGoogle. Click the big, blue Add to Google button. Your iGoogle page opens with the new spreadsheet gadget displayed. You can move, edit, or delete the gadget as you would any other gadget on your iGoogle page.

 When you put a spreadsheet gadget on your iGoogle page, the gadget remains in your spreadsheet as well. You can delete the spreadsheet version of the gadget without affecting the iGoogle gadget and vice versa.

Deleting a Gadget

If a gadget has outlived its usefulness, you can delete the gadget from your spreadsheet. Open the relevant spreadsheet and click the gadget to select it. Click the down arrow on the right side of the title bar and then select Delete Gadget. Immediately, the gadget disappears.

If you want to delete a gadget that occupies its own sheet, open that sheet and click More, Delete Gadget. When a gadget has its own sheet, deleting the gadget also deletes the sheet; Google asks whether you're sure you want to do that. Click OK, and Google removes both the gadget and its sheet from your spreadsheet.

 If you delete a gadget by mistake, click Undo immediately to bring it back.

Sharing and Collaborating on Spreadsheets

You don't have to keep your spreadsheets all to yourself. When you share them with others, you can share both the information the spreadsheet holds and the work of keeping it up to date. As with Google Docs word-processing documents and presentations, you can share spreadsheets with collaborators who can work on them simultaneously in real time. It's up to you how much access you want sharers to have—whether they can edit a spreadsheet or just view it, whether or not they need a Google account.

This chapter shows you how to share and collaborate on spreadsheets using Google Docs, covering these and other topics:

- Publishing a spreadsheet on the Web
- Inviting others to view or work on your spreadsheet
- Collaborating with others
- Creating a form to let others add data to a spreadsheet
- Analyzing data submitted via a form
- Viewing earlier versions of a spreadsheet

Sharing Spreadsheets

With Google Docs, you can share any spreadsheet you create. (In some cases, you can also share a spreadsheet you've been invited to help edit.) Share your spreadsheet with a select few—or with the whole world. This section tells you how to let others in on the spreadsheet fun.

Publishing a Spreadsheet on the Web

When you publish a spreadsheet on the Web, anyone with Internet access can see your spreadsheet. You can publish an entire spreadsheet or just one sheet within a larger spreadsheet. Publishing a spreadsheet on the Web is a lot like publishing a document on the Web (which was described in Chapter 5). To publish a spreadsheet, follow these simple steps:

1. Open the spreadsheet you want to publish and click its upper-right Share button.
2. From the Share menu, select Publish as a Web Page. This opens the Publish as a Web Page dialog box, shown in Figure 8.1.
3. Click Publish Now.

The Publish as a Web Page dialog box changes to look like the one shown in Figure 8.2. At the same time, Google assigns your spreadsheet a Web address (called a URL) and makes the spreadsheet available at that address. Simply copy the link and email it, send it by instant message, or link to it so others can find it.

At this point, you may be all set—your spreadsheet is published. If you're done, click the upper-right x to close the Publish as a Web Page dialog box. Before you do, though, take a look at the options offered by the expanded dialog box. There are a couple of settings you might want to adjust:

■   Automatically Republish When Changes Are Made—Checking this box means that as you make changes to a spreadsheet, those changes automatically appear in the published version whenever Google saves the spreadsheet.

■   What Parts?—If your spreadsheet is made up of multiple sheets, Google lets you choose which part of the spreadsheet you want to publish. Use this drop-down to choose All Sheets (the default) or the individual sheet you want to publish.

 Want to publish a chart or a gadget without the spreadsheet's rows, columns, and data in the background? Put the chart or gadget on its own sheet (Chapter 7 tells you how) and then publish just that sheet.

 When you publish a spreadsheet on the Web, Google marks it as "Published" on your Google Docs home page. The *Published* label appears in the Folders/Sharing section of the Docs list.

If you want to remove a published spreadsheet from the Web, open the spreadsheet you want to remove. Click Share, Publish as a Web Page. The Publish as a Web Page dialog box opens, looking like the one in Figure 8.2. Click Stop Publishing, and that's exactly what Google does. Your spreadsheet no longer appears on the Web.

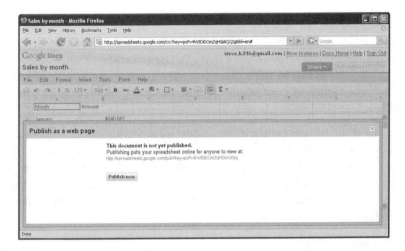

Figure 8.1
Click Publish Now to put your spreadsheet on the Web.

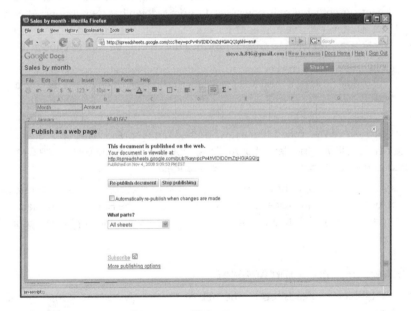

Figure 8.2
After you've published a spreadsheet, the Publish as a Web Page dialog box changes to look like this.

Embedding a Spreadsheet in Your Web Site or Blog

If you want to make a spreadsheet part of your Web site or display it in a blog post, instead of giving the spreadsheet its own page, you can do that by embedding the spreadsheet in a Web page or your blog. This is a good technique if you want to display a chart or gadget that shows (for example) your company's most popular products or your progress in writing the Great American Novel.

You need some HTML code to embed a spreadsheet (or a single sheet from it) in your Web page or blog. To get that code, open the spreadsheet you want and then click Share, Publish as a Web Page. If the spreadsheet isn't currently published, click Publish Now. When the Publish as a Web Page dialog box expands to look like the one shown in Figure 8.2, click the More Publishing Options link at the bottom of the dialog box. This opens the More Published Formats page, shown in Figure 8.3, in a new window.

Here, make choices for these sections:

- File Format—From the drop-down list, select HTML to Embed in a Web Page.
- What Sheet?—Use this drop-down to choose the sheet you want to embed. Even if your spreadsheet currently has only one sheet, this drop-down has two options: All Sheets or Sheet1 (or whatever you've named the sheet.) So if you want to add more sheets to the spreadsheet later and want to embed just the current one, be sure to choose it here.

 If you want to embed a chart or gadget, rather than a grid-formatted spreadsheet, put the chart or gadget on its own sheet (Chapter 7 tells you how) and then choose that sheet to embed.

- What Cells?—If you're embedding a rows-and-columns spreadsheet, you can input a cell range here. Stick with the default of All Cells, type in a cell range such as A2:G44, or use a named range (see Chapter 7 for naming cell ranges).

When you've chosen the options that tell Google what to embed, click the Generate URL button. Google cooks up some HTML code for you and displays it in the Here's the URL field. Now, simply copy that code and paste it into an HTML document (which you then upload to your Web site) or include in a blog post.

Inviting Others to Share a Spreadsheet

Of course, publishing a spreadsheet on the Web isn't your only option for sharing it. If you've got a spreadsheet that you want to share with a select group of people—up to 200 coworkers, family members, or friends—you can give them exclusive viewing and editing privileges for a spreadsheet. You can also add "Everyone"—that is, anyone with Internet access—to your list of sharers.

Figure 8.3
Google can generate HTML code that lets you embed a spreadsheet, chart, or gadget in a Web page or blog.

Sharing a Spreadsheet with Individuals or Groups

When you share a spreadsheet with other people, they can view or edit that spreadsheet (your choice) when they sign in to their Google account. So workers can see next week's schedule or update their time sheets, your project team can update their progress, or coworkers can submit travel expenses while they're on the road.

To share a spreadsheet with an individual or group, open the spreadsheet you want to share and click Share, Invite People. This opens the Share with Others dialog box, shown in Figure 8.4. In the dialog box, fill out these sections:

■ Invite—In this section, type or paste in the email addresses of the people you're sharing with. If you're sharing with multiple people, use commas to separate their email addresses. Below the Invite box, choose the kind of access you want these people to have:

  ■ To edit—Editors can view and make changes to the spreadsheet. If you grant permission, they can also share the spreadsheet with others (see next section).

  ■ To view—Viewers can see the spreadsheet but not change it in any way. They cannot share your spreadsheet with others, although they can export or copy it.

 You give editing *or* viewing privileges when you add a group of sharers. If you want some of the people you're inviting to be viewers and others to be editors, you have to invite them as two separate groups.

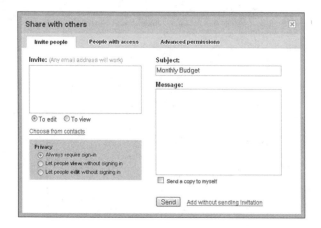

Figure 8.4
You can invite others to collaborate with you on a spreadsheet or simply to view it.

 If you use Gmail, Google's email program, you can quickly choose sharers from your Contacts List, Gmail's version of an address book. Click the Choose from Contacts link. In a new window, Google displays your Gmail contacts. Select the contacts you want to share with and then click Done. Google pops your contacts' email addresses into the Share with Others dialog box.

- Privacy—You've got three options here:
    - Always Require Sign-In—This means viewers or collaborators must sign in to their own Google account to have access to your spreadsheet.
    - Let People View without Signing In—Choose this option if some of your viewers don't have a Google account.
    - Let People Edit without Signing In—This option lets people edit the spreadsheet even if they don't have a Google account.
- Subject—This field, prefilled with your spreadsheet's name, specifies the subject line for the notification email Google sends.
- Message—Google's notification email to sharers includes a basic message that you've shared a file, as well as a link to your spreadsheet. If you want to customize that message, type your text in this box. Additionally, if you want to receive a copy of the notification email, check the box labeled Send a Copy to Myself.

When you've got your list of sharers, click Send. Google sends them an invitation email and, if they have a Google account, adds your spreadsheet to their Docs list. At the same time, it adds the new sharers to your People with Access list. From there, you can edit or remove sharers, as the next section, "Setting or Changing Permissions," explains.

If you prefer, you can add sharers without sending an invitation email. You might want to do this when you've just announced in a meeting that you're sharing the spreadsheet with everyone present (and you know that all sharers have a Google Docs account). When you add a sharer but don't send an email, Google simply adds the spreadsheet to that person's Docs list—just make sure he or she knows to look for it there.

To add sharers without sending the invitation email, click Share, Invite People. In the Share with Others dialog box (see Figure 8.4), fill in the email addresses and set permissions and privacy as you normally would. Don't worry about the Subject and Message sections; these apply only when you're sending out invitations. Instead, click the Add Without Sending Invitation link. Google opens another dialog box, asking you to confirm your choice. Click OK, and you've added your sharers—without sending a notification email.

Setting or Changing Permissions

After you've shared a spreadsheet with some other people, you may want to adjust the level of access those sharers have: give a viewer permission to edit (or vice versa) or restrict editors' ability to share the spreadsheet with still more people. This section explains how to tweak permissions in a shared spreadsheet that you own.

Info 4U *Owning* a spreadsheet means that you created the spreadsheet or that its previous owner has transferred ownership to you. (Chapter 5 discusses transferring ownership of a document—it works the same way for spreadsheets.) A spreadsheet's owner has the ability to delete a shared spreadsheet from all sharers' Docs accounts and can set the permissions described in this section.

Allowing or Restricting Others' Ability to Share

When you give other people permission to edit the spreadsheet, you may or may not want those editors to share the spreadsheet with more people of their own choosing. You can stop editors from sharing a spreadsheet with others by following these steps:

1. Open the shared spreadsheet. Click Share and then select either Invite People or See Who Has Access. Either option opens the Share with Others dialog box.
2. Click Advanced Permissions.
3. The Advanced Permissions tab has just one option: Editors Can Share This Item. This box is checked by default, automatically giving collaborators permission to share. If you *don't* want editors to have this permission, clear the checkmark from the box.
4. Click Save & Close.

When you revoke permission to share the spreadsheet, you're the only person who can give others the ability to view or edit the document.

Changing Someone's Sharing Level

Maybe you granted someone viewing privileges when you meant to give that person the ability to work on the spreadsheet. Or maybe you're regretting that you gave editing privileges to someone who's messing up your data. You can change a sharer's access level with these steps:

1. Open the spreadsheet and click Share, See Who Has Access to open the Share with Others dialog box to its People with Access tab, as shown in Figure 8.5.

2. Your name, as owner, appears at the top of the list. Below your name are the people who share the spreadsheet. Find the name of the person whose sharing level you want to change. To the right of the name is that person's permission level. Click the downward-pointing arrow next to the permission level.

3. From the menu that appears, choose the sharing level you want for this person: Can Edit, Can View, or None. If you want, continue changing sharing levels for other people.

4. Click Save & Close to apply your changes and close the dialog box.

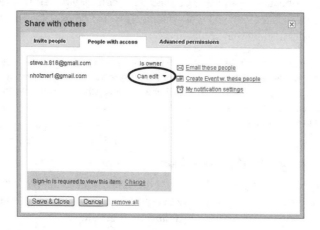

Figure 8.5
View, change, or remove sharing privileges here.

 When you set someone's sharing level to None, Google removes that person from your People with Access list and removes your spreadsheet from that person's Docs list.

Sharing a Spreadsheet with the World

When you publish a spreadsheet (or one of its sheets) on the Web or embedded in a Web page, you're publishing a read-only version—which means that viewers can see the spreadsheet data but not work on it. (If you've shared the published spreadsheet—see "Sharing a Spreadsheet with Individuals or Groups" earlier in this chapter—your collaborators can click a link to sign in to Google and edit the spreadsheet in their Docs account.)

Sometimes, though, you might want to publish a spreadsheet that anyone can edit. For example, say you have a spreadsheet that lets people sign up for the monthly neighborhood potluck dinner. You want anyone in the neighborhood to be able to sign up for a type of dish and a time slot—whether or not they have a Google account.

To publish a spreadsheet that anyone can edit, open the spreadsheet you want and click Share, Share with the World to open the Share with the World dialog box, shown in Figure 8.6.

In the dialog box, choose a privacy option:

- Always Require Sign-In—This option, the default, is how your spreadsheet is already set up. It lives on the Web but inside your Google Docs account. The only people who can view or edit it are those you've chosen to share it with (see next section), and they must sign in to see or work on the spreadsheet.

- Let People View without Signing In—Similar to the method of publishing a spreadsheet discussed in the section, "Publishing a Spreadsheet on the Web," this option lets anyone who finds their way to the spreadsheet's URL view the spreadsheet. In other words, viewers don't need a Google account to see the spreadsheet.

- Let People Edit without Signing In—For the neighborhood potluck sign-up example, this is the option you want. Your spreadsheet can be edited by anyone regardless of whether or not they have a Google account.

When you choose to let people view or edit the spreadsheet without signing in, Google displays a URL in the Link to Share in Email or IM field. Click the Preview link to open the spreadsheet in a new window; this is how others will see your spreadsheet:

- If you chose Let People View without Signing In, the spreadsheet looks just like it does in the spreadsheet editor, but all of the menu buttons (except Help) are disabled and grayed out. If a viewer clicks a cell, he or she cannot enter or change data in that cell.

- If you chose Let People Edit without Signing In, the spreadsheet opens in a spreadsheet editor, just as it does in your Google Docs account. Anyone can make changes to the spreadsheet, and those changes are recorded in your version.

Info 4U When you publish a version of the spreadsheet that anyone can edit, there are some restrictions. For example, people editing this version of the spreadsheet cannot share it with others or make a copy of it (although they can export or print it).

Copy the spreadsheet's URL so that you can link to it from a Web page or blog or send it to interested people by email or instant message. When you're finished, click Save to put a viewable or editable version of the spreadsheet on the Web.

Info 4U When you share a spreadsheet "with the world," as described in this section, Google adds Everyone to the Folders/Sharing column of your Docs list on the Google Docs home page.

Figure 8.6
Choose whether you want the spreadsheet to be viewable or editable by anyone—whether or not they have a Google account.

Collaborating on Spreadsheets

When you've shared a spreadsheet, giving editing privileges to some collaborators, you and those people can work on the spreadsheet together in real time. As long as you've all got Internet access and a Web browser, you can work on the spreadsheet from anywhere and at any time. As edits are made, Google updates everyone's version of the spreadsheet, so you can be sure that the version in your Docs list is always the most up-to-date version.

 With Google Docs, up to 50 people can edit a spreadsheet simultaneously.

This chapter gives you the ins and outs of working on a Google Docs spreadsheet with collaborators, including simultaneous editing, using a spreadsheet's built-in chat function, working with comments, and getting notifications of changes.

Working Simultaneously

You no longer have to get everyone in the same room to work on a spreadsheet as a team. When you're working on a shared spreadsheet, you and your colleagues can edit a document together, even when you're in the office, Chris is in a hotel room two states over, Sam is visiting a branch office, and Paula is working from home.

When you're working on a spreadsheet and someone else comes on board to work on it, you get a notification in the lower-right part of the spreadsheet. At the same time, the person's ID appears on the right side of the bar above the spreadsheet, as shown in Figure 8.7.

If several people are editing a spreadsheet at the same time, Google assigns each of them a different color, so you know who's making which edits. When a collaborator selects a cell, that cell is outlined with a color assigned to that collaborator, so you know where he or she is working. And if the collaborator clicks in a cell to enter or edit data, that cell becomes shaded in your spreadsheet.

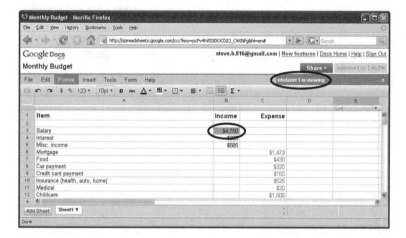

Figure 8.7
When someone joins you in editing a spreadsheet, Google tells you who's there and what they're working on.

Chatting as You Work

When you and some collaborators are editing a spreadsheet, you'll probably have a question or two about the data that you want to ask your colleagues. When that happens, you can start a chat session without leaving the spreadsheet.

To get the conversation going, click the right side of the bar above the spreadsheet (where it shows who else is viewing the spreadsheet, as shown in Figure 8.7). When you click the bar, a chat pane opens, as shown in Figure 8.8. At the top of the pane is a list that shows who's currently working on the spreadsheet, along with the color assigned to that person. (When an editor selects a cell, this color outlines the cell in your spreadsheet.) Below the list of editors is a chat box. Type your message into the text field at the bottom and then press Enter to send the message to your collaborators.

If a collaborator has the chat pane open, the message appears in the chat box. (If the chat pane isn't open, the Viewing Now section of the bar above the spreadsheet turns orange; this is a signal that a chat message is waiting. Clicking the orange bar opens the chat pane.)

Can't concentrate because there's too much chatting going on? Click the Viewing Now bar at the top of the chat pane, and the chat pane disappears. The bar will turn orange as your collaborators continue to chat, but you can keep the pane closed.

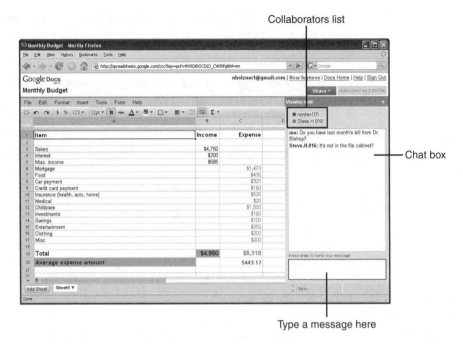

Figure 8.8
Open the chat pane to send instant messages to your collaborators.

Commenting on a Spreadsheet

Another way to communicate with your collaborators is through comments. When you insert a comment, Google puts a marker in the upper-right corner of the cell you're commenting on, as shown in Figure 8.9. When someone hovers the mouse pointer over the marker, your comment appears in a box. Your collaborators can read and respond to your comment in that box. Comments are useful when you have a question or point to make about a cell but no one is around for a chat. They're also great for leaving notes to yourself for future reference.

Inserting a comment requires just a few steps:

1. Click the cell you want to comment on to select it.

2. From the menu bar, select Insert, Comment. A small box opens for you to write your comment. This box is already stamped with your Google ID, the date, and the time.

3. Type your comment.

4. When you're finished, click outside the comment box. Google closes the comment box and marks the cell with an orange dot in its upper-right corner.

That's all there is to it. If you want to read your comment, put your mouse point on the cell's marker. The comment box appears. When you move the mouse pointer away, the comment disappears.

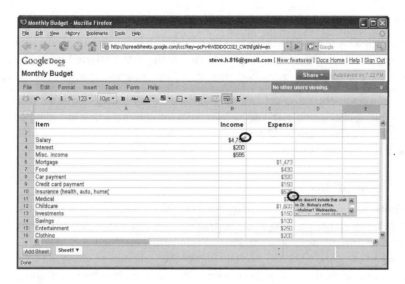

Figure 8.9
Hover the mouse pointer over a marker (circled) to see a comment on that cell.

 Tip 4U Windows users can take this keyboard shortcut to insert a comment: Select a cell and then press Shift+F2 and then type your comment in the box that opens.

Editing Your Comment

After you've left a comment, you may want to go back and edit it—clarify it in some way, add more information, or correct a typo. When you want to edit a comment, hover your mouse pointer over the relevant cell's marker. When the comment box appears, click inside it. Now you can type inside the comment box and edit your comment. When you're done, click outside the comment box to close it.

Responding to a Comment

When you read a comment left by someone else, you may want to respond to it: answer a question or explain the data, for example. You can respond to a comment in the same way you'd edit one (see previous section), but that method doesn't stamp your response with your ID, the date, and the time, but that may confuse your collaborators, who won't know who left the response. To keep everything clear, make sure that Google stamps your reply with your ID and the date and time you made it.

To do this, select the cell that holds the comment and then click Insert, Comment. The comment box opens. At the top of the box are the instructions "Type here," followed by your Google ID, the date, and the time. Type your response and then click outside the comment box when you're done.

Deleting a Comment

You don't want a lot of obsolete or irrelevant comments hanging around and cluttering up your spreadsheet. After a comment has been addressed or the data it referred to has changed, you can delete the comment, removing both its text and the comment marker from the spreadsheet.

To get rid of a comment, hover your mouse pointer over the comment marker. When the comment box opens, click inside it. Delete all the text in the comment box, including commenter IDs and any date and time stamps. When the comment box is empty, click outside of it. The box closes, and the marker disappears.

Receiving Notifications

When a bunch of people are working on your spreadsheet, you probably want to know about the changes they're making. Google makes that easy for you with automatic notifications. Depending on how you set things up, you can receive an email notification whenever a change is made, when someone works on a certain part of the spreadsheet, when the collaborator list changes, or when new data comes in via a form (the next section explains all about forms).

 Anyone who has access to a spreadsheet can set up notification rules. Whether you're the owner, an editor, or a viewer, you can tell Google to notify you about changes to the spreadsheet.

Before you can receive notifications about what's going on with a spreadsheet, you need to set up notification rules. To do that, open the spreadsheet you want and then click Share, Set Notification Rules. This opens the Set Notification Rules dialog box, shown in Figure 8.10. In the dialog box, choose the notifications you want:

- Notify Me When—In this section, select the conditions under which you want to receive a notification:
    - Any Changes Are Made—If you want to keep a close eye on each and every change someone makes to the spreadsheet, check this box.
    - Anything on this Sheet Is Changed—To watch changes made to a particular sheet within the spreadsheet, check this box and choose the sheet you want from the drop-down list.
    - Any of these Cells Are Changed—Enter a range of cells (you can use a named range), and Google will tell you when changes happen to that range.
    - Collaborators Are Added or Removed—This option keeps you aware of who's working on the spreadsheet. (Of course, if you haven't given collaborators permission to share a spreadsheet you own, you don't need to worry about this option.)
    - A User Submits a Form—The next section, "Creating a Form to Gather Data," tells you how to set up a form to get data into your spreadsheet—users fill out the form, and the information they submit goes straight into the spreadsheet. If you want notification when a spreadsheet receives data in this way, check this box.

■ Notify Me With—In this section, choose how often you want to receive notification emails:

■ Email–Daily Digest—Check this box to get a once-a-day email summarizing recent changes to the spreadsheet.

■ Email–Right Away—If you want immediate notification of a change, check this box.

When you've set up the notification rules you want, click Save to apply them to the spreadsheet. Then watch your Inbox.

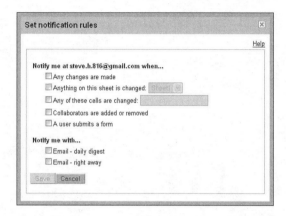

Figure 8.10
Use this dialog box to set notification rules so you'll know when a spreadsheet changes.

Creating a Form to Gather Data

If you collect data from different sources, such as travel expenses from sales reps or orders from customers, you can create a form to gather that data directly. A *form* collects data by asking a series of questions, which users answer; their answers become data in your spreadsheet. For example, as they travel, your company's sales reps can submit their expenses using the Travel Expenses form, and the information they submit goes directly into your Travel Expenses spreadsheet.

You can create a brand-new spreadsheet by designing a form to collect its data, or you can create a form for an existing spreadsheet. The next sections tell you how to do both.

Creating a New Spreadsheet by Designing a Form

To set up a form and create a new spreadsheet, you can start either on the Google Docs home page or from the spreadsheet editor:

■ From the Google Docs home page, click New, Form.

■ From the spreadsheet editor, select File, New, Form.

Either method opens a new window displaying the Edit Form page, shown in Figure 8.11. Here is where you'll set up the form by choosing options and setting up fields. In a form, a *field* collects a specific piece of information, such as user name, employee ID number, quantity, price, notes, and so on:

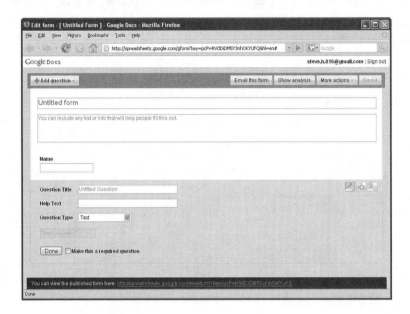

Figure 8.11
Build a form one question at a time.

- Title—A text field at the top of the page holds the words Untitled form. Click in this field and name your form. The title you use here becomes the title of the spreadsheet that collects the form's data.

- Description—This is optional, but it can be helpful to include a description that states the purpose of the form and any pointers that may help users fill it out. Type a description in the large text box under the form's title field.

- Name—Google has provided your form's first field for you. This field is a text box that collects a respondent's name. (If you don't want a name field—for example, if you're collecting anonymous customer feedback—you can edit or delete this field. See "Editing a Form" later in this chapter to find out how.)

- Question Title—Here's where you start setting up the first field for your form. What you type here labels the field and becomes a column heading in the spreadsheet that collects data through the form. For a form collecting travel expenses, for example, the Question Title might be *Employee ID*. For a customer survey, it might be something like *Customer Service*.

- Help Text—Whatever you type here appears beneath the question in gray text. Use this optional box to explain or elaborate on the question. For example, for the Customer Service question title, you might add this Help text—*Please rate your satisfaction with our customer service on a scale of 1–10.*

- Question Type—Choose the kind of information the question requires as an answer (in other words, choose the field's data type). As you choose an option here, the section changes to collect the information Google needs to set up the kind of question/answer you choose:

  - Text—This option, shown in Figure 8.11, presents users with a small text box.

  - Paragraph Text—When you choose this option, users see an expanded text box, suitable for lengthier responses.

  - Multiple Choice—Multiple choice presents users with several options, each marked by a radio button, from which they can choose one. When you select Multiple Choice as the Question Type, the section changes to show two text boxes, where you can type the user's options. When you click in the lower option box, Google automatically adds a new option box below it, and when you click in that box, another appears below that one (and so on until you've entered all the options you need).

  - Checkboxes—Checkboxes are another kind of multiple-choice question. Unlike radio buttons, which allow users to select only one option, checkboxes let users pick more than one option. When you choose Checkboxes, the section expands so you can type in the options the form presents to users.

Tip 4U Both Multiple Choice and Checkboxes let you offer an option called Other. Click the Add Other link, and Google adds a radio button or checkbox labeled Other, along with a text box that lets users enter their own answers.

  - Choose from a List—Use this option to create a drop-down list of choices. As with Multiple Choice and Checkboxes, the section expands so you can tell Google the choices you want.

  - Scale (1–n)—This option lets users rate something on a numeric scale. When you select it, first determine the range of the scale (1–5 or 1–10, for example). If you want, you can add optional labels to the lowest and highest numbers on the scale, such as *Poor* and *Excellent,* so that users understand how the scale works. You can have up to ten choices on a scale.

- Make This a Required Question—If the question is an essential one that the user must answer in order to submit the form, check this box. On the form, required questions are marked with an asterisk (*).

When your question looks good, click Done. To add another question to your form, click the upper-left Add Question button. A menu appears that lists the different question types just discussed. Choose one, and Google adds it to the bottom of the form. Once it's there, type in the question, any help text, and any answer options.

You can save time creating a form by duplicating an existing question and then tweaking the copy. To duplicate a question, move your mouse pointer over the question you want so that you see some icons appear to its right. Click the Duplicate icon, which shows two overlapping squares. Google inserts the duplicate question immediately after the original.

When you're finished setting up the form, click the upper-right Saved button. Google saves the form and adds it to your Docs list.

 The spreadsheet that Google creates to hold the data from your new form draws its column headings from your question titles. In addition, Google automatically adds a Timestamp column so you'll know when a user submitted data via the form.

 To see how your form will look to users, click the link at the bottom of the Edit Form page. The form opens in a new window.

Creating a Form for an Existing Spreadsheet

If there's a spreadsheet already in your Google Docs account that would benefit from receiving data through a form, you can create a form from that spreadsheet. (This can save you a lot of work—when you need to collect data from various people, those people can input the data themselves.)

To use an existing spreadsheet to create a form, open the spreadsheet you want and click Form, Create a Form. This opens the Edit Form page shown in Figure 8.11. Instead of an untitled, blank form, however, the form is prefilled with the spreadsheet's title and question titles that correspond to the spreadsheet's column headings. If that's all you need, click Save; Google creates the form and associates it with the spreadsheet. When someone answers the form's questions and submits the form, the data gets added to your spreadsheet.

If you want, you can tweak the form's questions. For example, you might want to change a text field to multiple choice to limit the options for data in that field. For example, you might prefer Yes and No radio buttons to the opportunity to submit a more long-winded answer. The upcoming section "Editing a Form" tells you how to change a form's questions.

 When you create a form to add data to an existing spreadsheet, the form does not affect the data that's already in the spreadsheet.

Emailing a Form

Now that you've created and saved a form, it's ready to receive data. But how are people going to find it to fill it out? For a form that a limited number of people will fill out, such as coworkers, club members, or students at your school, you can email them the form. The email Google sends has a link to the form (you can also include the form itself in the email message).

To email a form, open the Edit Form page. If you've just created the form, you're already on that page. At the top of the page, click Email this Form. If you created the form a while ago, open the spreadsheet that's linked to the form and click Form, Send Form.

Either method opens the Send this Form to Others dialog box, shown in Figure 8.12. In the dialog box, type or paste in the list of recipients (use commas to separate multiple addresses). Gmail users can choose contacts from the Contacts List. The subject line for the email is the same as the form's title; you can change it if you like. The checkbox labeled Include Form in the Email is checked by default.

 The email always includes a link to the live, online version of the form. It also includes the description of the form that you wrote (if any) on the Edit Form page.

When you're ready to invite people to fill out the form, click Send to send them the email.

Figure 8.12
Email a form to the people you want to fill it out.

 The Google Docs: Forms List gadget gathers all your spreadsheet forms together in a list and displays them on your iGoogle page. When new data comes in via a form, Google displays the name of that form in bold and tells you how many times data has come in via the form (both the total number and the number of new submissions). Click a form's name to open its associated spreadsheet. Chapter 1 explains how to add gadgets to your iGoogle page.

Embedding a Form in a Web Page or Blog

What about situations in which you want anyone to be able to fill out the form—not just people on your email list? For example, you may want visitors to your Web site to use a form to request product information or sign up for your company newsletter.

When you're collecting information from the general public, you can embed the form in a Web page or blog post. To do this, open the Edit Form page. Click More Actions, Embed. (Or if you're looking at the spreadsheet that's linked to the form, click Form, Embed Form.) The Embed dialog box opens, displaying the HTML code you need to put the form into your Web site or blog. The HTML is already selected; copy it to your computer's clipboard (press Ctrl+C in Windows or Cmd-C on a Mac). From there, paste the HTML into an HTML document or Web page editor and upload it to your Web site or blog. The form now appears in the page or blog post where you pasted the code.

 Want to know when someone has added data to your spreadsheet using a form? Set up a notification rule that tells Google to send you an email (either immediately or as a daily digest) when someone submits a form. "Receiving Notifications," earlier in this chapter, tells you how.

Editing a Form

If you need to make changes to a form, you can easily do so. When you edit a form, those edits are reflected in the spreadsheet to which the form is linked. For example, if you add a new question to the form, the question title appears as a column heading in the spreadsheet. Similarly, if you move around the form's questions, you change the order of the columns in the spreadsheet, as well.

When you want to make changes to a form, open the associated spreadsheet and select Edit, Form. The Edit Form page opens, with details for the current form filled in. Hover your mouse pointer over the question you want to change. As you can see in Figure 8.13, the cursor becomes a four-way arrow, and three icons appear to the right of the Question Title. Now, you can take any of these actions:

- Move the question—To rearrange the questions in your form (and the columns in the corresponding spreadsheet), click and drag the question up or down. Let go of the mouse button to drop the question into its new location.

- Edit the question—Click the Edit icon (which looks like a pencil), and the question changes so you can edit it. Change its title, help text, type, and whether it's required. Click Done after you've finished your revisions.

- Duplicate the question—Clicking the Duplicate icon creates an exact copy of the selected question and inserts it immediately after. From there, you can edit the duplicate question as you like.

- Delete the question—Click the Delete icon (the one that looks like a trash can) to remove a question from the form. A dialog box appears, asking whether you're sure you want to delete the question. Click OK, and it's gone.

When you've finished editing the form, click Save to apply your changes to the live form.

 When you delete a question from a form, Google removes the corresponding column heading but leaves any existing data in that column. In your spreadsheet, you can re-enter the column heading (this won't affect the form) or delete the column, depending on how you want to treat the existing data.

Figure 8.13
Select a question to move, edit, duplicate, or delete it.

Editing a Form's Confirmation Message

After someone's filled out a form, Google lets them know their submission was successful with this default message: *Thanks! Your response will now appear in my spreadsheet.*

This message is fine for many purposes, but you may want to change it. For example, for potential customers who are requesting product information, a more appropriate confirmation might be something like this: *Thank you for your interest in our products. The materials you requested are on their way.*

To change a form's confirmation message, open the relevant spreadsheet and click Form, Edit Form. On the Edit Form page, click More Actions and then select Edit Confirmation. This opens a dialog box that displays the form's current confirmation message. Click in the text box and make whatever edits you like. When you're done, click Save, and Google uses your new confirmation message.

Analyzing Form Data

Google offers a feature, currently experimental, that automatically summarizes and analyzes the data you collect via a form. Google looks at the data that arrives through the form and creates a summary for each question. It also automatically creates charts where applicable. For example, if one of your questions is multiple choice, Google creates a pie chart that shows how each choice contributes to total answers to that question. Figure 8.14 shows an example.

 Google analysis of form data applies only to data submitted through the form. Data entered directly into the spreadsheet and data edited within the spreadsheet do not appear in the analysis.

To see Google's automatic analysis of your form data, open the relevant spreadsheet and click Form, Show Analysis. Google does the rest, breaking down your data and opening a page that looks like the one in Figure 8.14.

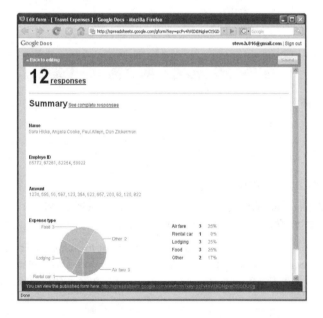

Figure 8.14
Google can create an automatic summary and analysis of data submitted through a form. This example shows how travel expenses break down into categories such as air fare, car rental, lodging, and so on.

Disabling or Deleting a Form

Disabling a form means that you prevent that form from receiving any data (usually temporarily). *Deleting* a form means that you get rid of the form altogether, removing it from the spreadsheet and destroying it. You might want to disable a form, for example, when there's a temporary freeze on spending and no new expenses can be submitted until the freeze is lifted. You might want to delete a form, on the other hand, when it surveys responses to a marketing campaign that has now ended.

 Neither disabling nor deleting a form affects the data that's currently in the spreadsheet, including the column headings.

Disabling a Form

Disabling a form is easy. Open the spreadsheet whose form you want to disable and click Form. When the form is enabled, the Form menu's Accepting Responses option shows a checkmark; this checkmark means that the form is live and can feed data into the spreadsheet. Click Accepting Responses. Google removes the checkmark and disables the form.

Now if someone tries to access the form, Google shows a message saying that the form is turned off. So no new data can be submitted using the form.

To reenable the form, open the spreadsheet and select Form. Notice that the Accepting Responses option does *not* have a checkmark; this means the form is disabled. Click Accepting Responses to turn the form back on.

Deleting a Form

If you want to remove a form from a spreadsheet (rather than simply turn it off), open the spreadsheet and click Form, Delete Form. A dialog box appears, asking whether you're certain that you want to delete the form. Make sure you really do want to get rid of this form—once you've deleted a form, you can't get it back, and that includes Google's analysis of the form's data. If you're sure you want to delete the form, click OK, and Google deletes it.

Working with a Spreadsheet's Revision History

Google knows that your data is important to you—so it keeps track of different versions of your spreadsheet as they existed at various moments in time. A spreadsheet's revision history lets you see previous versions of the spreadsheet and, if necessary, roll back to one of those earlier versions. Good to know when you've got a dozen different collaborators messing around with your data.

When you want to look at earlier versions of a spreadsheet, click File, Revision History. Google opens the most recent previous version of the spreadsheet. As you can see in the example shown in Figure 8.15, Google highlights cells that changed in that version, making it easy for you to focus on what's different about that version. Also when you're looking at a spreadsheet's revision history, the menu bar is grayed out, and a revision history toolbar appears. Here's what's on it:

- Back to Edit—Click this button to return to the spreadsheet editor (and the spreadsheet's current version).

- Revision—This shows the time stamp for the version you're looking at now. Versions more than a day old are stamped "1 day(s) ago," "3 day(s) ago," "2 week(s) ago," and so on. Click the button to see a list of edits, who made them, and when they were made. Choose any revision to view it.

- Older/Newer—Clicking these buttons displays the previous or the next version, respectively.

- Revert to This One—Click this button to make the version you're looking at now the current version of the spreadsheet.

Revision history toolbar

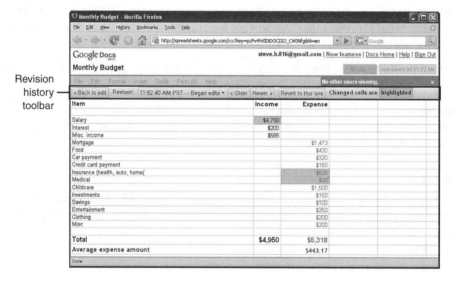

Figure 8.15
Google highlights changed cells when you view a spreadsheet's revision history.

Info 4U You don't lose the current version when you revert to an older version; it simply becomes its own version in the spreadsheet's revision history.

Introducing Presentations

Slideshow-style presentations, such as those made with Microsoft PowerPoint, have become a staple of meetings everywhere. When you're speaking to a group, a presentation gives structure to your talk, expresses your main points in a way that's clear and easy to remember, and provides visual interest to keep your audience's attention.

Google Docs presentations offer all these benefits, along with the ability to collaborate with others to develop a presentation and to give the presentation over the Internet (no special software needed).

This chapter introduces presentations, from creating and saving your first presentation to spiffing up your slides with themes, text formatting, images, shapes, and video. If you're used to working with PowerPoint, you may find Google Docs presentations a bit basic—no fancy animations, transitions, or sound effects here. Even so, you'll find everything you need to create, organize, and show attractive, informative slides. And that's what a good presentation is all about.

What's a Presentation?

Simply put, a *presentation* is a slideshow that you share with an audience. Individual slides hold text, images, shapes—even video. As you speak, you click from one slide to the next. Each slide supports a specific part of your talk. For example, if your presentation is about second-quarter sales, you might start with a slide that gives an overview of the company's sales, followed by several slides that break down sales numbers in various ways (by product, by region, and so on), followed by slides that analyze the quarter's sales trends and then use them to project future sales and recommend strategies. Each slide or set of slides corresponds to a specific part of the talk, supporting your points.

Why Use Google Docs for Presentations?

With Google Docs, you can invite others to collaborate on a presentation you're developing. Maybe you're great with figures but not so great with design—you can provide the content and then bring someone else on board to spiff up your slides. Or if you're part of a group giving a presentation, you don't have to wait around for a colleague to pass the presentation to you—everyone can do his or her part working on the same presentation, in real time. When you or someone else makes a change, it appears immediately, keeping everyone's version of the presentation up to date.

Additionally, Google Docs lets you give your presentation to a group of people who are in the room with you or to a scattered audience that connects to the Internet to join your presentation. You can even publish a presentation on the Web so that people can go through your slides on their own time.

 Chapter 10, "The Main Event: Sharing and Viewing Presentations" tells you all about sharing, collaborating on, and giving presentations.

Some Pointers for Designing a Presentation

If you've ever sat through a presentation where you missed half of what the speaker was saying because you were trying to make sense of his or her slides, you know that there's an art to designing an effective presentation. Fortunately, this art isn't hard to master. Follow the suggestions in this section to create a presentation that supports what you have to say—without undermining or overwhelming your points.

What's Your Presentation's Purpose?

Presentations can have many different goals: to inform, to sell, to teach, to persuade, even to entertain. What do you hope to accomplish with your presentation? Your answer to that question reveals the presentation's purpose. Now, think about how the design of your slideshow can support that purpose. Bright colors and goofy cartoon characters don't support a formal financial presentation to the Board of Directors but could be appropriate for a presentation about the upcoming neighborhood block party.

Keep Your Slides Simple

Cluttered slides are a distraction. Instead of listening to you, your audience is probably squinting at the slide, trying to understand it. Don't try to cram too much onto one slide—if a slide is looking crowded, present its information over several slides or, perhaps better, ask whether all this information really needs to be on slides. Remember that your presentation is what you have to say. Slides support your main points; they don't do your talking for you.

Also choose backgrounds that let your slides speak for themselves. Don't allow a slide's background or color scheme to make its text difficult to read.

Avoid Text-Heavy Slides

You want the text on your slides to have high impact, to present the main point or points of that part of your talk. So don't try to squeeze paragraphs onto your slides. Instead, use a single sentence, a sentence fragment, or a to-the-point bulleted list.

 It's a good general guideline to keep a slide's bulleted list to six items or less.

Don't Go Overboard on Graphics

Graphics include photos, charts, shapes (such as arrows, speech bubbles, and sunbursts), clip art, and other images. As with text, any graphics you use should support the point of the slide: a chart to illustrate sales trends, pictures of products, vacation photos to share with your family or friends—all these can work to support your purpose. On the other hand, the clip art that has become ubiquitous can easily distract viewers from a slide's information. Ask yourself, "Can I make my point without this graphic?" If so, leave it off.

Be Consistent

You'll give your audience a headache if you keep switching color schemes and fonts from one slide to the next. Choose the colors you want, choose the font you want, and then stick with them throughout the presentation. When you select a theme for your presentation (see "Adding Some Style with a Theme," coming up in this chapter), Google takes care of the fonts and colors for you—so you can focus on the presentation's content. And *that's* what your presentation is all about.

Your First Presentation

Ready to get started? This section gives you the very basics on how to start working on your first Docs presentation, whether you create it from scratch or upload an existing presentation into your Docs account.

Starting from Scratch

To create a new presentation, start from the Google Docs home page. Click New, Presentation to open the presentation editor, shown in Figure 9.1. (If you already have the presentation editor open, you create a new presentation by clicking File, New, Presentation.)

Figure 9.1 shows a blank, untitled presentation, ready for you to start working on it. On the left is the slide sorter pane; as you add slides to your presentation, this pane shows an overview of those slides, in order. Use this pane to add, copy, rearrange, and delete slides. On the right is the slide editor, where you work on individual slides.

When you create a new presentation, the first slide is always a title slide, with text boxes preinserted and preformatted for a title and subtitle. Click the sample text to reveal a text box, where you can type in your own words. When you've finished typing, click outside the text box.

On the first slide, give the presentation's title (indicating what the presentation is about) and a subtitle. The subtitle could give more information about the presentation's topic, or it might give other information, such as your name, your company name, or the date of the presentation.

Slide editor pane

Slide sorter pane

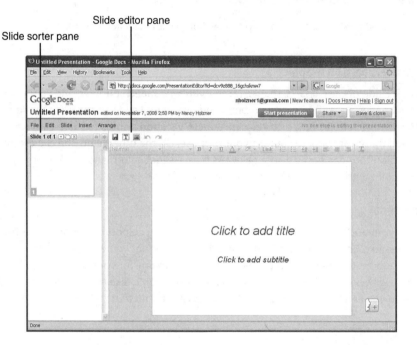

Figure 9.1
When you create a new presentation, the presentation editor looks like this.

Naming Your Presentation

Google assumes that the title of your first slide is also the title of your presentation. So when you click the words "Click to add title" and type your title in the text box, Google grabs what you type and uses it to name the presentation. The presentation title appears in the upper-left area of the presentation editor.

If you prefer, you can also name (or rename) the presentation using one of these methods:

- Click the upper-left presentation title. (If you haven't yet given the presentation a name, this says *Untitled Presentation*.)
- Click File, Rename.

Either method opens a dialog box for naming the presentation. Type in the name you want and then click OK. Google applies the name to this presentation.

Getting an Existing Presentation into Google Docs

Your first Google Docs presentation may not be one you create from scratch. Instead, you may have a presentation created and stored in another program, such as Microsoft PowerPoint or Apple Keynote, that you want to upload into your Google Docs account. To start from the Google Docs home page, click Upload. (From the presentation editor, click File, Upload a Presentation.) The Upload a File page, shown in Figure 9.2, opens.

 Google Docs accepts presentations in these formats: .ppt (Microsoft PowerPoint) and .pps (Microsoft PowerPoint Slideshow). If you created the presentation in OpenOffice.org Impress or Apple Keynote, be sure to save the file in one of these formats before you upload it to Google Docs.

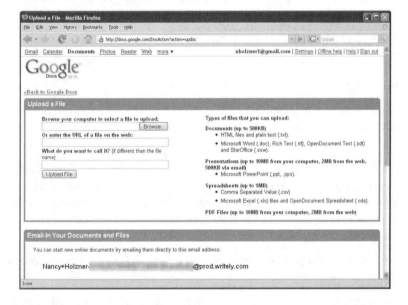

Figure 9.2
The Upload a File page gives you three methods for getting a presentation into Google Docs: upload from your computer, upload from the Web, or email as an attachment.

As with word-processing documents, you have three options for uploading an existing presentation into Google Docs:

- Upload a presentation from your computer. Browse for a presentation that's stored on your computer and then upload it to your Docs account. Using this method, you can upload presentations up to 10MB in size.

- Grab a copy of a presentation that's on the Web. Give Google the Web address (URL) of the presentation you want, and Google uploads it to your account. This method works for presentations that are 2MB or smaller.

- Email the presentation as an attachment. If the presentation is 500KB or smaller, you can email it into your Google Docs account as an attachment. (Use the email address at the bottom of the Upload a File page.)

The specific steps for uploading a presentation using one of these methods are the same as for uploading a word-processing document. If you want detailed instructions on uploading a file to Google Docs, refer back to Chapter 2, "Starting Word Processing."

 Compared to some other presentation programs, such as PowerPoint, Google Docs offers only limited effects for your slides. If you import a presentation that's chockfull of effects—transitions between slides, fancy animations, sound effects, and so on—these get stripped out of the presentation in Docs.

Adding a New Slide

As mentioned earlier in this section, when you create a new presentation, Google starts you off with a blank title slide. But one slide does not a presentation make. After you've typed in a title, naming your presentation, and perhaps added a subtitle, you'll want to insert a new slide to follow that first one.

To add a new slide, start at the top of the slide sorter pane, on the left side of the screen. Click the Insert a New Slide icon, a slide with a plus sign on it, as shown in Figure 9.3. Alternatively, you can either select Slide, New Slide or right-click (Control-click on a Mac) a slide in the slide sorter pane and select New Slide from the context menu.

The Choose Slide Layout dialog box opens. As you can see in Figure 9.3, five layouts are available for your new slide:

- Title—This slide layout has box for large-font text (36 points is the default) with a second for text with a smaller font (24 points) just beneath it.

- Text—This layout has a slot for a slide title at the top (formatted with 32-point font) and a large text box below it (the default font size here is 20 points).

- Two Columns—In this layout, the title at the top of the slide has two text boxes of equal size side by side below it.

- Caption—This layout places a text box at the bottom of the slide, which you can use to provide a caption for an image or chart.

■ Blank—No text boxes on this slide; you can insert your own (see next section) or fill the slide with other content, such as an image or video ("Adding Images, Shapes, and Videos" tells you how to do that).

 Tip 4U Layouts are all about the placement of text. Each style of layout has one or more preformatted text boxes placed on the slide. Use layouts to make your slides consistent, because text placement, sizes, and styles are standard throughout the presentation.

Click the layout you want to insert a slide with that layout. If you've chosen one of the five layouts with text boxes, click the sample text and start typing. If you've inserted a blank slide, read on to learn how to insert a text box, or jump ahead to "Adding Images, Shapes, and Videos" to insert one of those elements.

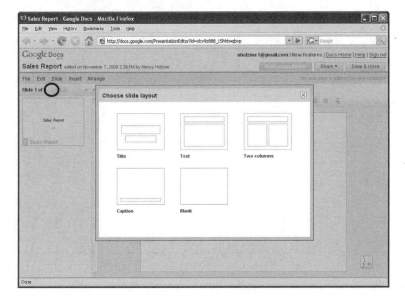

Figure 9.3
Click the Insert a New Slide button (circled) and then choose one of five layouts.

Selecting a Slide and Inserting Text

As you add slides to your presentation, you'll want to move back and forth among them, but the slide editor displays just one slide at a time. *Selecting* a slide means choosing that slide to be displayed in the slide editor. To select a slide, simply click the slide you want in the slide sorter pane. When you do, Google highlights that slide in the slide sorter pane (to show which slide is selected) and displays it in the slide editor. Now you can work on that slide in the slide editor.

When you insert a new slide, Google always puts it immediately after the currently selected slide.

If the slide you selected already has a text box inserted, you'll know because actual or sample text appears on the slide. Click the text to reveal the text box and start typing.

To insert a new text box, click the Insert a Text Shape button (it looks like the letter T surrounded by a dotted line). Google inserts a text box with a blinking cursor inside it, as shown in Figure 9.4. Start typing to enter some text. You can also format your text (see "Formatting Text") and move or resize the text box (see "Moving and Resizing Elements").

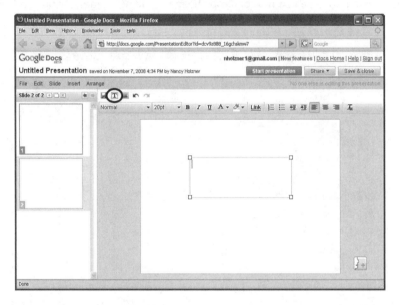

Figure 9.4
Click the Insert a Text Shape button (circled) to put a text box into a slide.

Saving a Presentation

If you've worked with Google Docs documents or spreadsheets, you won't be surprised to know that Google autosaves your presentation every few minutes. (Every once in a while, you'll notice a red *Saving* message appear in the upper-right part of the screen.) So saving your presentations is one less thing you have to worry about.

If you want to save the presentation at a particular moment—for example, maybe you want to be sure the current version gets saved in the presentation's revision history—you can click the toolbar's Save button or go to the menu bar and click File, Save. And to make sure that Google saves all changes before you close the presentation editor, click the upper-right Save & Close button. (Or if you prefer, click File, Save & Close.)

Giving Your Slides Pizzazz

Once you've mastered the basics of creating a presentation, inserting new slides, and adding some text, you may start to feel that your presentation could be a bit livelier. Maybe you'd like to add some color, try a different font, or insert images to add visual impact. This section explains ways to take your presentation beyond the basics, adding visual interest and working with the different elements (text, shapes, images, videos) you can put on a slide.

Adding Some Style with a Theme

If black text on a white background doesn't excite you, try using one of Google's available themes for your slides. A *theme* is a design that you apply to all the slides in a presentation: background, colors, fonts, and (in some cases) graphics.

To see the themes that are available and see how they look when applied to your presentation, click Edit, Change Theme. This opens the Choose Theme dialog box, shown in Figure 9.5. Google currently offers 15 themes (including Blank, the default for a new presentation); scroll through the Choose Theme box to get an idea of what each one looks like. When you see a theme you like, click it. Google closes the Choose Theme box and applies the theme to your presentation.

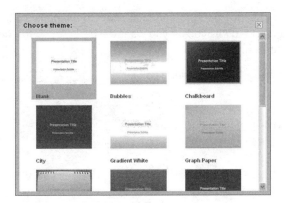

Figure 9.5
Click a theme to apply it to your presentation.

If you decide you don't like this theme after all, click Edit, Change Theme and choose a new theme from the Choose Theme dialog box. You can change a presentation's theme as many times as you like.

 Tip 4U If there's a theme you use in another presentation program, such as PowerPoint, that you want to use in Google Docs, create a slide with that theme in the other presentation program, save it as a .ppt or .pps file, and upload it to Google Docs. The presentation you uploaded has that theme as a background. Be aware, though, that Google treats this theme as an image; it won't appear in Google's Choose Theme box.

Giving Your Slides a Custom Background

If Google's presentation themes don't offer what you're looking for, you can create a custom background for your slides. You do this either by choosing a custom color or by uploading an image, such as your company's logo, to display. You can apply a custom background to just one slide or to all the slides in your presentation. So you might choose, for example, to show the company logo as the background on the title slide and then use a theme or a custom-color background for the rest of the presentation.

Choosing a Custom Color Background

Perhaps you don't want a fancy theme for your presentation, but you're not thrilled with Google's default white background (called Blank), either. You can add some color to your slides by choosing a custom background color.

Open your presentation and choose Edit, Change Background to open the dialog box shown in Figure 9.6. Click the Change Background button, which looks like a paint can on the verge of tipping over. A menu appears, showing a palette of colors. Click the one you want, and it appears in the left-hand preview section. If it's not quite the color you want, click the Change Background button again and pick a different color.

If you want this color to be the background for all slides in the presentation, check the box labeled Apply Background to All Slides. If you want the background for the currently selected slide only, leave that box unchecked.

All set? Click Save to apply the background color.

Figure 9.6
Use this dialog box to select a custom color or upload an image to use as a background.

You can change a presentation's theme as many times as you like.

You can also change a presentation's theme or a slide's background by right-clicking any slide in the presentation and choosing Change Theme or Change Background, respectively.

Using Your Own Image as a Background

If you want an image instead of just a color as a custom background for one or more slides, you can upload an image from your computer to use as a background. Any text, images, and so on that you add to slides appear on top of this image. That means, of course, that you don't want a background that's too bright or too busy—it'll make your slides hard to read. In other words, don't let a slide's background overpower its content.

 Because slides are horizontally oriented, it's best to choose a background that's also horizontally oriented. In other words, choose landscape orientation, not portrait.

To create a custom background using an image, open the presentation you want. If you're applying the image as a background to just one slide, select that slide in the left-hand slide-sorter pane. Click Edit, Change Background to open the Change Background dialog box (see Figure 9.6).

In the dialog box, click Insert Image. A text box and Browse button appear. Click Browse to open a new window where you can browse your computer's files to find the image you want. Select it and click Open to put the file's path in the Change Background box.

Next, choose whether you want the background to apply to all slides (check the Apply Background to All Slides box) or just the current slide (leave the box unchecked). Click Save to insert the image into your presentation. Figure 9.7 (in the "Formatting Text" section) shows a slide with a custom background.

 When you apply a custom background, you may need to change the font color of text on your slides to make the text show up clearly. "Formatting Text," coming up in this chapter, tells you how.

Removing a Custom Background

If you applied a custom background to your presentation and decide it's not working out, you can remove it by applying a theme to the whole presentation (see "Adding Some Style with a Theme," earlier in this chapter). When you apply a theme, Google assumes you want to apply it consistently throughout the presentation, so (after a warning that asks you to OK your choice) it removes any custom background you've created.

Formatting Text

You've put some text on a slide, and now you want to format that text: Use boldface or italics to emphasize a word or sentence or change the color or font style. This section tells you how to format the text that appears on your slides.

To change the appearance of the text on a slide, select the text you want to change. When you do, the box that holds the text appears, and Google enables the formatting toolbar, shown in Figure 9.7.

Formatting toolbar

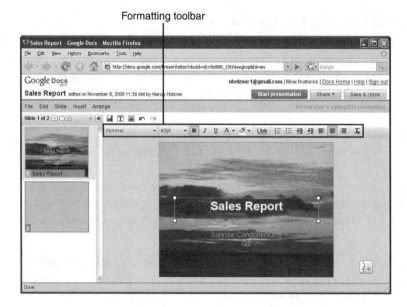

Figure 9.7
The buttons on the formatting toolbar change the appearance of text on a slide.

For text, the formatting toolbar offers these options (from left to right):

- Font—Click this button to see a menu of the six font styles Google currently offers for presentations.

- Font Size—You can select any size you want for your text. Google's built-in sizes range from 10 points to 96 points. If you don't see the size you want on the list, click Add. A dialog box opens where you can type in a custom font size (in points); click OK to apply the size you chose and add it to the Font Size list.

- **Bold**.

- *Italic*.

- <u>Underline.</u>

- Text Color. When you click this button, Google displays a palette of colors. Click any color to select it.

If you don't see the color you want, click the plus sign at the bottom of the palette. A dialog box opens, where you can give Google a custom color to use. For custom colors, Google accepts color names, such as *pink;* hexadecimal values, such as *#FFC0CB* for pink; or rgb values, such as *rgb(255, 192, 203),* also for pink. For a chart that gives more than 500 color names, along with their hexadecimal and rgb values, visit http://cloford.com/resources/colours/500col.htm.

- Text Background Color—To highlight text, click this button and then choose from Google's color palette or add a custom color.

- Add or Remove Link—An advantage of giving presentations online is that you can link to Web pages of interest. Click this button to open the Edit Link dialog box, shown in Figure 9.8. Select the kind of link you want to add—Web Address or Email Address—and then type or paste the URL or email address into the text box and click OK. Google inserts the link into the text you selected. To remove or edit a link, click this button again and make your changes in the Edit Link box.

 Exercise caution when inserting an email address into a presentation. If you plan to publish the presentation on the Web (see Chapter 10), you might find any email address you link to gets flooded with spam.

Figure 9.8
You can link text in a slide to a Web page or email address.

- Numbered List—This button converts the selected text into a list in which each item starts with a sequential number.

- Bullet List—If you want your list items to start with bullets, click this button.

- Decrease/Increase Indent—Click this button to move the selected text closer to or farther away from the left edge of the text box. The Increase Indent button is useful for creating subitems in bulleted or numbered lists.

- Left/Center/Right—These buttons align text.

- Remove Formatting—This button removes all formatting from the selected text with a single click.

Unlike some other presentation programs, Google Docs doesn't have a master slide that you can format to standardize slides throughout the presentation. Instead, create a slide and set up its formatting the way you like. Then duplicate that slide to insert a new slide with the same layout and formatting. "Copying a Slide," later in this chapter, tells you how to duplicate slides.

Adding Images, Shapes, and Videos

Sure, you can create a presentation that has nothing but text on its slides. But sometimes an image gets your point across with more impact, such as a chart showing sales figures or a photograph of a new product. This section shows you how to go graphic in your presentation, adding images, shapes, even video clips.

Adding an Image

To insert an image on a slide, select the slide you want and then click the Insert an Image button (or if you prefer, click Insert, Image). This opens the Insert Image dialog box, which lets you insert an image that's stored in either of these locations:

- On your computer—Select the radio button labeled "Browse your computer for the image file to upload" and click the Browse button. In the window that opens, find and select the file; click Open. The file's path appears in the Insert Image box.

 Google can upload images up to 2MB in size.

- On the Web—First, copy the image's Web address (URL). Then, in the Insert Image box, select the Specify an image URL radio button and paste the URL into the text box.

 Most of the images you'll find on the Internet are protected by copyright. Make sure you can legally use an image before you put it in your presentation.

After you've told Google where to find the image, click OK. Google uploads the image and inserts it into your slide.

 If the image you want to insert is on the Web, try this shortcut: Open the image in its own browser window and then resize that browser window so that you can see it and your Google Docs presentation editor at the same time. Click the image and drag it from its window onto your slide; let go of the mouse button to drop it into place. This method won't work with all images, but it's so quick and easy that it's worth a try.

Adding a Shape

Shapes can add emphasis to your presentation. For example, use an arrow to point to an important bullet point or a speech bubble to show a customer expressing typical feedback.

To insert a shape, select a slide and click Insert, Shape. A flyout menu shows the dozen shapes Google currently offers: square, circle, speech bubble, sunburst, and arrows pointing in different directions. Click the one you want to insert it.

If you don't see a shape you want, find or create a graphic of the desired shape and insert it as in image into your slide.

Formatting a Shape

After you've inserted a shape, you can format it. When you click the shape to select it, these options appear on the formatting toolbar, as shown in Figure 9.9:

- Fill Color—When Google inserts a shape, that shape is white with a black outline. To change the color of the shape's interior, click this button. Google's color palette appears; click a color to apply it or select None to make the shape's interior the same color as the slide's background (this works with themes as well as with solid-color backgrounds).

 To create your own custom color to fill in the shape, see the Tip in "Formatting Text," earlier in this chapter.

- Outline Color and Size—When you click this button, Google shows you its color palette so you can select a color for the shape's outline. If you don't want the shape to be outlined, select None. To change the outline's width, click Weight. A flyout menu appears, where you can select a width for the outline, from 1 to 6 pixels.

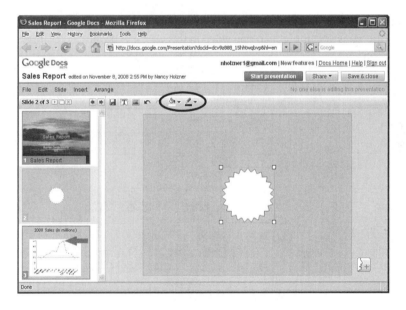

Figure 9.9
Select a shape, and the shape formatting buttons appear (circled).

To flip a shape, making an arrow point in the opposite direction, for example, select the shape you want to flip and then click Arrange and choose either Flip Horizontal or Flip Vertical. Alternatively, you can right-click the shape and choose one of those options from the context menu that appears.

You can also move and resize shapes, as an upcoming section, "Moving and Resizing Elements," explains.

Inserting a Video

Google has made it easy for you to find a YouTube video and put that video on a slide—nothing to copy and paste, no need even to leave Google Docs to find the YouTube video you're looking for.

To insert a video, select the slide you want and click Insert, Video. Google opens the Choose a Video From dialog box, shown in Figure 9.10. The title of your presentation appears in the Search box at the top, and videos that match that search term appear in a list. Scroll down the list to find a video or search for a different term to get new results.

 You can sort the video search results by relevance (the videos that best match your search term) or by view count (the most-watched videos related to your search term).

When you find the video you want to insert, click it. Google selects the video and checks the box to its left. (You can select more than one video in this way, if you want.) Click Insert Video to put the video(s) on your slide.

Figure 9.10
Select one or more videos and then click the Insert Video button.

After you've inserted a video, it shows a big, right-pointing Play arrow in the middle of the viewing area. To play the video, simply click the arrow.

If you insert more than one video on a slide, Google stacks them on top of each other. See the upcoming section "Moving and Resizing Elements" to find out how to spread out the videos so that each can be seen.

Moving and Resizing Elements

You're not stuck with Google's placement when you put an element onto a slide. Whatever kind of element you've inserted—text, image, shape, or video—you can move or resize that element. When you click an element to select it, a box appears around the element, with a small square, called a *handle*, at each corner. When you see that box, you can take these actions:

- Move the image—Hover your cursor over the element so that it becomes a four-way arrow. (If you're moving a text box, hover your cursor over the box's outline.) Click and then drag the element to move it. Let go of the mouse button to drop it in place.

- Resize the image—Put your cursor on top of one of the four handles at the corners of the selected element's box. Click and drag to resize the box. When you let go of the mouse button, Google resizes the element to fit the box.

Arranging Elements on a Slide

As you add text, images, and other elements to a slide, Google stacks more recently added elements on top of older ones. This means, for example that you can add a speech-bubble shape and then put a text box on top of it to show what's being said. You might find, however, as you add elements to a slide, resize them, and move them around, that one element obscures another in a way you don't want, as shown in Figure 9.11.

You can move elements forward (toward the top of the stack) or backward (toward the bottom of the stack) on a slide. Click the element you want to rearrange to select it and then click Arrange and choose one of these options:

- Bring to Front—Puts the element on top of all other elements. Windows users can also use this keyboard shortcut—Ctrl+Shift+up arrow.

- Bring Forward—Moves the element forward one place in the stack of elements. The Windows shortcut is Ctrl+up arrow.

- Send Backward—Moves the element back one place in the stack. In Windows, use Ctrl+down arrow as a keyboard shortcut.

- Send to Back—Puts the element on behind all of the other elements. The keyboard shortcut for Windows is Ctrl+Shift+down arrow.

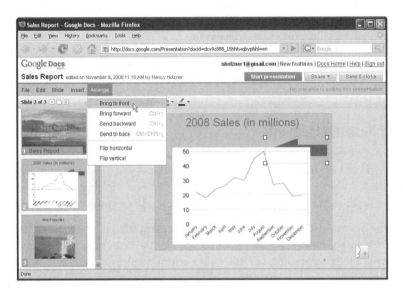

Figure 9.11
The arrow is obscured by the chart; the Arrange menu brings the arrow forward.

 Here's another option for moving an element backward or forward: Right-click (Control-click on a Mac) the element you want to rearrange and then select the option you want from the context menu.

Revealing Elements One by One

When you've got a slide listing several points—in a bulleted list, for example—you want your audience to listen to what you have to say about one point before you move on to the next. And that's the idea behind incremental reveal, which shows items on a list or elements on a slide one by one. When you click the mouse, the next list item or other element appears. So you don't have to worry about audience members reading and thinking about the sixth point on your list while you're still explaining the first.

To reveal list items (or other elements) one at a time, right-click (if you use Windows) or Control-click (if you use a Mac) the element you want, such as a bulleted list or a picture whose entrance you want to control. From the context menu, choose Incremental Reveal. Google shows that you've applied incremental reveal with a clock icon in the bottom-left corner of the element (the text box, for example).

 If you're revealing more than one element incrementally, such as several images, the clock shows a number to indicate the order in which each element is revealed (1 for first, 2 for second, and so on). To change that order, right-click (on a PC) or Control-click (on a Mac) an element's clock icon. From the context menu that appears, click the number you want for that element.

Now, when you present the slideshow, click the mouse when you want the next part of the incrementally revealed element to appear on the slide. For example, on a slide that shows a bulleted list, you must click when you want to show the next list item. Similarly, on a slide that stacks several images on top of each other, revealing those images incrementally, each mouse click shows a new image that covers up the previous one.

Deleting an Element

If you need to remove an element from a slide, select the element. Move the cursor so that it becomes a four-way arrow (anywhere on an image, shape, or video; on the border of a text box). From there, you can either right-click (Control-click) and select Delete from the context menu or simply press your keyboard's Delete or Backspace key.

If you delete an element by mistake, click Undo to bring it right back.

Working with Slides

As you build your presentation, creating and editing individual slides, you'll want to work with the slides themselves (not just what's on them). You do this in the slide-sorter pane, which appears on the left side of the screen and gives an overview of the presentation: showing small versions of the slides and the order in which they appear.

Importing Slides

If you've got a slide in one presentation that you'd like to reuse in a different presentation, you don't have to re-create that slide from scratch. Instead, you can import it. *Importing* a slide means copying a slide from one presentation and inserting a duplicate into another. Google Docs lets you import a slide from another Docs presentation or from a presentation that's stored on your computer.

The first step in importing a slide is to open the Import Slides dialog box, shown in Figure 9.12. To do this, start by selecting the slide you want the imported slide to follow and then click Insert, Import Slides. Alternatively, you can right-click (Control-click) the slide you're selecting in the slide-sorter pane and choose Import Slides from the context menu.

Importing from a Google Docs Presentation

The Import Slides dialog box (see Figure 9.12) displays a list of the presentations in your Google Docs account. Click the presentation you want, and the list changes to show the individual slides in that presentation. Below each slide is its slide number; check the box next to the slide number of any slides you want to import. Click Import to insert a copy of each selected slide into the current presentation.

Figure 9.12
The Import Slides dialog box lets you copy one or more slides from another presentation and put them into this presentation.

Importing from a Presentation Stored on Your Computer

If the slide you want to import is in a file stored in a presentation on your computer, you can use the Import Slides box (shown in Figure 9.12) to import that presentation into Google Docs and then select the slides you want to duplicate in the current presentation.

 Keep in mind that when you use the Import Slides box to import a presentation from your computer into Docs, that presentation is subject to the same limitations as any other imported presentation: It must be 10MB or smaller and in .ppt or .pps format. Additionally, any slide transitions will be discarded.

To import a presentation from your computer into Google Docs via the Import Slides dialog box, click the Browse button. A window opens listing files on your computer; find and select the file you want and click Open to put the file's path into the Import Slides dialog box. Click Upload.

Google uploads the presentation (adding it to your Docs list) and displays its slides on the right side of the Import Slides box. From here, proceed as you would when importing slides from another Docs presentation: Check the boxes of any slides you want and click Import.

Copying a Slide

There's no need to reinvent the wheel with each new slide you create. When you've created a slide that you want to use as the basis for another slide, simply duplicate the original and then tweak the copy as you like.

To duplicate a slide, select the slide you want to copy and then use one of these methods:

- Click the Create a Duplicate Copy icon at the top of the slide-sorter pane. (This icon shows two overlapping slides.) Google copies the slide and inserts a duplicate right after it.

- From the menu bar, select Slide, Duplicate Slide, and Google inserts a copy after the selected slide.

- Right-click the slide. From the context menu that appears, choose Duplicate Slide. Google inserts the duplicate immediately after the selected slide.

- Right-click the slide and choose Copy Slide from the context menu. Next, select the slide after which you want the duplicate to appear. Right-click that slide and choose Paste Slide. Google pastes in the slide in the location you indicated.

Moving a Slide

If you want to change the order of the slides in your presentation, you've got these options:

- To move a slide one slot—In the slide-sorter pane, right-click (Windows) or Control-click (Mac) the slide you want to move. A context menu appears. Select Move Slide Up or Move Slide Down.

- To move a slide several slots—In the slide-sorter pane, click the slide you want to move. Drag it to its new location and then drop it into place.

Adding Speaker Notes

Seasoned presenters know that attaching notes to a slide helps to ensure that you'll remember everything you want to say about that slide. Google Docs lets you attach speaker's notes to your slides, which you can view while giving the presentation.

To add notes to a slide, select the slide you want so that it appears in the slide editor pane. In the lower-right corner of the slide editor, click the View Speaker Notes button, which show's a speaker in profile and a plus sign. This opens the Speaker Notes pane, shown in Figure 9.13, on the right side of the screen. Type your notes into the large text box; click the pane's upper-right x to close it.

 Chapter 10 tells you how to view speaker's notes during a live presentation and how to show (or hide) speaker's notes when you print a presentation.

Deleting a Slide

If a slide isn't working out, you can delete it from the presentation. In the slide-sorter pane, select the slide you want to delete. Right-click (Control-click on a Mac) the slide—either in the slide sorter or the slide editor—and choose Delete Slide from the context menu. Google imme-diately deletes the slide from your presentation (but clicking Undo brings it right back).

If you prefer, you can select the slide and then click Slide, Delete Slide from the menu bar.

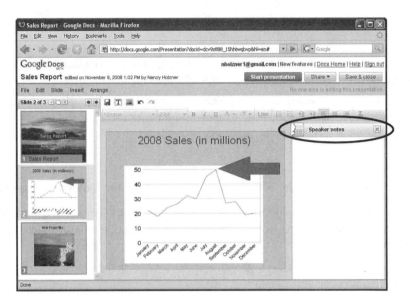

Figure 9.13
The Speaker Notes pane lets you add notes to individual slides.

 Here's an even quicker way to delete a slide: Select the slide in the slide sorter pane and then click the Delete the Current Slide icon at the top of that pane. This icon looks like a slide with an x in it.

Working with Presentations

You've finished your presentation—or at least you have a good working draft of it. This section shows you the next steps: previewing a presentation before you share it with others, exporting it to another program or to save on your computer, and deleting a presentation you no longer need.

Previewing a Presentation

It's always a good idea to do a few trial runs before you give a presentation to an audience. Does the order of your slides make sense? Are the slides attractive and consistent? Is incremental reveal working the way you want it to?

Previewing a presentation is essentially the same as giving it—except you're the only one present. To preview a presentation, click the upper-right Start Presentation button. Your presentation opens in a new window. Use the lower-left arrows to move through the presentation a slide at a time. If a slide reveals its elements one at a time (such as items in a list), click the right-pointing arrow (or anywhere on the slide) to reveal the next element. When you reach the last slide, click the slide, and a dialog box appears, asking whether you want to restart the presentation or exit it. Click Restart to go through the presentation again; click Exit to end the presentation and close its window.

 This section describes the bare-bones basics of viewing a presentation. For more detail, see Chapter 10.

 If you've got three dozen slides in your presentation and you want to preview slide 36, you don't want to click through all of the intervening 35 slides to view it. To preview the presentation beginning with a certain slide, right-click (Control-click on a Mac) the slide you want to preview in the slide-sorter pane. From the context menu, choose Start Presentation from this Slide.

Exporting a Presentation

If you want to transfer a copy of a presentation outside of Google Docs, you can export it. This can be helpful when, for example, you want to take a presentation you created in Docs and add some of the fancy bells-and-whistles formatting available in PowerPoint, such as slide transitions and animation of elements. (This formatting won't work in Google Docs, but you might want it in a separate, PowerPoint version of the presentation.)

To export a presentation, open the presentation you want and select File, Download Presentation as. A submenu appears, offering these choices:

- PDF—This stands for portable document format, which lets you see formatted slides in a PDF viewer such as Adobe Acrobat, Adobe Reader, or Foxit. This is a good format to choose if you want to print your slides (see next section).
- PPT—If you want to work on the presentation in Microsoft PowerPoint, choose this format.
- TXT—When you download a presentation as a text file, you get the text that appears on the slides but no images or formatting.

After you've selected a file format, a new window opens, asking how you want to handle the download: save the file to your computer or open it with an appropriate program. Make your selection, and you've exported the presentation.

 You can also export a presentation from the Docs list on your Google Docs home page. Check the box of the presentation you want to export and then click More Actions. From the More Actions menu, select how you want to export the file, PDF, PPT, or Text, and the download proceeds from there.

Printing a Presentation

When you give a presentation, it can be helpful to have a printout of the presentation to refer to as you go through the show slide by slide. Similarly, a printed handout of the presentation can be helpful to audience members as a takeaway.

To print a presentation, open the presentation and click File, Print. This opens the Print Preview dialog box, shown in Figure 9.14. The Print Preview box shows a preview of how the presentation will look when it's printed and offers these options:

- Layout—Use this drop-down to specify the number of slides to print on each page. Your options here range from one slide to a dozen on each page. (Figure 9.14 shows a layout of four slides per page.)

- Show Background—This box, checked by default, includes the presentation's theme or backgrounds in the printed slides. If you'd rather show just the slides' content and not their background, uncheck this box.

- Speaker Notes—Earlier in this chapter, the "Adding Speaker Notes" section told you how to append notes to slides in a presentation. If you want these notes to appear in the printed presentation, check this box.

When you're ready to print, click the Print button. Google exports the presentation in PDF format. Open the file in a PDF reader (such as Adobe Reader) and print it from there. How you do that depends on the PDF reader you use; if you're unsure, refer to the program's Help files.

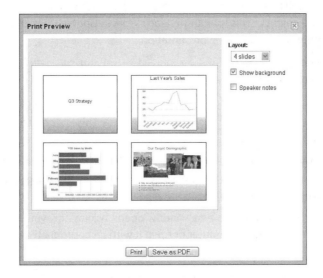

Figure 9.14
Use the Print Preview dialog box to determine how your slides will look when printed. Here, the preview shows four slides on a page.

Deleting a Presentation

Google Docs lets you store up to a combination of 5,000 documents and presentations and 5,000 images. So you may never need to delete a presentation. If you want to remove a presentation from Google Docs, however, you can do so in one of these ways:

- From the presentation editor—With the presentation you want to delete open, choose File, Delete Presentation. Google asks whether you're sure you want to delete this presentation; click OK.

- From the Google Docs home page—In the Docs list, find the presentation you want to delete and check the box to the left of its name. Then, click Delete. Google immediately moves the presentation to Trash.

When you delete a presentation, it's not really gone yet. Instead, Google moves it to the Trash. If you decide that deleting the presentation wasn't such a good idea after all, you can restore it to your Docs list. On the Docs home page, click Trash to open it (you may have to expand all items to find the Trash). Check the box of any files you want to restore and then click Undelete. Google reactivates your selection, taking it out of Trash and putting it back on your Docs list.

If, on the other hand, you want to delete a presentation once and for all, open Trash and check the presentation's checkbox. Click Empty Trash—and Google gets rid of the presentation for good.

The Main Event: Sharing and Viewing Presentations

Presentations are meant to be shared. Chapter 9, "Introducing Presentations," showed you how easy it is to create a professional-looking presentation using Google Docs. Now that you've created a presentation, this chapter focuses on sharing it—with a few select collaborators, with a live audience, or even with the world.

Sharing a Presentation

If you're part of a group giving a presentation, the entire group should be in on the action—helping to create the presentation or at least reviewing and critiquing it before show time. You can share any presentation you create with other people of your choosing. Those people can be either viewers (who can see the presentation but not make any changes to it) or collaborators (who can both view and edit the presentation).

To share a presentation, open the presentation and click its upper-right Share button to open the Share this Presentation page, shown in Figure 10.1.

If you've ever shared a Google Docs document or spreadsheet, this page will look familiar. That's because the methods and options for sharing a presentation are exactly the same as for sharing a document. Chapter 5, "Sharing and Collaborating on Documents," covers document sharing in detail, so please refer back to that chapter's "Sharing a Document" section to find out everything you need to know about sharing a Google Docs presentation.

After you've shared a presentation, you can email that presentation to the people with whom you've shared it. (If the presentation is unshared, you can use this method to email it to yourself.) You might want to do this, for example, to notify others of changes you've made to the presentation. Open the presentation and click Share, Email Presentation. A dialog box opens, where you can choose the sharers you want to email and add an optional message. When you click Send, Google sends an email with a link to the presentation.

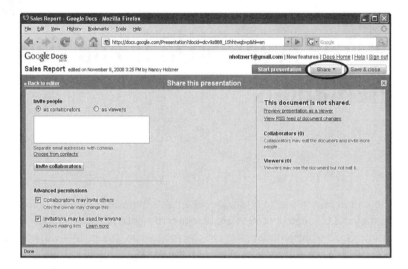

Figure 10.1
Click the Share button (circled) to open the Share this Presentation page.

Collaborating on a Presentation

When you and a collaborator are working on the same presentation at the same time, Google lets you know with a notification in the upper-right part of the presentation editor. Every minute or so, Google refreshes the presentation, and you see the changes your collaborator has made since the last refresh.

With two or more collaborators working on the same presentation simultaneously, Google does its best to merge the changes. Sometimes, though, a conflict arises. For example, maybe a collaborator deleted a shape five seconds ago, but the deletion hasn't yet showed up on your screen, and you're busy trying to resize the shape. When that happens, Google displays a dialog box that informs you of the conflict, as shown in Figure 10.2. In the dialog box, your only choice is to accept that your change is null and void: Click OK or the upper-right x to close the dialog box. (Then, if you want, pick up the phone and have a discussion with your colleague about who's editing what.)

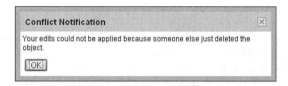

Figure 10.2
When there's a conflict between collaborators' edits, Google lets you know.

 Unlike Google Docs spreadsheets, presentations don't have a built-in chat function to use as you collaborate. If you want to be able to chat with colleagues as you work on a presentation together, use the Google Talk gadget, which allows multiuser chatting from your iGoogle page, and add a comma after chatting after you move it from your iGoogle page.

Giving a Live Presentation

You've created and organized your slides, given them clear bullet points and sharp-looking graphics. You've previewed the presentation and taken it for a trial run or two. Now it's time to give your presentation to an audience.

If you're giving the presentation to an audience who's gathered with you in one room, make sure the computer that's hooked up to the projector has Internet access so that you can sign in to Google, open the presentation, and show it. Otherwise, export the presentation as a .ppt file so that you can use a program such as Microsoft PowerPoint or OpenOffice.org Impress to show your presentation. Chapter 9 explained how to export a presentation from Google Docs.

If you're giving the presentation over the Internet to people in different locations, anyone who you've added to the presentation as a collaborator can join the presentation by signing in to their Google account at the appointed time, opening the presentation, and clicking its Start Presentation button. Viewers can open the presentation from their Docs list. Whether viewer or collaborator, once participants have opened the presentation, you can take control and start going through your slides.

 You can invite people to join the presentation by sending them the URL at the top of the live presentation's right-hand pane. If you invite someone with whom you had not previously shared the presentation, Google automatically adds that person to your list of sharers as a viewer.

Each member of your audience needs to have a Google account so they can sign in and view the presentation. If someone who's not signed in to Google tries to view a presentation, Google presents the Docs sign-in page; anyone who doesn't yet have a Google account can quickly create one from there. It takes just a minute to set things up, and then the new Google Docs account owner is on board for your presentation.

Starting the Show

To view a presentation, open the presentation and click its upper-right Start Presentation button. Google starts the presentation in a new window, as shown in Figure 10.3. As others join the presentation, their names appear in the chat pane on the right.

When everyone's present, start the presentation by clicking the upper-right Take Control of Presentation button. When you take control of a presentation, it means that as you move through the slides, all the participants see the same slide that shows on your screen. To move between slides, click the arrows in the lower-left part of the screen (you can see these arrows in Figure 10.3). Click the right-pointing arrow to move forward to the next slide; click the left-pointing arrow to go back to the previous slide.

Click here to start the presentation

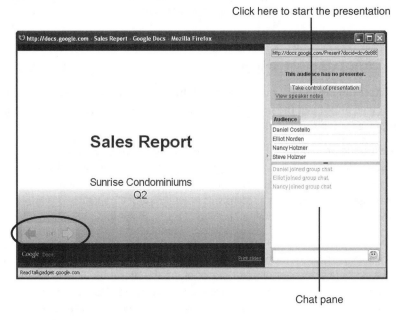

Chat pane

Figure 10.3
When everyone's present, click the Take Control of Presentation button to begin the slideshow.

During the Presentation

As you give the presentation, your audience can simply follow along. However, audience members also have the option of going through the presentation at their own speed; any audience member can use the lower-left arrows to page through the presentation. When an audience member gets out of sync with what the presenter is doing, the presenter's current slide appears in the audience member's right pane, as shown in Figure 10.4. Below the presenter's current slide is a link: Follow the Presenter. To get back in sync with the presentation, the audience member simply clicks that link, and the slide shown in the main part of the screen again matches what's on the presenter's screen.

Info 4U When you're the presenter, you have no way of knowing whether audience members are following you or going through the presentation on their own.

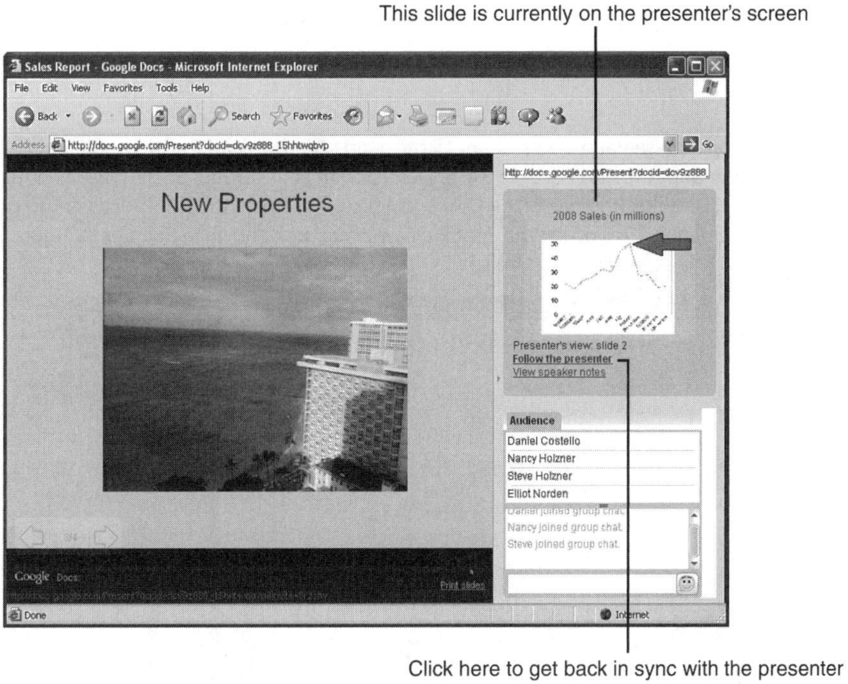

This slide is currently on the presenter's screen

Click here to get back in sync with the presenter

Figure 10.4
When a viewer is out of sync with the presentation, Google displays the presenter's current slide in the right pane. Click Follow the Presenter to get back in sync.

Anyone who has collaborator status is able to take control of the presentation. (Viewers, on the other hand, can only follow the presenter or go through the slides on their own.) A collaborator can take control of the presentation by clicking the upper-right Take Control of Presentation link, shown in Figure 10.5. Someone else might take control of the presentation if, for example, they have a question or comment about the previous slide and want to return to it for a moment.

So how do you know who's in control? Look in the top part of the pane on the right for one of these messages:

- You are presenting!—This means that you're the presenter and audience members are following what's on your screen. (Although, as noted earlier, they can go through the slides at their own pace.)

- You are following the presenter—This means that someone else has control of the presentation, and you're following what's on that person's screen.

You can take back control of the presentation at any time by clicking the Take Control of Presentation link.

 During a presentation, you (or any participant) can download the presentation in PDF format to print the slides or save the presentation to your computer. Click the lower-right Print Slides link (this link isn't visible if you press F11 to see the full-screen version of the presentation). This opens the Print Preview dialog box, shown in Chapter 9's Figure 9.14.

Figure 10.5
The top part of the right pane lets you know whether you're in control of the presentation or following someone else.

 During a presentation, use the F11 key to switch from normal view to full-screen view, maximizing the slide. If you want to go back to normal view, press F11 again.

Viewing Speaker Notes

If you created speaker notes to go with slides in your presentation (see Chapter 9), you'll want those notes available to you as you give the presentation. To see a presentation's speaker notes, click the upper-right View Speaker Notes link. A new window opens, displaying the notes for the current slide. When you click the navigation arrows to move to the next slide, the speaker notes also move to that slide. (When you click the navigation arrow, the speaker notes window gives up the focus; click that window's button on the task bar to bring it back.)

When you open speaker notes in a new window, those notes don't show on the audience's screens. Be aware, however, that anyone viewing the presentation—whether the presentation's owner, a collaborator, or a viewer—can view speaker notes in a new window. So make sure that any notes you attach to your slides are appropriate for everyone viewing the presentation.

Chatting During a Presentation

When you're giving a presentation over the Internet, chances are you'll set up a conference call so that you can talk to the other participants and answer their questions. But Google gives you another option for communicating during a presentation: sending instant messages, commonly known as *chatting*. Chatting can be useful during a presentation. For example, when you want to share some text that's not already on a slide, you can copy that text and paste it into the chat window. Even better, you can paste a video into the chat pane, and audience members can play it right there without leaving the presentation.

 To chat during a presentation you need to have Adobe Flash Player version 8 or above installed. If you use Linux as your operating system, you need version 9 or higher. To download the latest version of Adobe Flash Player, go to www.adobe.com/products/flashplayer.

When you type a comment in the text box at the bottom of the chat pane on the right and then press Enter, that comment appears in the chat box, where all participants can see it (as shown in Figure 10.6). If another participants type something in answer to your comment, that response appears below yours—and so it goes as the chat proceeds.

 If you don't need to chat during a presentation and you want to have more room for your slides, click the tiny right-pointing arrow to the left of the chat pane (it's circled in Figure 10.6); the chat pane collapses. If you want to make the collapsed chat pane visible, click the arrow again (it's now on the far-right side of the screen and pointing left).

Inserting Emoticons into Chat

When you're communicating online, it can be hard to get across nuances and tone. That's where emoticons can come in handy. An *emoticon* is a symbol meant to convey an emotion, such as :) for a smile or ;) for a wink.

Google takes emoticons one step further in chat, converting them into cute cartoon smiling, frowning, or surprised faces—whatever feeling you want to convey. There are two ways you can insert an emoticon into chat during a presentation:

▪ Type the keyboard-based version of the emoticon you want, such as :D for laughter or :-o for surprise. When you press Enter to display your comment, Google changes the emoticon into its cartoon-face counterpart. (Not all Web browsers can display the cartoon faces. In that case, the audience member sees the characters you typed.)

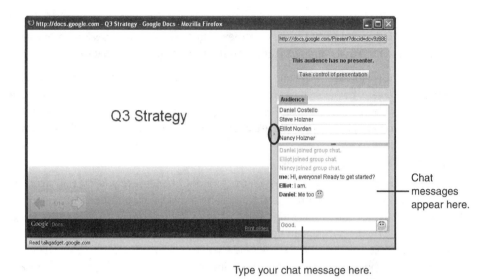

Chat messages appear here.

Type your chat message here.

Figure 10.6
Type into the text box and then press Enter to send an instant message to presentation participants. Click the circled arrow to collapse the chat pane.

■ At the bottom of the chat pane, click the Emoticon button to the right of the text box. This displays Google's library of emoticons, as shown in Figure 10.7. Click an emoticon to insert it. Google inserts the emoticon into the chat text box as text and then converts it to the cartoon face you chose when it displays your comment in the chat box.

Figure 10.7
You can insert emoticons into your chat messages by clicking the Emoticon button (circled) and then selecting the expression you want.

Google offers three styles of emoticons: round cartoon faces, square cartoon faces, and text-based emoticons. The style you choose determines how emoticons look in your own chat pane (other participants can choose their own styles). To choose an emoticon style, click the emoticon button to the right of the chat pane's text box. When the menu of emoticons opens, the three different styles appear above the menu of expressions. Click the style you want and then click the upper-right x to close the emoticons menu. Google applies the style you chose to all emoticons showing in your chat pane.

Copying and Pasting into Chat

Possibly the most convenient thing about having a chat pane available during a presentation is that you can copy something you want to share—some text, a link, an image, even a video—and then paste it into the chat pane, making it available to all participants. Obviously, you can have all these elements on the slides, but it's helpful to have the ability to paste such elements into chat in case something comes up that you didn't address on a slide.

Because Google uses Adobe Flash to make chatting work, copying and pasting may work a little differently than what you're used to (that's because of a quirk built into Flash). To copy something (such as a URL) to paste it into chat, first select what you want to copy and then try one of these methods:

- Right-click (Control-click on a Mac) and select Copy from the context menu.
- Follow this sequence, one key at a time—Press and release the keys one by one, using this sequence: Press the Ctrl key (Cmd on a Mac). Then, while holding that key down, press C. Next, let go of the C key. Finally, let go of the Ctrl (Cmd) key.

Now go back to your presentation-in-progress. Click in the chat pane's text box to put the cursor there. Then use one of these methods to paste what you copied into the text box:

- Right-click (Control-click on a Mac) and select Paste from the context menu.
- Follow this sequence—Press and release the keys one by one, using this sequence: Press the Ctrl key (Cmd on a Mac). Then, while holding that key down, press V. Next, let go of the V key. Finally, let go of the Ctrl (Cmd) key.

After you've pasted your selection into the text box, press Enter to display it in the chat window.

Copying and Pasting Images and Videos into Chat

Google's chat function is smart enough to recognize certain Web addresses (URLs) as belonging to videos, images, or photo slideshows. So when you paste in the URL for, say, a YouTube video, Google recognizes that the URL is for a video and puts the video itself into the chat box. Your audience members can either play the video right in chat or click a link to go to the video on YouTube, as shown in Figure 10.8.

Google can perform this nifty trick with these URLs:

- Google Video and YouTube videos
- Picasa Web Albums and Flickr images, albums, and slideshows

Simply open a window that shows the video or image you want and copy that page's URL from your Web browser's address bar, paste the URL into your ongoing presentation's chat text box, and press Enter. (Use one of the copying and pasting techniques described in the previous section.) And presto! The video or image appears in the chat pane.

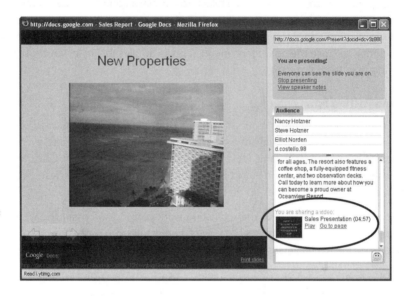

Figure 10.8
In this example, the presenter has copied the URL of a YouTube video and pasted it into chat. Participants can click Play to see the video in the chat box or Go to Page to view the video in a new window.

Ending a Presentation

When you've come to the end of a presentation, click anywhere on the final slide. Google displays a dialog box telling you that you've reached the end of the presentation. Click Exit to end the presentation. That closes the presentation on your computer and tells your audience you've left chat. Audience members can look through the slides again or close the presentation's window to leave the presentation.

Publishing a Presentation on the Web

Most presentations are designed to be given live, but when you've worked hard to put together a good presentation, you don't necessarily want to put the presentation in mothballs after you've given it a time or two. Instead, you can publish the presentation on the Web. When you do this, anyone can view the presentation, going through it at his or her own pace.

Making a Presentation Public

When you make a presentation public, Google gives the presentation its own Web address (URL). Anyone can view the presentation when they go to that URL.

To make a presentation public, open the presentation and click Share, Publish/embed. This opens the Publish this Presentation page, which tells you that the presentation currently is not published. To make the presentation public, click the Publish Document button. Google publishes your presentation, and the page changes to look like the one in Figure 10.9.

At the top of the page is the presentation's URL: Click the link to view presentation or copy the link and post it on the Internet or email it to people who might want to view the presentation themselves.

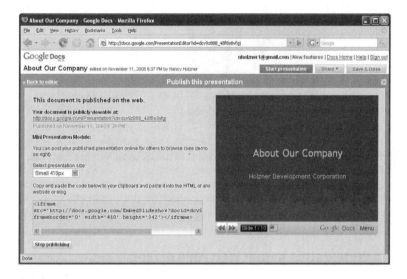

Figure 10.9
When you've made a presentation public, Google shows you this page.

When someone follows the link, he or she lands on a Google Docs sign-in page, as shown in Figure 10.10. But a person doesn't have to have a Google account to see the presentation. On the left is an image of the opening slide of your presentation. Below that image is a link: View published presentation in a new window. Anyone can click the link to view the presentation.

 Anyone viewing your published presentation can download the presentation as a PDF file and save or print the presentation (as they can during a live presentation) by clicking the lower-right Print Slides link.

Figure 10.10
Whether or not viewers have a Google account, they can click the circled link to view your published presentation.

Embedding a Presentation in Your Web Page or Blog

Besides publishing a presentation on its own Web page, you can *embed* the presentation, that is, you can make it an element in a Web page or blog post. When you embed a presentation, the presentation appears in a mini-viewer, like the one shown on the right side of Figure 10.9. People can click through the presentation using the arrow buttons in the lower-left part of the viewer. They can also open the presentation in its own window or embed the presentation in their own Web pages or blogs.

To embed a presentation, open the presentation and click Share, Publish/embed. If the presentation is not yet published on the Web, click the Publish Document button. The Publish this Presentation page, shown in Figure 10.9, opens. The right side of the page shows a preview of the embedded presentation. This preview works just as the embedded presentation will work in your own Web page or blog. If you want, try it out—click the lower-left arrow buttons to move through the presentation, for example.

On the Publish this Presentation page, you need to tell Google how big the embedded presentation should be. Use the Select Presentation Size drop-down list to choose one of these:

- Small—410 pixels wide × 342 pixels high
- Medium—555 pixels wide × 451 pixels high
- Large—700 pixels wide × 559 pixels high

The size you choose affects the HTML code in the text box. After you've selected a size, copy the HTML code. Paste the code into an HTML document and upload the document to your Web site or paste it into a blog post and publish the post. Your presentation appears in its viewer.

What can visitors do with the embedded presentation? Take a look at Figure 10.11, noticing the buttons at the bottom of the viewer. From left to right, here's what they do:

- Arrow buttons—These move the presentation one slide forward or one slide back.

- Open in New Window—This button opens a full-sized version of the presentation in a new window. For collaborators who are signed in to their Google account, it opens the presentation in the Docs presentation editor.

- Google Docs—If the person viewing the presentation is signed in to his or her Google account, clicking this button opens the Google Docs home page in a new window. Otherwise, a new window opens to the Google Docs sign-in page.

- Menu—When someone viewing the embedded presentation clicks this button, the presentation changes to look like the one in Figure 10.11. Then the viewer has these options:

  - Embed—The person viewing the presentation can copy its HTML code to embed the presentation in his or her own Web page or blog.

  - Create your own!—Clicking this link opens a new presentation in the Google Docs presentation editor (if the person is signed in) or the Google Docs sign-in page.

  - Open the public presentation—Below the slide is a link with the presentation's title. Clicking this link opens the published presentation in a new window (as in Figure 10.10).

Clicking Menu again toggles back to the presentation's original display.

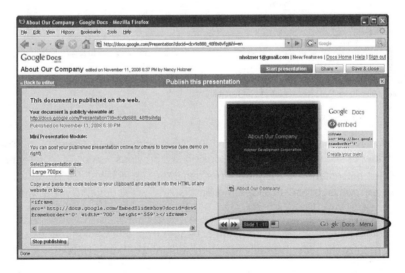

Figure 10.11
An embedded presentation's viewer gives people several options for viewing your presentation.

Working with Revisions

As it does for documents and spreadsheets, Google saves your presentations every few minutes as you work on them and stores the different versions of your evolving presentation in the presentation's revision history. You can view previous versions of a presentation and, if you want, revert back to an earlier version.

To see a presentation's revision history, open the presentation and click File, Revision History. This opens the Revision History page for that presentation, as shown in Figure 10.12. This page shows a list of all the different versions of the presentation identified by revision number, along with when each version was last edited (and by whom) and a summary of what changed in that version.

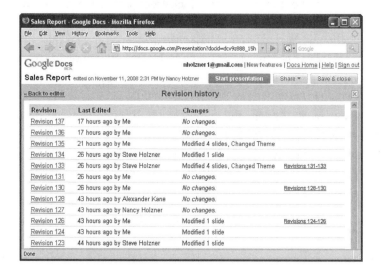

Figure 10.12
Click any Revision number to see that saved version of a presentation.

If you want to take a look at a particular revision, click its revision number. That version opens in a new window, as shown in Figure 10.13. Looking at a previous version of a presentation is like looking at the presentation in the slide sorter pane: You see all the slides in that version, the first slide at the top with subsequent slides in order below it. Scroll down to see all the slides in that version.

With presentations, Google doesn't highlight changes from one version to the next, so be prepared to scrutinize the slides carefully to find the differences between versions.

To revert to a version, click Revert to this Version. If this isn't the version you're looking for, close the window that displays the version, go back to the Revision History list, and try again. (Unlike with documents and spreadsheets, there are no Older and Newer buttons to move from the version you're viewing to other versions.)

Reverting to a previous version opens that version in the presentation editor; it's now the current version (and what was the current version has been added to the revision history). If you decide not to revert to a previous version, go to the Revision History page and click the upper-left Back to Editor link to go back to the current version in the presentation editor.

Figure 10.13
Read the previous version from top to bottom. If you want to make this version the current one, click Revert to this Version (circled).

Index

J - K - L

Q - R

S

U

Create and Share Your Work Online

Google Docs 4 Everyone

Steven Holzner and Nancy Holzner

que

FREE Online Edition

Your purchase of **Google Docs 4 Everyone** includes access to a free online edition for 45 days through the Safari Books Online subscription service. Nearly every Que book is available online through Safari Books Online, along with more than 5,000 other technical books and videos from publishers such as Addison-Wesley Professional, Cisco Press, Exam Cram, IBM Press, O'Reilly, Prentice Hall, and Sams.

SAFARI BOOKS ONLINE allows you to search for a specific answer, cut and paste code, download chapters, and stay current with emerging technologies.

Activate your FREE Online Edition at www.informit.com/safarifree

> **STEP 1:** Enter the coupon code: RVWFKEH .

> **STEP 2:** New Safari users, complete the brief registration form.
> Safari subscribers, just log in.

If you have difficulty registering on Safari or accessing the online edition,
please e-mail customer-service@safaribooksonline.com

O'REILLY Peachpit Press PRENTICE HALL QUE Redbooks SAMS SAS Publishing Sun microsystems WILEY

Addison Wesley Adobe Press ALPHA Cisco Press FT Press FINANCIAL TIMES IBM Press lynda.com Microsoft Press New Riders